CW00801250

# LIVING DEMOCRACY

TIM HOLLO is Executive Director of the Green Institute and wrote this book while a visiting fellow at the Australian National University's RegNet. A musician, environmentalist and community activist, he was the Communications Director for Greens Leader Christine Milne and a board member and campaigner at Greenpeace Australia Pacific. He is the founder of Green Music Australia and has recorded seven albums and toured globally with FourPlay String Quartet. Living in Canberra with his partner and two kids, Tim established the city's flourishing Buy Nothing groups, set up a little library, spearheaded a campaign to keep the city free of billboard advertising and has run for election with the Greens.

# LIVING DEMOCRACY

## AN ECOLOGICAL MANIFESTO
## FOR THE END OF THE WORLD
## AS WE KNOW IT

# TIM HOLLO

NEWSOUTH

**A NewSouth book**

*Published by*
NewSouth Publishing
University of New South Wales Press Ltd
University of New South Wales
Sydney NSW 2052
AUSTRALIA
https://unsw.press/

© Tim Hollo 2022
First published 2022

10 9 8 7 6 5 4 3 2 1

This book is copyright. Apart from any fair dealing for the purpose of private study, research, criticism or review, as permitted under the *Copyright Act*, no part of this book may be reproduced by any process without written permission. Inquiries should be addressed to the publisher.

 A catalogue record for this book is available from the National Library of Australia

ISBN    9781742237251 (paperback)
        9781742238449 (ebook)
        9781742239347 (ePDF)

*Internal design* Josephine Pajor-Markus
*Cover design* George Saad
*Printer* Griffin Press, part of Ovato

All reasonable efforts were taken to obtain permission to use copyright material reproduced in this book, but in some cases copyright could not be traced. The author welcomes information in this regard.

# CONTENTS

# INTRODUCTION

## To not simply survive but thrive

Here, at the end of the world as we know it, two very different realities stretch out in front of us.

Looking one way, we see fires, floods and heat like never before. We see a pandemic upending the world, and deep racial, social and economic injustices flaring to the surface. As ecosystems collapse, their magnificent complexity reduced to impoverished, disconnected remnants, so too the political systems that we've come to imagine as natural and permanent are riven with cracks and crumbling before our eyes. If we continue down this path, we face a bleak, and possibly short, future.

And, as the old world dies, a new world is being born.

Look the other way. Watch as people reach out to each other, with explosions of mutual aid in every corner of the globe. Witness renewable energy cooperatives in Newcastle, community-supported urban agriculture in Canberra, Barefoot Patrols replacing police in Aboriginal communities, and sharing and repairing groups everywhere. See the extraordinary models of grassroots democracy evolving from Barcelona to Wangaratta to Kurdistan. In the face of disaster, humanity's astonishing capacity for care, our instinct to help one another, is blossoming in myriad wonderful ways.

The choice is ours.

We could continue down the path to catastrophe, accelerating as we tear each other and the living world apart. Or we could learn from those living systems. We could choose to cultivate living democracy – democracy understood as a living entity embodying our collective coexistence; democracy as a conscious practice of living well together and co-creating our common future.

If we choose that future – and this book provides some of the what, why and how of doing so – we won't just survive. We'll thrive.

Between July 2019 and February 2020, as vast fires on a scale never seen before rage across Australia, neighbours are working together to get their communities fire-ready, preparing meals for each other, supporting those out fighting fires and those who've lost everything. Volunteer fire-fighters risk their lives to save others', to protect homes and animals. Crafters knit socks for burned koalas. People donate clothing and food, and, amid the trauma, a festival atmosphere grows in the parks where people gather to sort and distribute it all. They're demonstrating the cooperation, creativity and generosity that has made humankind such a successful species. By living democracy, they're making life more worth living, even in the teeth of tragedy.

When the COVID pandemic hits in early 2020, mutual aid groups spring up as communities self-organise to support each other, finding joy and connection amid the fear and isolation. They letterbox neighbourhoods and get groceries or medical supplies for those in need. Phone trees are organised to check in with older neighbours or new arrivals. Working around the physical distancing, people world-wide Zoom to share their experiences, learn from each other, and simply feel connected.

In May 2020, George Floyd's murder by police is filmed on a phone camera; the Black Lives Matter movement erupts into action. With the slogan 'defund the police' echoing around the globe, millions learn about community protection programs as effective alternatives to militarised policing. Economic and racial injustices exposed by the pandemic jump-start conversations about combined solutions to all three issues.

Craving ideas for action, people from all walks of life form discussion groups and community forums. Some launch practical projects like community-owned renewable energy cooperatives, walking school buses, or bulk purchases of e-bikes. Some feed into the new democracy movement, evolving into citizens' assemblies, cooperative enterprises, electoral projects, or even new systems of government. Some join protests, from the huge School Strikes for Climate to burgeoning Invasion Day marches, from blockading coal ports to occupying the offices of politicians, lifting their voices together and demanding action from governments.

Governments aren't listening.

Most aren't just failing to act but, hand in glove with powerful corporations, are making things worse.

Peaceful protesters are aggressively dispersed by riot police to allow fossil fuel CEOs unimpeded access to conferences. The protesters are threatened with ever more serious gaol terms. Australia's treasurer smirks as he fondles a lump of coal in the parliament; when he becomes prime minister the following year, he makes the lobbyist who gave him the coal his chief of staff. Governments taking millions in 'donations' from fossil fuel companies with one hand, and providing subsidies and royalty holidays with the other, draft laws making it harder for advocacy groups to do their jobs.

Those in power suppress information, prosecuting whistleblowers while simultaneously underfunding public broadcasting. They reduce funding to fire services while handing gigalitres of water to coal mining and gas fracking. They gut support for community programs, crying poor while cutting taxes for the rich and handing billions in pandemic funds to massively profitable corporations. They facilitate logging in the few remaining forests and approve new coal and gas extraction, all while mouthing care for the environment.

If we continue down this path, extinction looms.

Extinction.

That threat is new and confronting for many of us. But, for First Peoples, the end of their world began centuries ago, and their struggle against genocide continues. And they survive. Any project for survival, and for a better way of living, must learn from, listen to, and follow Indigenous people. One of the vital concepts we can and must learn from them, as we'll explore, is what I think of as 'ecological thinking': recognising the fundamental interconnectedness of all things, appreciating that each of us is a precious part of a grand interdependent whole. And, at this moment in history, we are all getting an object lesson in that fact.

During that horrific summer of 2019–20, the first thing to waft in each day before the wave of choking smoke is the gorgeous aroma of eucalyptus; we are reminded we're breathing in the ghosts of gum trees. When the pandemic arrives, we learn that our health is dependent on the health and actions of those around us. It heightens our awareness of our vital need, as social beings, to stay connected to each other while keeping physically apart. The impacts of fires and the virus, and then the economic impacts of the lockdowns, bring to the surface the intersections between human health, environmental health, social and economic inequity, racial injustices, family violence, politics, the media, technology ... the whole shebang. All the crises and challenges we face weave together in a web of interconnection, underpinned by the same root causes, and exacerbating each other in a multitude of feedback loops. The crashing of confidence in our democratic systems and institutions is a stark symptom of all these crises and the abject failure of governments to address them.

What if we treated the abject failure of our systems of government as a liberating opportunity to reinvent them?

They're clearly not up to the job. They created the crises we face and, as such, they cannot enable the solutions. It's not that the demands of activists, school kids, First Nations people, scientists and doctors, of the great mass of humanity, haven't been heard, or just need to get louder. They are being heard, and deliberately shut out by a set of anti-democratic, anti-ecological systems structured to maintain power and protect the status quo.

What's worse, these systems are spectacularly ill-suited to enabling human survival in the world of rolling crises that they have created. As ecological collapse triggers ever worse extreme weather events, diseases, and food and water shortages, systems based on disconnection and domination, individualism and adversarialism will only increase the chaos. While they may briefly enable survival for a select few, as the intersecting crises deepen, extinction would seem the likeliest outcome.

But here's the thing: we invented these systems and, like everything else in our ecological world, they're subject to change. Indeed, they're already collapsing around us.

What a time to be alive!

At times of emergency, our human instinct for mutual aid, self-organising to help each other, comes into its own. What if we used this moment of global emergency to institutionalise that instinct, to build systems that bring out the best in us? That, fundamentally, is what this book argues we can and must urgently do.

The challenges we face now require us to see and organise the world in a different way. To turn around ecological collapse and generate the resilience we need to survive and thrive, we will need more networks of support, more social cohesion, more layers of redundancy, more cooperation and generosity – all those aspects of society which ecology teaches us create resilience but which, in our anti-ecological system, are unvalued, marginalised and often outright erased.

But they're still here. They've always been here. Like plants growing through cracks in the pavement, they're living things, always chafing at their bonds, remarkably resilient, and incredibly regenerative when given the opportunity to flourish. That's why, although this transformation might be difficult, it's entirely possible. It's why, although it will be seen by some as impractical, it is actually the only practical option we have. It's why I believe that, although life will inevitably be hard as our destabilised planet shakes and judders its way into the next equilibrium, in some ways it will also be better as we pull together and work cooperatively and creatively for the common good.

It's the end of the world as we know it. It doesn't have to be the end of the world.

'You have stolen my dreams and my childhood.'

So said the remarkable Greta Thunberg in her blistering speech to the 2019 United Nations Climate Action Summit.[1] Thunberg's raw honesty about the climate science and her fears for the future have reverberated around the globe, inspiring millions to participate. The School Strikes for Climate have been the most encouraging innovation in this space in the 20 years I've been involved. They highlight how unprepared we are for what's coming. They put a steely focus on the failure to act, and the urgency and scale of the transformation we need.

There's a problem, though: like almost all activism, the strikes demand action from the existing system. And that is no longer a credible demand.[2]

Without a believable pathway forward, this approach is extraordinarily demotivating – indeed, it can be utterly depressing. Climate anxiety is becoming an epidemic.[3] Many student climate strikers, including my younger child, find the activism powerful but, after being belittled and told to get back to school, after successive disappointments from governments, they're left with little hope. And it's not just students. As 'natural' disasters roll one into the next, talk of survivalism is becoming commonplace among adults.[4] A defeatist attitude has become palpable, as campaigners mobilise people to demand action from governments, knowing in their hearts that governments won't do what's necessary.

The same is true across much of progressive politics. There's a mounting sense of desperation in the face of rising authoritarianism, obscene economic inequality and racial injustice, the backlash against progress on equal marriage, abortion rights and multiculturalism, and the arrival of a post-truth politics absolutely divorced from reality.

Across the community, people are searching for hope, seeking answers, looking for a way forward, and finding precious little on offer from contemporary politics.

If this strikes a chord, this book is for you.

Whether you're already active, or a concerned community member wondering how best to contribute, I'm hoping this book will give you ideas and energy. While it sets out an ecological politics, it's by no means only for or about capital G Greens, though I hope it will help many Greens to think deeply about our politics. We'll learn lessons for communities, organisations, political parties and individuals, and a recipe for combining all those ingredients – taking the development of alternatives at the margins and baking them into transformative collective action. This book isn't about giving you hope – it's about guiding you towards your own hope.

The book takes us on a journey. In Part 1, we'll look around at where we are and how we got here. Part 2 sets out a vision for the future based on existing examples. And in Part 3 we discuss how transformative change happens, and happens fast.

It's important to emphasise that this has been a tremendous journey for me. I've been lucky enough to go through the generative, creative process of listening to diverse views, reading widely, working in a broad range of spaces, and talking with numerous people, both in writing the book and in becoming the person who wrote it. I draw on my experiences actively making change in communities through sharing groups and mutual aid projects, as well as discussing ideas in universities and as executive director of the Green Institute; working for non-government organisations as large as Greenpeace and as small as the musicians' environment group I set up from my kitchen table; communing with nature and playing music with people all around the world; growing up as the child of refugees and grandchild of Holocaust survivors, learning very young that none of us is safe until we are all safe; walking the corridors of parliament as a staffer for the Australian Greens and walking the streets talking to people as a candidate for election.

Through it all, like a bowerbird, I've picked up shiny ideas and brought them back to my nest. Through an evolutionary process of testing, challenging, and cross-fertilising, many have morphed into something else as they've found a niche in the ecosystem of my mind. And this book, far from a final word, is intended for others to use in a similar way. Evolution has no end; the journey *is* the destination.

The book is about making big political ideas accessible and useful to anyone by linking them to practical projects we can all do, but there will be a bit of theory, interspersed with stories. Because it's impossible to cover everything, I've chosen examples that build a framework of thought which can then be applied to other issues. Though I keep jargon to a minimum, some of it is necessary. And I do, frankly, want to take you out of your comfort zone a little. Part of being ecological is learning to live with a dash of ambiguity, a dose of confusion, a bit of tension.

I also want to make clear that this book does not rehearse the well understood facts of the crises we face, nor detail the technical steps we need to address them. It's understood that we need a rapid transition to ecologically sound and socially just practices, technologies, and ethics. The book asks what a political system capable of enabling that looks like, and how we can bring that system into being.

Hang on, aren't we in an emergency!? Is this scale of change even worth contemplating? Is there enough time?

There's no time to lose. Because there's no alternative.

Continuing to hope that corporate-captured governments will change if enough of us shout loudly enough is magical thinking. Survivalism, where those with the means run for the hills and burn the bridges behind them, shuts off the possibility of action and, dividing us even further, makes societal collapse more likely. Emergency responses that suspend democracy are no solution, as they open the door to a very grim future. Our problem is not too much democracy – it's too little.

The years ahead will be hard. The only way we'll survive is if we survive together, building social cohesion while learning to live in harmony with the natural world: living democracy. The wonderful thing is that this is a joyful path! If we follow it, we won't just survive – we'll thrive.

The two futures laid out in front of us aren't new choices. They're repeated throughout history. But the stakes right now are as high as they get. There's no guarantee that we'll take the right path in time. But I believe we will.

I'm often asked where I find such hope.

I find it firstly in the miracle of ecology. Life, against all odds, finds a way.

Ecosystems have a remarkable capacity for self-organising regeneration. I'll always remember bushwalking with friends in the Royal National Park at Sydney's southern edge in early 1995, a year after massive bushfires had devastated the park. The sight of green shoots popping up from blackened trunks and soil fills me today with the same ecstatic relief and hope that it did when I was 19.

And here's the corollary to the hope in ecology: we humans are part of the natural world. We're part of those ecosystems. Don't ever let anyone tell you humans are the problem. Like anything else in the glorious complexity of ecology, we can be destructive and creative. But unlike any other organism that we know of, we can choose to be deliberately regenerative.

Through bush regeneration and regenerative agriculture, we've shown it's possible to take degraded land and rebuild its health and resilience. Surely we can do the same with our degraded democracy. Indeed, people and communities are doing it every day. With a regenerative approach, we can plant the seeds of trust, social cohesion, cooperation and generosity, tend them with care, weed out our destructive tendencies, and reap the harvest of a healthy, resilient, joyful, beautiful, ecological, living democracy.

Now turn the page and let's start the journey.

PART 1

# WHERE ARE WE COMING FROM?

# AN ECOLOGICAL MANY-FESTO

A spectre is haunting the world – the spectre of living democracy, of living interdependent with each other and the natural world we are part of; the spectre that the changes we need in order to survive involve making our society more just and our lives more sweet. All the powers of the old world have entered into an alliance to exorcise this spectre, to divide and conquer those seeking change. Creatures of the world, reconnect! We have a world to wean![1]

In 1848, the world teetered on a knife's edge.

Wars and revolutions were reshaping maps, monarchies were falling, fields turning into battlefields. Workers in grinding poverty, living in slums surrounding new factories, were confronting the ballooning wealth of a new ruling class as industrialists challenged the landed gentry. This urbanisation and industrialisation disconnected people from the land, from each other, from the fruits of their labour. Foetid air, the potato blight, and rivers-turned-sewers brought 'nature's revenge'[2] into people's lives. And, around the globe, people were coming together to plan and build better ways of being.

At this moment, two little-known German philosophers, Karl Marx and Friedrich Engels, brought together the ideas of numerous others into *The Communist Manifesto*: 'Workers of the world, unite! We have a world to win.'

It was a statement of their movement's beliefs, an analysis of how the world became as it was, and a guide for change. Communism evolved from a 'spectre haunting Europe' – disparate ideas, defined more by its opponents than its proponents – into a coherent political project. It paved the way for an extraordinary era of change, of liberation and new oppression, democratisation and disaster, whose consequences are still playing out.

Almost 200 years later, again we're on a knife's edge.

With insurrection in the Capitol, armed white-supremacist parades and mass racial justice uprisings in the USA, with Brexit and nationalist authoritarianism tearing Europe apart, political certainties are collapsing. People don't believe that existing governing systems are working – according to one reputable analysis, confidence in democracy in Australia plunged from 86 per cent in 2007 to 41 per cent in 2018.[3] Amazon's Jeff Bezos has accumulated a grotesque $200 billion while his workers are peeing in bottles to avoid unpaid toilet breaks. Social, economic and racial injustices are bursting to the surface, most powerfully through the Movement for Black Lives (M4BL). The epidemics of loneliness and mental illness, and the widely held view that our labour is meaningless, show alienation plumbing new depths.[4] Above it all looms ecological collapse – fires and floods, polluted air and water, the deaths of rivers and extinction of species – an ever-present threat intersecting with all the others, and making them worse, more urgent, and harder to tackle.

Just as the mid 19th century was a crucible for extraordinary social, political and economic innovations, now around the planet countless people, communities and organisations are experimenting with living democracy. As we'll explore through Part 2, people are rediscovering old forms of collective decision-making and inventing new ones; we're sharing, caring and repairing, finding ways to avoid and subvert the economic system that treats the land we walk on, the water we drink, and our very bodies as resources to extract value from; we're developing creative, peaceful ways of looking out for each other instead of submitting to state coercion; and we're reclaiming land in cities for food, for flora and fauna, and for having fun together. We're learning anew that through cooperating, constructive contestation, and embracing coexistence, we can all live better, healthier, happier lives.

And yet the political movement we need in order to bring the alternatives from the margins into the majority, to replace the systems that are destroying life with ones that cultivate life, is disparate and divided, defined more by those trying to stop it than by those building it. Too often, we're fighting separate fights against separate problems.

That's why we need an ecological many-festo.

A manifesto is, literally, about making something manifest – making it clear.

Manifestos usually present a homogenised, pasteurised,

one-size-fits-all approach: follow this path or you surely will be lost. This 'many-festo' intends instead to offer an array of paths to manifest a different way of seeing and being in the world, and helping you find your own way.

Playing with the word like this underscores the inter-sectional nature of this project;[5] whether you come to this primarily concerned about the climate crisis or racism, economic injustice or sexism, the rise of authoritarianism or simply with a sense of unease about the state of the world, what I hope will become clear is that they all stem from the same root. Each of our struggles is the same struggle, each destruction – of lives, of forests, of communities – is the same destruction, manifest-ing in different ways. Each extraction of value – from the land, from our bodies, from our minds – is the same extraction. And our tasks in addressing these injustices and cultivating a better world are, at their core, the same task, to be put into action in myriad diverse, intersecting, complementary ways – the task of living democracy.

That's also why I've used the indefinite article 'an', with a nod to Ursula Le Guin, in my view one of the 20th century's most underrated political philosophers. Just as her *A Wizard of Earthsea* implies that there are many wizards, many stories, this book presents one approach to contribute to the larger whole.

Then there's 'ecological'.

Where the word 'capitalist' signifies a political system guided by the accumulation and control of wealth, and 'socialist' implies a prioritisation of collective human society, the word 'ecological' conjures a political philosophy emerging from and valuing living systems.

Such an approach seeks to ensure the ongoing health of

the natural world. And surely that must be at the core of any politics that wants a future.

More profoundly, it recognises that we, and everything we have ever made, from communities to cities, cellos to computer chips, are part of the natural world, inextricably intertwined and interdependent with every other part. We're not just individuals in constant competition for resources. Neither are we a uniform collective with individuality erased. Ecology implies a politics of and for interdependent individuals, coexisting as part of an interconnected whole.

Deepest of all, it's a system of governance that learns from ecology, and which is designed around ecology's principles and metaphors.

Before we dig into detail, living democracy needs ecology to be made manifest.

Let's give that a go.

# WHAT ON EARTH
# IS 'ECOLOGY'?

Ecology is life.[1]

Ecology is the birds, the bees, the bushes, the bugs in the soil, the burrowing beasts, the burbling babies of human beings, the bugs in the bellies of the beasts which help them digest the remains of the birds and expel the nutrients which nourish the bushes, whose flowers are pollinated by the bees, and whose fruit the birds eat, expelling the seeds further up the mountain as they fly, enabling the bushes to grow higher up as the climate warms because humans have cut down so many trees and burned the metamorphosed remains of so many ancient buried bushes and beasts.

Ecology is the whole and its parts and the connections between them and the patterns they make as they connect and reconnect, from the smallest microbe, made up of even smaller atoms, to the whole lifeform of the biosphere itself, which ecological philosopher Timothy Morton defines as 'a total system of interactions between lifeforms and their habitats (which are mostly just other lifeforms) ... a network of relations between beings ... that is an entity in its very own right'.[2]

Ecology is the complex adaptive system of life itself as well as of each individual and recombinant being which is part of the web of life. You are an ecosystem, a complex adaptive system made up of countless lifeforms, changing as you eat and breathe. I, too, am an ecosystem, and as you read these words the ecology of me meets and interacts with the ecology of you, and the coffee I drank years ago is now stimulating your metabolism, altering your appetite and your mood such that, who knows, you may decide to set up a veggie patch, join a renewable energy cooperative, or run for parliament.

Ecology is coexistence; it's cooperation and competition combining in complexity which isn't always comfortable. Ecology is interdependence, the health of the whole and its constituent parts dependent on the others, and the connections between them. Ecology is ambiguity, even contradiction; it looks different depending on which direction you're observing it from and where you think its edges lie. Ecology is ephemeral; point to it and, like the whale breaching or the sea eagle diving, it's moved on before you can exhale. In ecology, the only thing that stays the same is change.

So far so poetic. But what does this mean for our manyfesto?

After much discussion with ecologists, I think we can distil these ideas into three words to help us conceptualise living democracy: interdependence, diversity and impermanence. We'll keep returning to these words, so it's worth teasing them out a little to see if we can make something manifest.

## Interdependence:
## Everything is connected

In ecology, everything is connected. But not like replaceable cogs in a machine, pieced together in a given order. In ecological interdependence, the parts are as meaningful as the whole. Each part is a whole and each whole a part, connecting and reconnecting with every other.

Whether it's bees pollinating trees, or those trees drawing in the carbon dioxide we exhale and expelling the oxygen we inhale, or mycelia and microbes mobilising the nutrients and minerals in the soil, feeding the trees and connecting them to each other, none could survive without each other. We powerful humans can be felled by mosquitos or micro-organisms before being digested by mushrooms. Complex, multi-directional interdependence is what makes systems resilient.

Consider what this means for relations of power in human society.

We can replace hierarchy with horizontality; instead of seeking to dominate each other, people cooperate and contest across society. We can drop both atomised individualism and centralised control and build relational coexistence. And we can uproot established social order of classes, castes and 'knowing your place', introducing instead recombinant social cohesion, 'knowing we belong'. In an ecological system, we all work together, equal and different, to co-create our common future.

This, in turn, has implications for how we make decisions. True interdependence needs deep democracy, based on mutual trust, where everyone can take part. We'll dig deep into participatory practices throughout the book, looking at how to make them work, and how doing them well creates better outcomes.

We can learn from evolution here. But not the old-school idea of pure individual competition, red in tooth and claw. Evolution is increasingly understood as group selection; species, communities and ecosystems evolve together, forming niches and networks, and it's at this group level that fitness for survival is most relevant. Being altruistic might disadvantage you against someone domineering at a purely individual level (against a playground bully or a sociopathic CEO), but cooperation makes the whole group more likely to survive.

Charles Darwin himself wrote of how 'those communities which included the greatest number of the most sympathetic members would flourish best, and rear the greatest number of offspring'.[3] A politics built around group selection has institutions that support and enable people and communities to find their own way together, guided by norms which emphasise stewardship – the recognition that we are responsible for each other, for all other beings, and for future generations.

Can this work at scale, beyond small and local? Well, ecosystems operate at every level from your gut microbiome to continents, from catchments to the whole planetary system, with constant inter-relation between them. If we're to replicate this in democracy, the challenge of scale is one of effective interconnection.

## Diversity:
## Thinking differently about difference

In ecological interdependence, we still have walls that separate us. But we need to reimagine the walls as permeable, changeable, cell walls rather than the concrete walls of a prison cell.

Consider your skin. It's the boundary of your body. And it's permeable in both directions. And that boundary is also the habitat for whole ecosystems of other creatures coexisting with you.

Ecosystems, populations and species are all more resilient with greater diversity. Unlike authoritarian forms of collectivism, then, ecological interdependence doesn't want us goose-stepping in formation, reciting pledges of allegiance, worshipping at the same altar, reporting on our neighbours' aberrant behaviour. It *needs* diversity.

But diversity in ecology requires us to think differently about difference. As Timothy Morton explains, 'it's obvious that a slug is different from a panda. But it's different in the way that a distant family member is different; not different in the sense of black vs white, or here vs there, or good vs bad'.[4] The same goes for other humans with different skin colour, languages, or opinions.

This has tremendous implications for how we live democracy.

Neither seeking to erase differences between people, nor dividing us on the basis of those differences, nor even encouraging 'toleration' of difference, ecological politics embodies coexistence. If our fitness for survival operates at the group level more than the individual, we're all better off when we work out how to live together well. Just as 'toleration' implies that we cannot tolerate intolerance, interdependent diversity means that we respect all differences except the refusal to respect difference. Weaponising difference extinguishes the interconnection, the information flows, the multiplicity of voices and testing of ideas that we need for group level fitness. Ecology, then, implies equality of opportunity while accounting for both historical wrongs and the multitude of ways people participate.

What does this mean for how we make decisions? Instead of adversarial models – combatants seeking to defeat opponents, seeing compromise as weakness – we need to work constructively and creatively towards consensus. This doesn't mean everyone magically agrees! It's hard work, shifting the way we disagree towards respectful deliberation built on trust, with the aim of reaching a solution that everyone is okay with.

What about structures? Corporations or governments grown large and powerful are like monoculture crops planted over huge areas – incredibly unhealthy and fragile. The more centralised and dominating institutions are, the less responsive, responsible and resilient they become. This is why ecological politics is more attracted to decentralised, community ownership than to nationalisation and centralisation. As for the idea of a corporation 'too big to fail', the ecological reality is that growth is only beneficial up to a point. Anything grown too big is ultimately destined to fail.

Together, interdependence and diversity create complexity.

Consider doing a multiple-choice survey. How often do you feel you'd give one answer in some circumstances and another in others? How much more frustrating when it's bureaucracy which, however well-meaning, is standing in the way of good outcomes? There's a tension between the reality of complexity and the desire of our culture to simplify. Ecological governance means respecting complexity, uncertainty and ambiguity. It requires replacing simplistic solutions to specific problems with systemic approaches that recognise a plurality of issues, causes and solutions, to be finessed by each community. Instead of the single-minded focus on efficiency, it understands the need for redundancy and the imperative to let go of control. It shifts us from democracy as machine to living democracy.

## Impermanence: Change is the only constant

Change is reality. Seeking to stop it, or standing still in the face of it, is a recipe for disaster. From trilobites to triceratops, the geological record is littered with examples of species that were unable to survive as circumstances changed.

The more we humans have sought to control the world, the more we've come to dangerously insist on permanence. This has led to the Thatcherist claim that 'There Is No Alternative' and constant calls from business lobbyists for 'certainty', but also to ideas of constitutionalism and utopianism, both of which imply a permanent, perfect state. The ecological recognition of impermanence liberates us from the chains of the status quo, but it's challenging to give up our belief that anything – social norms, institutional structures, towering statues, continent-spanning forests – will last forever.

The lesson for politics, especially now, is to cultivate adaptable, resilient systems which can enable us to ride the waves of change in ways that improve lives. We need systems which can help us facilitate industrial transition from fossil fuels to renewable energy, which can guide urban development in a changing climate, and can bring us together as social norms change and as millions of people are forced to relocate.

Fundamentally, we have to recognise that government and economy are no more than tools that we invented and can reinvent; institutions and even constitutions need to transform, both to keep up with changing circumstances, and because successive generations will be well advised to revisit them to evolve their own models of trust. And, vitally, not just over generations. Every system of governance needs constant feedback and readjustment – which brings us back to interdependence and diversity. The more interconnected and diverse a system is, the better its feedback systems will be and the better it's able to manage change.

We also need to relearn not just *that* change happens but *how* change happens. We've already discussed how the stories we've been told about evolution being a bloody battle for survival don't reflect reality. Neither do the ideas of linear, incremental change and clear cause and effect we find comfortable in our predictable Newtonian world. There are crucial lessons here for how we govern, and how we work for change.

Individuals, species and ecosystems evolve together in ways that are mutually or reciprocally beneficial, with cooperation at least as important as competition. This happens between as well as within species. Thanks to biologist Lynn Margulis, we know that eukaryotic cells – the basic building blocks of all multicellular life on Earth – are the product of symbiotic coevolution between separate living entities, merging so as to bring their specific abilities together, compensate for each other's weaknesses, and find new niches. The same process led to the coevolution of humans and our microbiomes – a complex array of organisms which cannot survive without us and without which we cannot survive. We see this in spectacular rainforests and reefs, where countless species – predator and prey, habitat and inhabitant – evolved to coexist for mutual benefit; and we see it in less fertile areas, where survival is more tenuous. It's there that we see more starkly that too much competitive behaviour is harmful to everyone's interests: if one species outcompetes others to the extent that it substantially reduces the diversity of the system, it undermines its own capacity to survive along with all others'. The adaptive cycles of this process create the tendency towards equilibrium in ecosystems.

But what we see in ecosystems is a dynamic, punctuated equilibrium. Things change; and when change happens, it can happen fast. This is a factor of the multi-layered complexity of systems, as we'll explore in Part 3. One level of a system can be relatively stable while another changes, leading to a tipping point, a non-linear change known as a trophic cascade. Consider a waterway where the slow, incremental removal of fish has no noticeable impact on the system at large until suddenly it triggers an algal bloom with devastating effects. Or how a human body can effectively fight an infection until it is overcome, leading to cascading organ failure. Cascades also run upwards. Famously, the reintroduction of wolves to Yellowstone National Park triggered a spectacular and rapid flourishing; the wolves reduced the population of grazing animals, which enabled more young trees to grow, which attracted more diverse birdlife and reduced erosion on the banks of rivers and streams, supporting healthier aquatic life.

Analogously, growing discontent in a society due to economic inequality can be managed effectively when feedback to a governing class leads to stabilising reforms. However, if such feedback is ignored or stifled, it can explode, triggering revolution or violent suppression (or both). Conversely, increasing support for a cause, like marriage equality, can seem impossible to implement politically until, suddenly, the change becomes inevitable.

The recognition of impermanence means we need to manage the relationship between stability and change. And that means managing systems instead of just their parts, learning to find the points of intervention that will create the possibility of the changes we need. As the great systems thinker, Donella Meadows, articulated, seeking to control individual elements of a system will frequently make matters worse; we have to shift the paradigms and power structures of the system.[5]

Ecology teaches us that change emerges from context. So we can see our task as cultivating the right context for the outcomes we need to emerge. In a way, cultivating the context is all there is. Just as there's no end point to evolution, there's no final political outcome. The journey is the destination. Our task is to cultivate the best possible context for a diverse, interdependent society to evolve, continually readjusting based on feedback from our interdependent and diverse networks.

## It's alive!

Living democracy is a living practice.

Through practical projects and protest, electoral politics and new modes of democratic and economic participation, neighbourhood groups and communities of interest, all working towards better ways of living, we can cultivate the circumstances for the world we need to emerge extraordinarily rapidly.

It starts with a shift in mindset, understanding democracy as the living extension of our lives. It develops through a practice of living well together. It institutionalises by rewarding and encouraging our best instincts instead of our worst.

I'm convinced, from decades of observation and experience as well as studying an immense body of research, that these are practices we humans feel in our guts. We crave connection and agency. We resent not being allowed to participate or contribute. We hate feeling shut out or railroaded. We thrive when we play an active part in something bigger than ourselves.

A key moment of realisation for me came when, having spent six years working as an adviser in the federal parliament, one of the first things I did after stepping down was set up a local sharing group for people to offer things they no longer need or ask for things they want and would rather not (or couldn't afford to) buy. Within weeks, the group was flourishing, and people across my community with dramatically different life experiences and worldviews were expressing delight at this fantastic, non-transactional, cooperative, friendly practice. While I learned an inordinate amount working for the legendary Senator Christine Milne, and believe I contributed to real, positive change, the sense of joyous achievement I got from establishing the Buy Nothing group eclipsed all of it.

This is what it is to live democracy. The way people's faces light up when sharing home-grown, home-cooked food. The way we spark together when marching and chanting as part of a protest crowd. The bone-weary contentment at the end of a day with friends planting trees or tending a garden. The way we glow when having a great conversation, building off each other's ideas, finding solutions we can all be satisfied with. The energy buzzing in a participatory planning session, people leaping out of their seats with excitement to scrawl ideas on a sheet of paper, nodding vigorously, eyes shining. The inexpressible joy and relief in the voice of an elderly neighbour calling to thank you for dropping a message in their letterbox offering support during pandemic lockdown.

This is what it is to be a member of society, one special part of an unimaginably complex whole, listening to, respecting and coexisting with all that surrounds us, building trust and cohesion. This is what we humans do.

But, starkly, it's not how our systems of government and economics work today.

Why not? How did our systems come to stray so far from this ecological approach we instinctively love?

The ecological perspective gives us a lens through which to see the world as it is run now as anti-ecological. It gives us the tools to see how our governing systems have been built on foundations of disconnection (from each other and the natural world), domination (of each other and the natural world) and the illusion of permanence.

One thing's for certain: we can't tackle the crises we face through existing anti-ecological systems. If we're to survive and thrive in the decades ahead we need deep, systemic change. Next we'll skip through millennia of history and thought to see why this evolution is so critical.

Ready?

# THE EVOLUTION OF ANTI-ECOLOGY

Sixteenth and 17th century England must have felt like the world had turned upside down.[1]

Devastating waves of plague, which had killed over a third of the population in some of its deadliest outbreaks over previous generations, repeatedly swept the country. Compounding this, traumatised communities faced frequent food and labour shortages, huge economic and industrial transformations, and extraordinary socio-political changes as people challenged religious and feudal power.

Peasants revolted, demanding more rights. The expansion of the wool and cloth trade drove people into cities as the land they had worked in common for centuries was enclosed for large-scale agriculture and sheep grazing. Forests were cleared and fens drained. 'New worlds' suddenly appeared over the horizon. Democratic religious and political ideas spread like wildfire, aided by social mobility and the printing press. Communities launched local utopias, and civil war and unrest wracked the country. Revolts turned into revolution – the king was executed!

This world birthed three men whose ideas cast long shadows, accelerating and strengthening the anti-ecological culture of separation and domination that had been simmering for millennia and was soon to boil over.

There's no doubt Francis Bacon, Thomas Hobbes and John Locke helped shape some of the positive aspects of today's world. But they also contributed to its darkest.

For Hobbes, horrified by the English civil war, the world was a fearful place. He believed that people will naturally fight among themselves in a 'war of all against all' unless they submit to a powerful state. This concept of the 'Leviathan' influenced the growing political philosophy underpinning the secular state – an entity that no longer derives its power from divine right, but remains separate from the citizens it rules. Hobbes' conviction that human nature is entirely individualistic is encapsulated in his famous statement that life in the 'state of nature' was 'solitary, poor, nasty, brutish and short'.[2]

Locke was less pessimistic, believing human nature to be governed by reason and tolerance, and his rational individualism was immensely influential in the revolutions and reforms that saw the rapid rise of liberal democracy. But where Hobbes drove thinking towards domination, Locke embedded disconnection into political theory. He focussed on individual liberty at the expense of interdependence, with each other and the natural world. Writing that 'people must become effectively emancipated from the bonds of nature', and 'land that is left wholly to nature ... is called, as indeed it is, waste',[3] Locke provided the philosophical justification for the enclosure and wholesale destruction of the natural world that early industrialism was already triggering, as well as for the colonisation and genocide of peoples who didn't work the land in the same way as Europeans did.

Locke was influenced by Bacon, who is considered the father of the scientific method. But Bacon's vital ideas are embedded in a worldview of extreme separation and domination: 'I am come in very truth leading you to Nature with all her children to bind her to your service and make her your slave ... Nature must be taken by the forelock',[4] he wrote, explicitly linking patriarchy, colonialism and the rape of nature.

These ideas form the cornerstone of what I call anti-ecological culture. This isn't simply behaviour destructive of the natural world; it's the worldview, the pervasive network of ideas of who we are and how we relate to one another, which drives this destructive behaviour, and which makes ecologically sound behaviour unimaginable.

If ecology is characterised by interdependence, diversity and impermanence, anti-ecology is defined by disconnection, domination, and the pretence of permanence. It starts by separating 'man' from 'nature', 'man' from 'woman', 'white man' from 'other', defining each as a binary, and establishing a relationship of dominance. It becomes the white man's 'burden' to subdue the 'other', including women, colonised peoples, and nature. Separating 'us' from an objectified 'them', anti-ecological culture erases the respectful 'we/ they' interdependence, depicting us as fundamentally selfish individuals in constant competition. Anti-ecology sees land, plants, animals, and even other humans, as resources to be owned and from which to extract value. Refusing to accept limits to extraction, it invents the myth of eternal growth. It replaces a complex adaptive system with a simple machine, creating a mechanistic, deterministic mode of thought, valuing efficiency and disdaining uncertainty. By unleashing competition and driving expansion, it ironically leads to homogenisation, erasing difference by creating monocultures.

If this is our story, no wonder white supremacy, violence against women, homophobia and transphobia, economic inequality and environmental devastation developed.

But this wasn't always the story we told about ourselves. It's not a 'state of nature'. It evolved, in fits and starts, in tension with more ecological stories, over millennia, through the interaction between material circumstances, behaviour and ideas.

Remember, evolution emerges from context – from circumstances and behaviour; living things find niches to inhabit and, in doing so, shape and reshape the world around them. We humans, as a highly social and perhaps uniquely imaginative species, add the layer of ideas, of culture, to circumstances and behaviour. Culture improves our ability to find niches, and reshapes the world in its image. Our mythologies, creation stories and beliefs embed social norms, impose acceptable behaviours, guide the way we relate to one another and, in so doing, change the material reality of our world. They are crucial to establishing and sustaining the institutions and relations of power by which we govern ourselves, determining things like who can do what to whom, what gets built and what dismantled, and whose voices are heard. Historian Yuval Noah Harari articulates this beautifully in his book *Sapiens*:

> Much of history revolves around this question: how
> does one convince millions of people to believe
> particular stories about gods, or nations, or limited

liability companies? ... Just imagine how difficult it
would have been to create States, or churches, or legal
systems if we could only speak about things that really
exist, such as rivers, trees or lions? ... As time went by,
the imagined reality became ever more powerful, so that
today the very survival of rivers, trees and lions depends
on the grace of imagined entities such as gods, nations
and corporations.[5]

This isn't a new idea. Antonio Gramsci, an early 20th century
political philosopher who we'll return to in Part 3, wrote of
how political power is a combination of institutional and
cultural power, where control of institutions – parliaments,
executive government, police and military, big business –
exists in interplay with control of the political common sense
– shared understandings of the world. Influential stories
of how the world is and where we belong in it – stories like
those Bacon, Hobbes and Locke told – are central to power
and change. They're how the 1 per cent maintains control over
the 99 per cent without having to resort to violent coercion
of the majority most of the time: through mythologies of a
'natural order', reinforced by enough of a show of force against
a minority frequently enough to remind everyone of the
consequences of noncompliance.

Culture, by informing our actions, shapes material reality,
which informs and shapes culture. How we believe we can act
influences how we act, and vice versa.

We'll explore this much more in Part 3, but in the
meantime consider this in one life. I was brought up by refugee
parents who, having become relatively affluent in Australia,
encouraged and supported my passions for music and nature.

From music, I learned about the rules of harmony, and when to bend them; about how the whole becomes greater than the sum of its parts when we listen to each other; about transcendence, in those moments when you lift out of yourself and melt into the greater-than-human. In the bush, I learned how fallen trees, decomposing on the forest floor, nurture new life, providing homes and food for birds, mammals, insects and fungi, and a cradle for new forest giants to emerge. Stumbling across sunbathing snakes, I learned to look and listen as I walked respectfully in the world, to understand that another creature's wish not to be disturbed corresponds with my own wish not to be bitten. Staring across the snow-covered high country, into sparkling waters running through a canyon, into the vastness of the Milky Way, I found another lesson in transcendence. From my Holocaust-survivor grandparents, I learned how people in power in the most 'civilised' countries in the world have been responsible for unimaginable atrocities, while ordinary people do extraordinary things to help each other.

My worldviews were shaped by where we lived, our socio-economic status, the activities I took part in, the things others did around me, and the stories I was told about those who came before me. Those worldviews shaped my actions, which shaped my worldviews.

At the societal level, what's possible can be fashioned by the actions of powerful people and by mass grassroots movements, by cultural leaders like writers and artists, and by external factors such as fires and pandemics. Through contemplating the world Bacon, Hobbes and Locke lived in – plague, enclosure, industrialisation, political and religious upheaval, colonisation – we see how they were moulded by their circumstances, and how the ideas they contributed shaped the anti-ecological

WHERE ARE WE COMING FROM?

culture of disconnection and domination that accelerated in their wake.

To trace the evolution of this culture, and come to appreciate that we have to make change at a deep level if we're to survive, we have to acknowledge that this was not always the way we thought.

## 'Country owns us': Indigenous democracy and the commons

> Emu is a troublemaker who brings into being the most destructive idea in existence: I am greater than you; you are less than me. This is the source of all human misery. Aboriginal society was designed over thousands of years to deal with this problem ... [using] massive checks and balances to contain the damage it can do. ... All Law-breaking comes from that first evil thought, that original sin of placing yourself above the land or above other people.[6]

This is how Tyson Yunkaporta, in his book *Sand Talk: How Indigenous thinking can save the world*, described how Indigenous cultures institutionally suppress anti-ecological thinking. They acknowledge that humans are complex, and that the egocentric tendency towards disconnection and domination exists in all of us alongside our instinct for mutual aid. So, in a strategy replicated the world over, in a tremendous array of different structures and approaches, they work to contain the will to domination.

For the vast majority of our existence, humans have

understood our place as part of nature. This is not to say that we didn't always have an impact. Like every living organism, we are niche builders. Birds build nests; wombats dig burrows; trees grow seed pods that use fire to open them; insects burrowing into trees mobilise sugars which attract birds, which eat and distribute seeds, which grow to attract grazing animals, all of them co-evolving to fit their niches. There's no such thing as non-disturbance, no way of living in an ecosystem and not having an impact on it.

Uniquely, as far as we know, humans developed a consciousness which enabled us to recognise this interdependence. And, having recognised it, we could cultivate cultures which learned to live respecting interdependence, seeking to prolong our healthy coexistence by suppressing our worst instincts and supporting our best, actively institutionalising group selection over individual competition.

The continent we now call Australia is home to the oldest continuous human cultures on Earth. We have the opportunity to listen to peoples who, through cycles of disturbance and disruption, developed ways of living sustainably and peacefully for countless millennia. It's been my immense privilege to learn from a number of brilliant Indigenous thinkers. As I scratch the surface of their lessons about living ecologically, I emphasise that any errors are mine, and I acknowledge that their cultural ownership in these ideas persists, but that they want us to learn from them.

The central concept is that 'country owns us'.

The idea at the core of modern political economy – that we can and should own land and seek to control it – is anathema to Indigenous cultures. People and the land exist in a complex pattern of relationships, where rivers, animals, locations, are literally family members. Certain people might hold stewardship responsibility for parts of country – a river bend, a species of animal or plant – but it's a mutual caring relationship, like being an aunt or grandchild, and in no way possession. This understanding of where we belong in the interconnected world underpins the structure of Aboriginal society.

As Dr Mary Graham, a Kombumerri and Wakka Wakka woman and brilliant comparative political philosopher, has articulated it, 'the land is the law':

> The two most important kinds of relationship in life are, firstly, those between land and people and, secondly, those amongst people themselves, the second being always contingent upon the first. The land, and how we treat it, is what determines our human-ness. Because land is sacred and must be looked after, the relation between people and land becomes the template for society and social relations.[7]

What becomes clear (remember: think differently about difference) is that there is both a distinction between people and land *and* a blurring of that distinction. Where anti-ecological culture divides the world into 'me' and 'other', 'human' and 'nature', 'individual' or 'collective', Indigenous culture springs from the ecological recognition that we are all interdependent autonomous beings.

I learned the most beautiful encapsulation of that from Megan Williams, a Wiradjuri woman and assistant director of the National Centre for Cultural Competence at Sydney University. Williams shared the Wiradjuri word *wundirra* which means 'standing in one's own light' and moving forward in life from there. It conveys 'I am in my light, I have my part to play, and it's connected to your part'.[8]

Dr Tjanara Goreng Goreng, a Wakka Wakka and Wulli Wulli woman and founding secretary of the Australian Greens First Nations Network, set out this principle of autonomy within interdependence in her explanation of Aboriginal governance: 'Decisions are not made for the individual but are communal, and community is considered above the individual need; however individual growth in the law is important as we become "boss of ourselves", spiritually and culturally.' There are, she explained, three laws of respect: 'respect and honour the self; respect and honour everyone else; respect and honour Ngungynateea, our mother, the Earth'.[9]

There's a constructive tension that Yunkaporta has pointed out between the determined autonomy in the common phrase 'nobody boss for me' and the deep understanding of 'relatedness and communal obligation'. This translates into culture, philosophy and institutions. 'Indigenous models of governance are based on respect for social, ecological and knowledge systems and all their components or members ... The whole is intelligent, and each part carries the inherent intelligence of the entire system.'[10] The institutionalisation of interdependence goes for interpersonal relationships within groups and for intergroup relationships. Skin groups and language groups are different, but not separate, relational not hierarchical.

Goreng Goreng has told me there's no relevance of the idea of straight lines, in time or in space. Both follow the curves of hills and rivers, the cycles of seasons, with no beginning and no end. The intergenerational responsibility entailed in this worldview is reflected in every Indigenous culture, as well as

Taoism, Hinduism and essentially every culture until very recently. With this view of time, the anti-ecological urge for 'efficiency' is nonsense. Kate Harriden, a Wiradjuri woman at the Australian National University's Fenner School of Ecology, explained to me that the word *yindyamarra* means both respect and going slowly. The language conveys that being respectful means taking time.

Both Goreng Goreng and Graham have emphasised that these practices are laws, not just traditions or 'lore'. They entail binding obligations, embedded in culture, language and institutions. But they don't exist within a state, within Hobbes' Leviathan where people are subservient to a common power. From that perspective, Indigenous communities co-governed in this way exist in what Hobbes would call a 'state of nature'. And they were treated as such by colonisers, in declaring the land to be *terra nullius*: if you don't govern yourselves in a manner we can call a state, you don't exist.

The consequences of this are laid out in Bruce Pascoe's *Dark Emu*.[11] Pascoe hasn't just exposed the lies of *terra nullius*, detailing the extensive evidence of a complex, continent-wide culture. He also revealed the deliberate erasure of this culture, with evidence scrubbed from official records and history books. In order to avoid having to treat with Aboriginal peoples as sovereign, or accept evidence of a different way of living being successful, the colonisers engaged in one of the most thorough genocides in history, trying (and failing) to erase both the people and any knowledge of their culture.

Here's something else that has been erased: all human communities have, for most of our history, lived as Indigenous peoples do, with a rich understanding of ourselves as complex creatures living as part of a complex world, evolving various systems of governance to manage that interdependence. Some have been more hierarchical and others more egalitarian; some more aggressive and others more peaceful. But Graham, Pascoe and others described a system like countless others that operated, and continues to operate around the globe at the margins of dominating and colonising cultures everywhere: the commons.

We'll discuss commons governance throughout the course of this book, and one of our main guides will be Elinor Ostrom, the first woman to win a Nobel Prize for Economics. It's a concept that has been drastically misrepresented, so it's vital that we take the time to understand it.

The commons is often represented as a field where anyone can graze their cattle. In fact, it's the field, and the cows, and the people, and the ways in which the people come together to manage it all. Commons involve clear rules, boundaries, conflict resolution processes and sanctions for breaches, all developed democratically by the participants. Like ecosystems, commons are highly organised, but it's a dynamic self-organisation, not an unbending set of rules imposed from above.

Ostrom undertook detailed research with Indigenous, peasant and modern communities around the globe, through which she developed a set of principles that underpin every successful long-term project to jointly steward 'common pool resources'. Commons governance, she identified, is all about institutionalising interdependence; it requires mutual trust, open communication, and respect for limits; it necessitates involving all those who agree to be bound by rules in the process of setting them; and it's a system of shared custodianship of land and resources, not of property.

As Ostrom and the researchers who followed her have

shown, we all have the capacity to do this. Communities around the globe have held to these ideas since time immemorial through to the present day, developing similar systems of governance as the only model that can enable survival without endless expansion.

Those last three words – 'without endless expansion' – launch the evolution of anti-ecology. Once you take more than you put back, you launch yourself down a very slippery slope. The only choice is to enclose and extract value from ever more land, ever more people. And once you start the material process of enclosure, you have to shape culture in that image to maintain control.

Recorded history can be read as a struggle between cultivation of and enclosure of the commons. The enclosure stretches from the first city states, through the brutality of the Highland Clearances, the Irish Famine, and the industrial urbanisation of Europe, to appalling acts of colonialism and genocide on every inhabited continent. It continues to this day, with public parks sold to developers and streets to advertisers, hostile architecture used to exclude homeless people from public space, and the privatisation of the online world. It severs interdependence with each other and the natural world, destroying trust, extracting value. And, always and ever, it faces resistance. Always and ever, commons persist.

The rise of anti-ecological culture isn't some dastardly plot by evil geniuses. Nor is it some inevitable trajectory of progress. It's an uncertain, erratic, evolutionary process that feeds on ideas of separation and dominance which have always existed as one element in us, but which communities repeatedly developed sophisticated cultures and institutions to keep in check. The problem arises when the constraints are reversed, creating a system that rewards rather than suppresses our destructive impulses.

Various stories, from Pandora's box and the expulsion from Eden to theories about farming grains, explain this as a simple 'fall from grace'. It's far more complex than that. As the late, great anthropologist David Graeber and his colleague archaeologist David Wengrow have put it, 'human history is ... more full of playful possibilities than we tend to assume'.[12] They've detailed numerous social models that humans have developed, including agriculture without hierarchies or private property, and dominating hierarchies without agriculture; enormous networks of non-urban settlements stretching across vast areas; and even large non-hierarchical urban communities without authoritarian or bureaucratic control.

For millennia, we moved in and out of these different models, exploring options, experimenting with how to balance autonomy and interdependence, 'assembling and disassembling hierarchies on a regular basis'.[13] But then, somehow, we got stuck in one with the settings jammed in the wrong direction. How?

The most plausible explanation starts with the slow, unsteady appearance of city states, where people for the first time were made subservient to a common power, beginning around 5500 years ago, but only getting a firm foothold as recently as 3000 years ago, setting off a self-reinforcing cycle of expansion.

## City states and god kings: Enclosure begins

People kept running away.

All over the world at various times, individuals and small groups of people have tried to dominate their communities. Sometimes they've succeeded. Using violence and fear to control people, these proto-Trumps built walls both to keep others out and to make those inside subservient. But people kept resisting.

Anthropologist James C Scott, who specialises in the history of agrarian communities, examined archaeological and historical records and found that early city states lasted a handful of generations at most before they collapsed, and people returned to commons-based lives. It took 100 generations of repeated growth and collapse for this hierarchical structure that we think of as obvious 'progress' to become entrenched.

The thing is, we humans don't like being controlled. On the occasions when hierarchical city states arose, as Scott has uncovered, there is 'massive evidence of determined resistance'.[14] Early legal codes such as Hammurabi's were overwhelmingly 'preoccupied with escapees and runaways and the effort to return them to their designated work and residence'.[15] Coercion bred more coercion.

And enclosure bred more enclosure. The crops farmed within and just outside city walls needed to be carefully tended to control what became known as 'weeds', increasing time spent on labour, and distinguishing 'man'-made simplicity from complex nature. The rulers discovered that, thanks to their regular planting and harvesting seasons, monocultures made taxation and population management easier.

But forcing people and animals into closer proximity and reducing nutritional diversity led to sickness, shortened lifespans and increased child mortality. Intensive farming and logging depleted soils and caused erosion, making land and food systems less resilient. So city states needed to constantly expand in order to enclose more people for labour and more land for farming.

When you take more than you put back, the need to expand arises. This becomes self-perpetuating ... and creates the conditions for its own destruction, pushing against limits and stimulating opposition.

Rulers soon learned that expansion can suppress opposition by reducing people's alternatives. Agricultural economist Ester Boserup put this in terms that we will return to repeatedly: 'when ... land can be controlled it becomes unnecessary to keep the lower classes in bondage; it is sufficient to deprive the working class of the right to be independent cultivators'.[16] A favourite strategy was razing forests and salting the earth, destroying the possibility of self-provisioning and making conquered peoples reliant on trade with (and indebted to) the imperial centre.

But, as the failure of early states shows, internal control and external expansion are impossible to manage through coercion alone, because coercion always breeds resistance. It works better when cloaked in paternalistic language to convince those subservient within the walls that they're better off than those outside. In other words, states and their rulers needed to develop cultural as well as institutional control. The rulers learned to disparage those outside the walls as 'barbarian', beginning the transition from interdependent 'we/they' to anti-ecological 'us versus them', setting the precedent for nationalism and racism.

This is when animistic spirituality began to be replaced by god kings and anthropomorphic deities. Cultural values of interdependence were replaced by religions valuing subservience and disparaging non-believers. A cyclical understanding of time was replaced by the promise of a better hereafter (for the obedient), since life here and now was unpleasant. It was also marked by the appearance of patriarchal societies, correlating, as historians like Marija Gimbutas have noted, with the subjugation of women through constant child-bearing to counterbalance rising child mortality.

Driven by the cycle of expansion, and once they worked out how to effectively combine coercion and culture, city states grew into empires. In the Middle East, North Africa, China, India, Southern Europe and the Americas, empires rose ... and then fell, as they hit ecological and social limits and some form of commons governance was embraced again.

Wherever states appeared, commons practices, ethics of interdependence, continued, in some ways helping to stabilise growing empires, extending their capacity to grow by tempering individual selection with group selection. The Golden Rule in every institutional religion – some version of 'treat others as you would have them treat you' – helped people cooperate and work towards a common purpose, even if within subservience to a greater power and an 'us versus them' mentality towards other religions. Ancient Greek democracy bolted on some commons decision-making processes (although limited to adult male citizens) to an imperialist model, giving Athens an edge over its more authoritarian neighbours. Commons management of land under feudalism embedded within an authoritarian structure a degree of mutual responsibility between lord and serf, people and land, giving it greater resilience.

Then, after several thousand years, enclosure took off.

## The Great Transformation: Enclosure accelerates

Plague! Factories! Urbanisation! Revolution! Remember that period in Europe when Bacon, Hobbes and Locke wrote the political philosophy of disconnection and domination, depicting and directing what was happening around them?

This was the beginning of what Karl Polanyi called 'The Great Transformation'.[17]

Polanyi, a Hungarian Jewish economic historian who fled to England in the 1930s, studied the extraordinary changes through early modernity that enabled the world he found himself in – a world of capitalism, communism and fascism – to evolve. He described a process of 'disembedding', progressively removing all social, religious or moral constraints from the behaviour of the selfish individual.

Think about something like the impact on language, as people were increasingly forced off the land and into cities. We began to lose our very vocabularies of nature. How could we care about plants or animals at all, let alone as family members, if we never saw them, and couldn't even name them? Imagine the impact of this on our relationship with nature, especially when new fables, such as those of the Brothers Grimm, told us to be afraid of the forest, and the wild animals (and scary women) who lived in them.

Concurrently the Enlightenment's tremendous increase in scientific knowledge gave rise to the idea that the world is ultimately knowable and controllable. No doubt Enlightenment thinking brought us enormous benefits, but replacing respectful recognition of a complex living system with the model of a simple machine also caused major damage.

The author and activist Naomi Klein has suggested that our current crises find their roots in the 'core civilizational myths' of Enlightenment culture – 'myths about humanity's duty to dominate a natural world that is believed to be at once limitless and controllable'.[18] Ecological philosopher Wendell Berry wrote of how this 'machine civilisation' led to determinism and fatalism.

It disembedded us. It severed our interdependence. It replaced mutual trust with subservience or transactionalism. Institutionalising anti-ecology triggered a devastating feedback loop. Physical disconnection and domination fed cultural disconnection and domination, which fed more physical disconnection and domination.

Over just a few generations, vast tracts of forest were cleared; carefully managed commons were declared 'waste' and enclosed for private profit, forcing people into labour in the new factories; industrialism hardened social hierarchies of class, sex and race; and colonisation ran rampant, forging a path of slavery, genocide and environmental destruction across the globe. An unimaginable wealth transfer (theft of spices, cloth, timber, precious metals, human bodies and labour) from Africa, Asia, the Americas and eventually Australia to European elites created a comfortable middle class, and a working class that could look down on the colonised as lower even than them. Capitalism and class, racism and environmental destruction co-evolved, through dispossession, subjugation and slavery, first within Europe and then around the globe.[19]

People constantly resisted. In Europe, and in the colonies, protests, revolts and experiments with alternatives persisted. But the rate of enclosure and expansion across whole new continents, aided by the wealth it generated and appropriated and by the astonishing asymmetric coercive power of modern weaponry, saw much of that resistance violently suppressed and much of the rest co-opted into the growing culture of anti-ecology, enabling its expansion across the globe.

It's so telling that, just as the reality of the complex Australian Aboriginal cultures was erased by the invaders, the mainstream history of early modernity in Europe erases the complexity of the extraordinary contest of ideas that bubbled through the period. The array of truly radical thinking through peasants' rebellions, religious struggles and social upheaval as some people tried to reinstate commons practices while others fought over dominance is reduced to tales of simple fights between 'Great Men'. A deeper investigation shows the Reformation democratising religion, the Enlightenment democratising knowledge, revolutions democratising political power, each a predictable response to enclosure, and each response splintering between those seeking to seize power for themselves, those looking to develop new forms of power, and those wanting to dissolve dominating power altogether.

The English Revolution of the 1640s and '50s is an extraordinary example of this splintering, although we wouldn't know it from the history most of us were taught, boiling it down to Oliver Cromwell versus Charles I, parliament versus king, Protestant versus Catholic. The reality was so much more complex, with numerous groups working for different outcomes in 'revolt[s] within the Revolution'.[20]

While Cromwell and the royalists were fighting over the levers of power, radical groups like the Diggers, Ranters and Levellers were claiming parcels of land to build their utopias. Combining their anti-enclosure struggle with democratic readings of the Bible, opposing the authority of both king and parliament, they argued for and set about creating a world without top-down, coercive authority, with common ownership of land grounded in communal cultivation and decision-making. Informed by a pantheistic philosophy seeing god in everything and everyone, they identified that the enclosure project so enthusiastically embraced by both monarchy and parliament was designed to control both people and the natural world, turning them into a resource from which to extract value. Almost 400 years ago, the Digger Gerrard Winstanley saw enclosure as the cause of environmental disasters, writing that 'the risings up of waters and the breakings forth of fire to waste and destroy are but that curse, or the work of man's own hands that rise up and run together to destroy their maker'.[21]

Cromwell's forces defeated the Levellers. Then, after Cromwell's death, the monarchy was restored. But the ideas continued to evolve, opposing, tempering, being co-opted into and reinforcing anti-ecology. The radicals provided the seeds of socialism, communism and anarchism, while their democratisation of religion also evolved into hyper-individualistic theologies when co-opted by burgeoning American capitalism. The Cromwellians built the foundations for parliamentary liberal democracy, but it developed inter-twined with oppressive colonialism and industrial capitalism. Both contributed to the American primacy of 'life, liberty and the pursuit of happiness' – a declaration of independence, not interdependence.

In the brave new world of industrial capitalism, the material reality and cultural ideas of separation and domination led to a fetishisation of competition as the driver of all that is good. Through the Great Transformation's disembedding, a new 'state of nature' was declared: *homo economicus*, a purely selfish creature with nothing but the calculation of self-interest to guide him.

Capitalism arrived as the first social organising principle based on selfish individualism, the first system to make greed and non-cooperation its credo.

And it generated immense opposition.

## Revolution: Repeating enclosure differently

People gathered in public halls, coffee houses and theatres in Paris to discuss and debate how to manage their city together. Universal-access public schools were established. Factories were taken over and run cooperatively by their workers. Urban farms were dotted around the city, tended communally by people between work shifts elsewhere. Military conscription, the death penalty and child labour were abolished. A vibrant atmosphere of cooperative, creative democracy flared in the City of Light, shining around the globe as a beacon for 72 days.

In 1870, the Second French Empire had collapsed in disarray, having suffered a humiliating defeat in the Franco–Prussian War. While wealthy and powerful people made plans for a Third Republic, workers, soldiers and refugees gathered in Paris, under siege by the Prussian army, and set about establishing self-government. Building on a history of radical organising, the Paris Commune was established in March 1871, putting into practice the ideas of commoners and communists in one of the world's largest industrial cities. With no leader, with distributed decision-making among communities, and sending deputies to democratic coordinating councils, they created the modern world's first city-scale anarchy.

Here's another word we'd better define. Like the commons, anarchism has been misrepresented as disorganised chaos by those who benefit from domination. But 'an archy' means no rulers, *not* no rules. In fact, opposing all coercive power, anarchism must be highly organised. Like the commons, anarchism relies on democratically developed rules to cultivate interdependence, to support the relationships of mutual aid which form its basis. Anarchist societies like the Paris Commune, Indigenous societies, and others we'll explore through Part 2, need to be highly organised to ensure that every voice matters. Otherwise they end up as a libertarian mess – no rules, with everybody thinking they're a ruler.

In the mid 19th century, anarchism was one of several mainstream branches of anti-capitalism. With the Industrial Revolution and colonisation having created immense divides of wealth, class and power, this period bubbled with ideas and action, as the English Revolution had 200 years earlier. Some worked to temper the worst impacts of the system, organising workers to win basic rights and a share of profits, for example. Some worked towards a radical vision, underpinned by a different understanding of the world. Some sought power for themselves, co-opted or corrupted by anti-ecological culture.

The anarchist view of the world is a fundamentally ecological one, based on interdependence and diversity. Indeed, one of the leading anarchist thinkers, Piotr (Peter) Kropotkin, was a highly regarded natural scientist, studying evolution at the same time as Darwin, and seeing quite different drivers at play. Although Darwin recognised that cooperation can contribute to fitness for survival,[22] his theory is underpinned by competition, and it emerged just as anti-ecological separation and domination were becoming moral imperatives. So it's no surprise that his work was swiftly co-opted and twisted, thanks to the efforts of men like biologist Thomas Huxley, into poisonous ideas of social Darwinism and eugenics.

Kropotkin responded to this directly and deliberately by publishing detailed analyses of evolution as a process of mutual aid, whereby ecological communities co-evolve to improve the chances of their collective survival. His research, which informs current understandings of group selection and symbiosis, examined the 'instinct that has been slowly developed among animals and humans in the course of an extremely long evolution, and which has taught animals and humans alike the force they can borrow from the practice of mutual aid and support, and the joys they can find in social life'.[23] He translated this into social and political dynamics, articulating an evolutionary basis for:

> the unconscious recognition of the force that is borrowed by each person from the practice of mutual aid; of the close dependence of everyone's happiness upon the happiness of all; and of the sense of justice, or equity which brings the individual to consider the rights of every other individual as equal to their own.[24]

It was a world on this model that the Paris Communards were seeking to build. Tragically, although the Commune demonstrated the possibility of anarchist organising at city scale, it also highlighted the extraordinary danger of doing so amid forces of domination at the peak of their coercive and cultural power. Like the Diggers and Levellers two centuries earlier, like Indigenous societies around the globe facing colonial invaders, the Commune was brutally and ruthlessly destroyed by the forces of a Leviathan state. And its defeat and aftermath had enormous implications for what followed.

As Republican forces threatened Paris, the Commune was divided between those wanting to focus on their work of social and economic reorganisation and those insisting on the need to prioritise military defence. The military side won ... and then lost disastrously. And the schism went on to split the entire anti-capitalist movement.

Communists, including Karl Marx and Vladimir Lenin, saw the Commune's destruction as evidence of the need for strong centralised control to combat counter-revolution, and the anarchist wing of the movement was expelled or sidelined for objecting to this approach. The concept of the 'dictatorship of the proletariat' morphed from a metaphor into a horrible irony as a political movement based on opposing domination embraced it whole-heartedly. Half a century later, Kropotkin warned on his deathbed in 1921 that the Soviet revolution was playing out in this dangerous coercive way and therefore 'bound to end in failure'.[25] The same year, another influential anarchist, Emma Goldman, having been deported to the Soviet Union from the USA, left in disgust. Their warnings were ignored.

This is how anti-ecological communism arose, coming

to repeat enclosure in a different way. The fear of counter-revolution led to centralised authoritarian power, purges, neighbours encouraged to report on neighbours. Enforcing the collective at the expense of the individual eroded the interpersonal trust that's vital for any effective collective society in the same way that the capitalist idea that humans are entirely competitive destroys any capacity for mutual trust.

And, when the tendency towards domination and centralisation combined with the drive to lift up the downtrodden through rapid development, the revolutions also repeated capitalist enclosure's destruction of nature. Marx had written of 'metabolic rift', explaining how capital extracts value from the land, converting it into something else somewhere else, reducing the reproductive capacity of the Earth. But, from black snow around coal mines in Siberia to unbreathable air in industrial cities, from desertification in China to the emptying of the Aral Sea, communist revolutions continued the rift, causing immeasurable devastation.[26]

The 20th century became a battleground between different forms of domination and separation. Alongside capitalism and communism, a third anti-ecological system arose as anti-democratic anti-communist forces evolved into fascism, with its violent division of the world into 'us' and 'them' and explicit embrace of authoritarian power. Italian fascist dictator, Benito Mussolini, argued for 'Everything in the State, nothing outside the State, nothing against the State'.[27] And his northern ally, Adolf Hitler, turned the state into the most grotesquely efficient machine of mass murder of a dehumanised 'them' in history.

In the battle between capitalism, communism and fascism, capitalism came out on top because it bolted itself onto liberal democracy. This allowed it to successfully cloak its coercive nature in the garb of a cultural idea of freedom. And there was a certain truth to it. In liberal democracies, civil society was able to struggle for and win the welfare state, certain environmental protections, some regulation of corporations, and other limitations on the destruction, helping capitalism outcompete communism and fascism. For a time.

But now it is hitting hard limits. It's run out of commons to enclose.

## Reaching limits: The tragedy of the enclosure

Okay, with all this talk about the commons, we'd better name the elephant in the room. Chances are that, if you think about the commons, the word that springs to mind is 'tragedy'.

The tragedy of the commons is a powerful cultural idea that gained enormous traction from a 1968 essay of that name by American zoologist Garrett Hardin. The essay set out Hardin's contention that individuals who, for some unexplained reason, can't or won't talk to each other, can't or won't cooperate, will fail to manage commonly held resources, inevitably leading to over-extraction and collapse. This is, of course, true. But it's not a description of a commons. Commons are all about constant communication, negotiating and renegotiating agreed ways to steward shared resources. Hardin was describing capitalism, and the disconnection and competitive urge to dominate at its core.

Unlike Elinor Ostrom, Hardin conducted no actual research into commons management. Like Hobbes, traumatised by the English Civil War and convinced that life without a strong state must be a 'war of all against all', Hardin extrapolated from the capitalist world around him, decided that cooperation isn't possible, and helped to embed that idea into culture. Since he was a eugenicist and white supremacist,[28] the bleak view of human nature in *The Tragedy of the Commons* is no surprise.

What might be more surprising is that, although Ostrom's painstaking research into commons management was already well underway in the 1960s, it was Hardin's evidence-free essay that became central to economics curricula, and remains there today, long after Ostrom's complete debunking of it won the Nobel Prize in 2009.

Why? Because it fitted the culture that was coming to dominate so overwhelmingly during the Cold War. Capitalism is underpinned by the assumption that competition between self-interested individuals is what leads to good outcomes. Back in the 18th century, capitalism's original philosopher, Adam Smith, had tempered this assumption with nuance around people's morality and the guidance of the church. But the mid 20th century architect of neoliberalism, Friedrich Hayek, insisted that 'the sphere where material circumstances force a choice upon us is the air in which alone moral sense grows and in which moral values are daily re-created in the free decision of the individual'.[29] There is no morality but pure individual competition. In this context, evidence that cooperation leads to better allocation of scarce resources than free self-interest was always going to be deemed suspicious. A story that says we humans are irredeemably selfish was much more suited to the zeitgeist.

This is far from the only example. Around the same time, two hugely influential psychological experiments purporting to demonstrate the inescapable nastiness and brutishness of humans were undertaken. In the 1971 Stanford Prison Experiment, psychology professor Philip Zimbardo locked participants into a fake prison, allocating them into guards and prisoners, and observed how they supposedly descended rapidly into abuse. In the 1960s, American social psychologist Stanley Milgram set up a fake shock machine and tested how participants supposedly willingly administered more and more severe shocks to strangers, even to the point of apparently killing them.

Both 'experiments' have since been exposed as academic frauds. Records of participants resisting strongly, objecting, walking out, having to be coerced into behaving as Zimbardo and Milgram believed they should, were omitted and buried.[30] And yet, like *The Tragedy of the Commons*, they continue to be taught and referred to as truth. Indeed, they've become archetypal stories, encapsulating anti-ecological culture's depiction of human nature.

This powerful mythology of selfish individualism created the space for British Prime Minister Margaret Thatcher to absurdly declare that there's 'no such thing as society'[31] and be taken seriously, while attacking unions and the welfare state. As the ideas grew ever more dominant, they created feedback loops. Consider the impact of constantly being referred to as 'consumers' rather than 'citizens'. Consider the obsession in politics and policy with the 'prisoners' dilemma', positing two prisoners in separate rooms, unable to communicate, and removed from any cultural or relational context, asked to rat each other out. In supposedly testing human behaviour, but assuming complete disconnection, it is a test from within anti-ecology designed to annihilate the concept of cooperation.

This is where we arrived, at the end of the Cold War, in an era of triumphalist capitalism. The enclosure of the commons, having run out of new land to colonise, enclosed human nature as private property, claiming it as entirely selfish and competitive, and erasing the very idea of altruism or mutualism. A social norm of self-interest gained credence, insisting that any non-selfish behaviour must be underpinned by selfish motives.[32] This culminates in the invention of the slur 'virtue signalling' – the offensive idea that behaving considerately is purely about showing off and seeking praise.

In this worldview, only capitalism can improve people's lot, because it's the only social system that embraces our entirely competitive nature. In reality, capitalism has consistently made life harsher for the majority of life on Earth, expropriating resources – from colonised peoples, from lower classes, from future generations, from the Earth – and claiming it as 'wealth creation', pretending that the wealth trickles down. It was the new waves of organising – unionism, feminism, environmentalism, racial justice movements, pro-democracy movements – that sprang up in response, demanding that the benefits which capitalism accords to the few are shared with the many, that improved lives.[33] The welfare state, for instance, was created by capitalist liberal governments, adopting some of the ideas of radicals in their midst, as a means of preventing revolutions they feared were building.[34]

If Hardin demonstrated anything, it's the tragedy of enclosure. It's that competitive individualism will eventually devour everything if allowed. The logic of ecology means that any system based on anti-ecological behaviour – taking more than it puts back, severing interdependence, smothering diversity with homogenising domination – must eventually collapse. Anti-ecology takes constant effort to maintain, and it inevitably sows the seeds of its own destruction, no matter how long delayed.

As we reach the end of this thumbnail sketch of history through the lens of ecological and anti-ecological culture, cultivation and enclosure of the commons, we can see that the system has only managed to continue this long because it has worked out, time and again, how to extend enclosure. Now we've hit the limits of our finite planet; the logical conclusion of enclosure looms in front of us in the form of the climate crisis, ecosystem collapse, spiralling inequality, social unrest that takes ever more blatant coercion to suppress, and threats to hard-won democracies. If we continue down that path, our future will be nasty, brutish and short.

But we also see how ecological culture has always chafed at its enclosure, physically, institutionally and culturally, and how anti-ecology creates new impetus and new ways for it to do so. As Donella Meadows reflected, 'self-organization is such a basic property of living systems that even the most overbearing power structure can never fully kill it'.[35] We humans, as part of living systems, extend this through the flight of people from the first city states, internal and external struggles against early empires, numerous peasant rebellions, and constant Indigenous resistance and anti-colonialist struggles. It continues through libraries and workers' cooperatives, mutual aid projects, direct action protests, and new democracy movements. Indeed, the 21st century is seeing an extraordinary flourishing of commons-based ecological thinking and practice, partly due to the increasingly obvious reality of ecological, economic and social catastrophe, and partly because science and technology have created the opportunity for it to blossom.

The Enlightenment has, in a way, proven its own limitations: evolutionary biology is showing that cooperation is as important as competition; neuroscience is establishing through rational means that human behaviour is not actually rational;[36] biology is recognising that the human individual is itself an ecosystem containing multitudes of organisms in symbiosis, with more than half of our cells not containing human DNA;[37] quantum physics is demonstrating that disconnection is truly impossible, as observation changes reality.

And information technology creates new commons![38] The infinite replicability of information creates abundance in an economy designed around scarcity. For data, the value is not in the individual pieces, but in the connections between them, the patterns they make – a fundamentally ecological value system. In addition, by connecting across the entire globe, not only are we better able to share feedback than ever before, but we can experiment together with open source and creative commons approaches, demonstrating that cooperation can create more value for us all to share than competition will. In the online world, property is evolving back from individual and exclusionary to inextricably interdependent.

Of course, like every previous innovation, the online commons is being colonised, co-opted and controlled by capitalists and authoritarians. But in this new world, leaks spring open faster than they are plugged, demonstrating the pull to self-organising that Meadows celebrates. It's harder than ever before for those seeking control to suppress the alternatives that most of us want.

Ecological culture lives within us all. We evolved with it, and societies across the globe institutionalised it until a minority sought to erase it. That attempt has reached its end. They might stomp on the shoots and buds enough to ensure that the human future is nasty, brutish and short. But I believe life will find its way.

We are in crisis. Our choice is how we respond. Conditions are ripe for a flowering of ecological democracy.

# SEEDS:
# THE MEANS OF
# REPRODUCTION

Why go through this history?

Firstly, to show that the crisis we find ourselves in hasn't sprung from nowhere, and can't be fixed with tweaks to individual aspects of the system.

The climate crisis didn't just appear, and it can't be solved by simply swapping energy technologies. It's the most recent stage of a millennia-long process of treating the Earth as a resource for our use, living creatures as expendable, the oceans, atmosphere and land as dumping grounds. It's interwoven with our economic and political systems, in its history, causes and structures. The new authoritarianism hasn't arisen from a vacuum, and it can't be fixed with a bit of public interest journalism or punching the occasional fascist. It's the logical consequence of systems of dominating power and social and economic alienation. Economic inequality, racial injustices, the devaluation of democratic norms, environmental destruction – all are intertwined in a complex adaptive system.

Secondly, history shows that we humans aren't irredeemably bad. It isn't all war and genocide any more than evolution is all red in tooth and claw. Neither is it a shiny story of progress. It's complex. It's push and pull, give and take and share.

Both ecological and anti-ecological culture can evolve, as they both have, repeatedly. Both can be institutionalised and embedded through culture. But we need to understand the implications of the way anti-ecological culture has become so dominant. Our current governing systems evolved based on hierarchical power instead of trust-based horizontal power, making compromise a dirty word, promoting transactional deal-making over negotiated mutualism, obsessed with growth, only able to imagine leadership as domination instead of bringing people together.

We need a different theory and practice of government. Urgently. Only through structural and cultural change can we genuinely tackle the entangled crises we face, let alone thrive through what we know is coming. We need to be radical, in its true, ecologically-derived meaning: go to the roots.

Mainstream political discourse insists that there are only three possible options for political change: tweaking capitalist liberalism, swinging to the extreme right, or reinvigorating social democracy. In my view, these three are in turn naive, abhorrent, and insufficient, and we need to think beyond them. They, and the arguments between them are all embedded in anti-ecological thinking. False dichotomies abound, such as in the common assumption that the only alternative to capitalism is authoritarian state communism or, conversely, that because capitalist regimes opposed such autocratic communism, capitalism must be inherently democratic.

Frustration with these false dichotomies led some early Greens to declare that they were neither left nor right, but out in front. And indeed there are conservative conservationists, and there's a disturbing history of ecofascism.[1] But a truly ecological politics is definitively of the left in that it seeks to distribute power and resources rather than concentrate them in a few hands.

Many people remain convinced that capitalist liberalism is fine and, with a few tweaks here and there, can solve every problem from climate change to racism. Here's why I call this naive.

Capitalism and liberal democracy have always existed in an uncomfortable tension, with the people seeking democratically to tax and regulate capital, and capital using every means at its disposal to resist those constraints. It's important to recognise that capitalism, which is fundamentally about the accumulation and control of wealth and power, isn't democratic. Liberalism may start with democratic desires but, due to the underlying assumption of competitive individualism that it shares with capitalism, government becomes disconnected from citizens thanks to the enclosure for private profit of everything from railways to post offices, medical services to unemployment services.

And, when capital itself is granted democratic rights, when corporations can buy access and influence over political decision-makers and are seen as more important constituents than voters, democracy cannot survive. Financial power increasingly drowns out the people's voices. The relationship between citizen and government becomes one of customer and service provider, mediated by corporations, in which citizens have ever less capacity to play any active role, while the participation of corporations, through donations, lobbying, media control, and presence in political offices is welcomed.

In this supposedly best of all possible systems, a tiny minority has accumulated unimaginable wealth, buying the right not to pay taxes while people in the same cities are skipping meals, going without dental care, and living in their cars. Housing has become an investment, a wealth generator rather than a basic right. Food isn't grown to feed people – it's produced and distributed to make profits. The social welfare and criminal justice systems are designed to be punitive warnings to people not to deviate from the norm, instead of helping people to live better lives. Cities are designed around cars and shops, not communities and the natural world. Governing systems are so captured that climate action is impossible, even by progressive governments, leading to astonishing hypocrisy. The Biden Administration, while professing commitment to climate leadership, declares that the Intergovernmental Panel on Climate Change report calling for an urgent end to fossil fuel use 'does not provide sufficient cause' to end fossil fuel extraction.[2] The Australian Labor Party, while trumpeting the need for climate action, proudly says the country will be mining coal 'for decades to come'.[3] Climate activists are increasingly gaoled and surveilled, while police cars are emblazoned with fossil fuel corporate logos. And cynicism about politics grows apace.

In this context, improving civics education, supporting public interest media, banning corporate political donations and improving transparency are necessary but insufficient. They don't confront the disconnection and domination that are the foundation of both liberalism and capitalism, normalising selfishness and greed, and convincing us that altruism and cooperation don't exist.

Corporate structure institutionalises this norm, and politics follows, to the extent that we now expect politicians to be corrupt, we expect the system to destroy the environment, and we cannot envisage an alternative. Within this structure, tweaks won't help. Indeed, it's difficult to imagine them even being implemented.

The capitalist liberal democratic project was always an uncomfortable tension. But the capitalist tail is now strangling the democratic dog. It's time to acknowledge that this system has reached its logical conclusion and take the opportunity to reinvent it.

Currently, the extreme right is most effectively seizing the opportunity of the unravelling of liberal capitalist certainty. I don't need to explain that a politics of authoritarianism and hate is utterly anti-ecological, but we should briefly reflect on this extraordinarily dangerous phenomenon whose siren song attracts some of our fellow travellers, as many have been shocked to see at anti-lockdown protests.

As the 'Convoy to Canberra' disrupted my hometown in early 2022, with anti-vaccine mandate protesters aggressively confronting retail workers about masks and causing the cancellation of community events, debate raged in the community about how to respond. While most of us were justifiably angry, some pointed out that many of the attendees were finding in the convoy a deeper sense of community and connection than they were offered by mainstream society.[4]

That's the serious point we must address. The neofascists are, ironically, more honest about the alienation and disenfranchisement rampant in our society than many capitalist liberals, although they are deeply dishonest about its causes and solutions. In a classic bait and switch, they bring people together on the basis of legitimate concerns about the state of politics and how it's been corrupted, and then misdirect the anger away from the real causes, turning the group into the mob, primed and ready to fight those even worse off. Witness how Australian mining billionaire Clive Palmer, following Donald Trump's example, presents himself as a hero of the oppressed, when his business decisions have been the cause of so much misery for working class people.

Understanding the rise of the far right as the weaponisation of disconnection gives us a very clear direction as to how to respond. The brilliant philosopher Hannah Arendt articulated this in *The Origins of Totalitarianism*, explaining that, when a society is riven by atomisation and disconnection, when social bonds are breaking, it's possible for authoritarians to come to power through a combination of a powerful mythology of unity, attacks on a scary 'other', and continually feeding mistrust.[5] We will only beat it by replacing its exclusionary 'us' with a more attractive, inclusive, interdependent 'we', cultivating connection and trust.

The various forms of socialism that have re-entered mainstream political debate in the last decade are a serious step towards that inclusive 'we'. But I described them as insufficient. Why?

For starters, the word 'socialism' has begun to lose meaning, stretched so far by both adherents and opponents that it now means almost anything that seeks to rein in neoliberalism. You can be labelled a socialist for wanting stronger planning laws or an increase in welfare payments. US politician Bernie Sanders calls himself a socialist but his campaigns have been about making the capitalist system fairer, while some of his British counterpart Jeremy Corbyn's politics owe as much to the Diggers and Levellers as to Marx. My critique isn't a repudiation of socialism if that implies repudiating any alternative to capitalism. But we need to find a new language to convey specific ideas.

And it's vital to distinguish these ideas from the problematically anti-ecological aspects in too much socialist thought and practice. A centralising tendency and distrust of people have been evident since the 1870s. As the anarchist theorist David Graeber wrote, 'both traditional Marxism and contemporary social theory have stubbornly dismissed pretty much anything suggestive of generosity, cooperation, or altruism as some kind of bourgeois illusion'.[6]

Another core distinction is that ecology sees the struggle for justice in far broader terms than the great majority of socialism. The tendency of many socialists to divide people into 'workers' and 'bosses' is both exclusive of people outside the formal workforce, whether by choice or by rejection, and fundamentally outdated in a world where fewer and fewer people identify with their labour. As ecofeminist scholar Ariel Salleh wrote, 'it is false to reduce all power to the economics of class'.[7] Ecological thinking understands that there are many intersecting inequalities across our society, such as gender, race, class and sexuality, with complex interplays between them, and which need to be addressed systemically. Salleh explained that 'the oppression(s) of Man over Man, of Man over Woman and of Man over Nature ... will only be dismantled together'.[8]

One stark example of the perils of socialist reductionism is its problematic misreading of climate justice, epitomised in a few revealing lines from the generally brilliant socialist writer Jeff Sparrow:

> Climate change will devastate the poor – and the rich
> and the powerful will barely notice. Insulated by money,
> you can still treat nature as an inexhaustible resource to
> be endlessly abused ... The politicians and tycoons with
> their stock options and property portfolios will still
> find pleasant locales for their holidays, no matter how
> degraded the oceans become.[9]

This is, of course, patently untrue. Yes, wealth will insulate tycoons from climate change for a short time but, if scientists are correct, there will soon enough be no 'pleasant locales' to run to. This argument foolishly gives the wealthy an excuse to continue to refuse to act. It's true, though, that poverty and pollution are closely correlated, both in their underlying causes and in location. Class is an important lens through which to view the drivers and responses to environmental destruction, but it fails unless understood in an ecological, intersectional way.

There is a lot in socialist thought that is valuable in cultivating an ecological politics, and there's a good reason why so many people seeking alternatives to capitalism are drawn to it. But while it remains caught in binary, disconnected, dominance-driven, anti-ecological thinking, it cannot solve the crises we face. Rather than 'seize the means of production', replacing one dominating group with another, perhaps our rallying cry should be to 'distribute seeds: the means of reproduction!'

Democracy needs to be alive.

We do not face a choice between the invisible hand of the market, the dead hand of centralised control, or the fascist fist in our face. We can use our own living hands, we can join hands together, we can dig them in the soil, and clap them in joy. Under capitalist liberalism, nothing is connected, everything is atomised, all is fungible. Under socialism, the collective trumps the individual, tending towards centralised power and erosion of trust. Under fascism, an exclusive 'us' is united, erasing individual identity in the struggle against a hated 'them'. In living democracy, everything is connected, in its grand interdependent diversity, as we negotiate our coexistence.

For the right, government should get out of the way of business while maintaining strict social order. It's a rhetoric of freedom with an undercurrent of authoritarian control. For the old left, government knows best. It's a rhetoric of democracy with an undercurrent of paternalism or, worse, coercion. Fascism combines the worst of both. None of them give people back control over their own destiny. None of them confront the disconnection and domination at the heart of the crises we face.

At this moment in history, with ecological collapse bearing down on us, and social and economic injustices boiling to the surface, the mainstream paths presented to us are dead ends.

But a wonderful array of interwoven paths is available to us, mapped out by people shoved aside by anti-ecology: the deep tradition of Indigenous governance of interdependent autonomous beings; Elinor Ostrom's work on the commons, and the radical anti-enclosure voices of the English Revolution; and the anarchism of Kropotkin and others.

In Part 2, we'll learn from these philosophies as we dig into the practices of living democracy from four different angles, the four pillars of Greens politics: grassroots democracy, economic justice, peace and nonviolence, and ecological sustainability. We'll look at the need to move from exclusion and adversarialism to participation and deliberation in our democratic systems, from extractivism to cultivation in the way we manage our economy, from coercion to coexistence so as to cultivate peace, and from disconnection from nature to re-embracing our interdependence with the natural world. We'll discuss ideas, proposals, and things people are already doing. As we do so, we'll find that the ecological system we need to cultivate is already there. Wherever humans, with our remarkable capacity for communication and creativity, come together, we give birth to these amazing systems of interdependence.

As the extraordinary Indian novelist and democracy activist, Arundhati Roy, has said, 'Another world is not only possible, she is on her way. On a quiet day, I can hear her breathing'.[10] I hope we've realised, through Part 1, how contingent our current world is, how the pretence of permanence is how it maintains control, and how we humans have never stopped believing in the possibility of another world. In Part 2, we're going to listen for her breath. In Part 3, we'll learn how we can breathe life into her.

## PART 2

# WHERE ARE WE GOING?

# DOING DEMOCRACY

## From exclusion to participation
## and from adversarialism to deliberation

One hundred and twenty eyes were trained on me. Some betrayed cynicism, others showed interest. Some were sceptical, others warmly encouraging. But they'd all chosen to be here in this community hall in Canberra – uni students, aged pensioners and disabled people, people living in poverty and people who were comfortably off – on a chilly autumn evening, for a meeting we'd called 'Their Budget, Our Lives'.

The Federal Budget is the most exclusive of inside-game politics. A plan developed behind closed doors for months is formally delivered in the parliament after journalists and select corporate and civil society representatives have been privately briefed in what is unironically known as the 'lock up'. The Press Gallery breathlessly reports 'winners and losers', while ministers and shadow ministers schmooze wealthy business people who've paid for the privilege of attending Budget night shindigs.

In May 2021, the Green Institute teamed up with the Australian Unemployed Workers' Union and several other grassroots organisations to flip that story. We wanted to put on an event where people with lived experience of the impact of government budget decisions about tax and welfare could share their stories and discuss how to respond.

We also wanted to give people a decent feed and a good time – because that's what vibrant democracy should be. And it certainly was on this night!

After we heard moving presentations from people about their experiences dealing with job agencies, living on disability support, struggling to make ends meet, I stood up and asked everyone to gather around tables while volunteers distributed butcher's paper and pens.

As I explained what we were about to do, I could feel anxiety and tension in the room. But, moments after I asked the groups to start discussing mutual aid – what we can do together to make life better, without waiting for uncaring governments to act – the room was abuzz with energy and ideas. Eyes were shining. Heads leaned in, listening intently. Pens zipped over paper. I felt terrible interrupting these animated conversations 30 minutes later, but after sharing a few ideas with the room, we shifted into discussing how, working together, we can change politics.

It took quite an effort to send people home, with boxes of leftover pide, a full hour after we were scheduled to finish! Some of the ideas, including a community tool library, have already been acted on. Others, like blockading job agencies with barbecues, are still in planning. Relationships were built.

Greens policy was informed. People felt heard, in a week when they're traditionally most excluded.

What we did was far from unique. In rooms and halls, squares and parks around the globe, communities excluded from politics are gathering together to cultivate their own living democracies.

Before we go any further, we'd better define this word.

From the Ancient Greek *demos*, people, and *kratos*, power or rule, democracy literally means 'rule by the people': government where the people make the decisions. That opens up more questions than it answers, though, doesn't it? Who are 'the people', and how do they make the decisions? Does 'the people' mean only adult male citizens, as it did in Ancient Greece? In Australia, voting rights now extend to all adult citizens, but should we include often thoughtful and well-informed adolescents? What about permanent residents who aren't citizens? When we make our decisions, are we doing so directly together, or do we delegate to representatives to make them for us? In either case, does a plurality (the largest number) win, do we need a simple majority (50 per cent + 1), or do we work towards consensus?

To help us consider the implications, consider planning a dinner with 20 people.

We might find that 15 prefer pizza while the five who want kebabs don't mind being outvoted. In this case, a clear majority leads to an acceptable outcome. But what if two of those who wanted kebabs made that choice because they needed a halal meal? If it's just one meal, they can make their own choice. But if 75 per cent of a population votes to ban halal certification, suddenly pure majority rule can be disastrous for minorities.

One option might be for our diners to sit down, present their preferences and reasons, and see if they can reach consensus. Doing this, they might find their way to a mutually acceptable outcome that's something altogether different – maybe they try out a new Indonesian restaurant. Let's say, instead, they decide to vote for one of their number to make the choice of what to eat. Decision-making takes a very different tack. Instead of working to find agreement, the nominees begin to fight for their case and against the others. Four of them make pitches to be elected, two get three votes each, one gets six and one gets eight. Should the person with eight votes out of 20 win? Should there be a run-off or preferential vote? What if one diner, flush with cash, offers to shout their friends' meals to secure their votes? Do children in the group get a say? If a dozen of the group have a long-standing habit of going for pizza and the eight others are newcomers, should the newcomers have to tag along with the established group until they prove themselves in some way? What if the person elected doesn't know that two of their number need a halal option? Once one is elected, do others still have the opportunity to try to influence their decision?

All of a sudden, this word we thought we understood – democracy – becomes complex. And these 'who' and 'how' questions aren't abstract. Process matters – not just for the sake of fairness, but because the process influences the result. People come to very different conclusions if told to pick a side or if given the opportunity to discuss their choice. Both are democracy, but they're radically different practices and their outcomes are poles apart.

More and more people are looking at politics today and finding it not a particularly good version of democracy. They're asking whether shouty adversarialism is the best way to get good results. They're questioning 'winner-takes-all' majority rules. Indeed, seeing increasingly blatant corruption, they're wondering whether we actually have majority rules if a powerful minority can drown the majority out. Ideas with massive popular support but powerful opposition, like a rapid transition to renewable energy or ensuring that the super-wealthy pay their fair share of tax, simply don't get acted on.

The collapse of confidence in governments reflects a growing recognition that they aren't particularly democratic. And this is feeding discussion and experimentation, challenging the idea that democracy just means turning up to vote for the least-worst option every few years. As food and democracy advocate Frances Moore Lappé has written:

> [L]et's acknowledge what's more and more obvious:
> that our idea of democracy is just way too weak for
> the job. Then we can get on with the work of bringing
> to life an emergent, more powerful understanding
> of democracy that does work because it's creating a
> context that reflects what is now clear about human
> nature: our capacity for cruelty when power is too
> concentrated, secrecy prevails, and scapegoating
> ensues, as well as – under the opposite conditions –
> our capacity for fairness and cooperation as we leave
> behind the status of whiners and blamers and share in
> power as doers and creators.[1]

If we're to survive this century, let alone thrive, our task begins with cultivating a living practice of democracy based on ecological principles.

In his beautiful book about Australian birdlife, *Where Song Began*, ornithologist Tim Low has provided an unintentionally perfect metaphor for the state of our democracy.

Low described how the magnificent diversity of Australian bird species co-evolved with each other and with the continent's diverse plants and climates. The diversity of birdlife depends on the interconnected diversity of plantlife, and vice versa. Some birds specialise in acacias, others in eucalypts or casuarinas; the mix of grasses, shrubs and mature trees provides the healthy ecosystem at various scales needed for a range of birds to thrive.

But over large parts of Australia, that diverse inter-dependence has been trashed. Small stands of mature eucalypts remain around the edges of monoculture paddocks, playing fields and lawns. In this impoverished, disconnected landscape, one particularly aggressive species of bird thrives, chasing away many of the others.

The name of this bird?

The noisy miner.[2]

I mean, really. Could you ask for a better metaphor for Australia's fossil-fuel dominated democracy?

A healthy democracy, like a healthy ecosystem, is diverse, interdependent and everchanging. Where the ecosystem has a diverse range of species, wide variation within those species, and inextricable interconnection between them, the democracy has a wide range of participants, and a broad array of different fora in which they participate, share ideas and co-design their common future.

In a healthy democracy all voices are listened to, building trust in each other and in the system. The small number of voices which will inevitably be noisier than others, or even occasionally aggressive, can be managed, making the discussion creative and enjoyable. Like the voices, the fora themselves need to be interconnected in order to coordinate efforts, face up to shared challenges and extend trust. And the structures and rules need to be revisited frequently to make sure they remain fit for purpose and to rebuild active trust.

Like ecosystems around the globe, however, the self-organising, trust-based democratic commons humans developed over millennia have been enclosed for private profit and personal power. Their diversity has been diminished, different voices and opinions chased away, opportunities to be heard and fora for discussion narrowed and, like the Monty Python sketch, constructive debate has withered into yes-it-is-no-it-isn't argument. With only ministerial offices and boardrooms remaining for major decisions to be made in, we shouldn't be surprised that noisy miners have come to dominate our politics as their namesakes dominate our suburbs, leaving us with government of the fossil fuel industry, by the fossil fuel industry, for the fossil fuel industry.

But it's amazing how quickly you can bring wildlife back to the suburbs with a bit of bush regeneration. Plant appropriate, diverse shrubs, trees and grasses, and see an explosion of joy and beauty as parrots, pardalotes, kookaburras and wrens join the noisy miners!

We need to do this regeneration with our democracy. Where the anti-ecological culture of separation and domination has seen the establishment of the state as an entity separate from us, ruling us, and bringing out our worst instincts, we need to re-learn interdependent self-governing in order to bring out our best. Where that culture has brought us to the brink of catastrophe, living democracy can help us survive.

We're going to explore four interconnected steps to do this: ensuring that everyone can participate in decision-making; shifting our decision-making from adversarial shouting matches to constructive, creative deliberation; rebuilding our governing bodies based on integrated, bottom-up organising instead of centralised, top-down control; and respecting impermanence by cultivating adaptable systems. Through inspiring examples from around the world, we'll look at how democracy breathes.

## Participation: Every voice matters

In north-east Syria, on the Turkish border, the people organise their own rubbish collection. They fix their own water supplies, develop school curricula, settle their own disputes, and clean up after the bombs drop. They have abolished the death penalty and child marriage, and promote gender equity. They manage their farms and industry through cooperatives. And they organise it all in meetings of each local community, each carefully co-facilitated so that everyone can participate, each sending delegates to regional councils to work through questions that need more coordination.

The Kurdish people of this region, persecuted by the governments of both countries, had been fighting for independence for decades, led by the charismatic Abdullah

Öcalan in a Maoist revolutionary struggle. But Öcalan, reading widely while imprisoned in Turkey, came across the work of the American anarchist, Murray Bookchin, on municipal confederalism. He sent word home about this exciting idea of self-organising self-government based on coordinated local assemblies: in their struggle for independence, they could simply start building the nation they wanted. And the people set about doing so.

In the Autonomous Administration of North and East Syria, also known as Rojava, they are living into being a multi-ethnic, feminist, environmentalist, democratic society. It's imperfect. It's struggling to survive. It's extraordinary that it exists at all.

Election day in Australia rocks. I love how we turn voting into a festival, with democracy sausages and school bands. I love how we can trust our independent Electoral Commission to run a fair process, and count every vote accurately.

And I sometimes wonder if our trustworthy voting system hasn't distracted us from the fact that our other avenues for democratic participation, from consultation to lobbying, whistleblowing to protest, are increasingly constrained. Thinking about Rojava, even that is too narrow a view of democracy. All of those are still forms of what I think of as supplicant politics – ways in which the people seek to influence our rulers, the state Leviathan we are subject to, rather than the people coming together to jointly make decisions and build a common future.

Supplicant politics evolved because our representative

democracy arose through a series of compromises extracted from monarchs to give more people a say. Remember that living democracies were widespread before monarchies and similar systems of absolute power seized control, while the people continually struggled against them. Representative democracy is a crucial step in that struggle, but voting is only one aspect of democracy.

The big step is to finally dissolve the dominating power of the separate state and ensure that power is truly shared among the people. While in a large, complex system, some degree of representation will remain necessary, the basic unit of ecological living democracy must be the people themselves acting together, with a diversity of voices, in many different spaces.

The basic practice, then, is participation.

Let's talk about the ideas behind this before we get our teeth into more examples.

For Kropotkin, participation is an emergent property – our instinct for mutual aid is the glue that holds society together, and his vision of anarchist self-organising stems from the concept that people naturally want to work together.

For Ostrom, it's a practical point. The people on the ground have the best information, from various perspectives, and the greatest capacity to manage that information and those perspectives. Ostrom's research showed that, when more voices are involved, decisions are more likely to be long-lasting as they are built on trust; and they are more likely to be high-quality as they are stress-tested, scrutinised, challenged and improved through a process of 'learn[ing] how to dissect and harness complexity, rather than eliminate it'.[3] The basis of her model of commons governance is that the clear rules, boundaries, processes and sanctions that communities agree to be bound by must be developed and managed democratically by all those agreeing to be bound, using processes that enable all voices to be heard.

Tyson Yunkaporta has made the same point about the 'generative cultural practice of yarning' in Indigenous governance, which is about ensuring that every voice is heard, including those who 'make me feel uncomfortable. I yarn with those people because they extend my thinking more than those who simply know what I know'.[4] 'Every viewpoint is useful,' he explained, 'and it takes a wide diversity of views for any group to navigate this universe, let alone to act as custodians for it.'[5]

And Bookchin and Öcalan's municipalist confederalism is designed on this principle. Community assemblies, accessible to all, are the basic governing unit, ensuring local management, encouraging engagement and building social cohesion. Actively involving all people, across gender, ethnicity, class and beyond, is both about improving the quality of decisions and about building justice and mutual trust into the architecture of the system.

For participation to work, democracy has to be relevant to people's everyday lives. One of the key successes of anti-ecological culture is that it has turned us off democracy. It distracts us from it by keeping us busy, and convinces us to ignore it as irrelevant or repellent, a game for the powerful to play at our expense.

If we are to counter that, democratic participation has to be fulfilling, enjoyable, fun – it has to live. That's why making its basic unit the level closest to the action is vital, because people get involved (and stay involved) when they can influence things that really matter to them. Often the entry point will be place-making activities, like planning issues, landcare or schools – things which give people a sense of belonging. But being 'closest to the action' doesn't have to be geographically local – it can be geographically dispersed communities of interest, co-governing anything from a union to a sports club or a publishing house.

Making participation the core of democracy will, over time, radically restructure democratic institutions. But part of its beauty is that it can, and must, grow from the grassroots up. The more of it we cultivate, the harder it is to stamp out, and the more the people will demand it, enabling it to flourish. It starts by expanding democratic space, reclaiming the commons, building positive experiences for people, so they come to enjoy and respect democracy. Then that community democratic space can become an effective political space.

London's Borough of Barking and Dagenham has seen an explosion of cooking co-ops and knitting groups, pop up shops and tool libraries, parents' support groups and community gardens. And it's no accident. The Participatory City program,[6] which I was lucky enough to visit in 2017, is gently, subtly and brilliantly supporting the community to develop these urban commons. They have drop-in centres on high streets, staffed by people who help locals find ways to participate, set up something new, navigate local government processes, or manage tricky interpersonal relationships. They're doing this partly because each project is wonderful, but largely because of the overarching benefits across the community.

They've already found that these projects reduce a range

of social ills, from homelessness to substance abuse to family violence, by making people feel included and valued, giving them more agency in their lives. One of the reasons they chose Barking was that the combination of poverty and ethnic diversity had seen a terrifying rise in far-right politics and racist attacks. Both have dropped since the project took off.

Participatory City is doing democracy differently, cultivating democratic space outside politics and, by giving people this positive experience, changing politics. It's one of the purest examples of living democracy that I know of.

You can do the same thing and be highly political. Take a look at Barcelona en Comú – Barcelona in Common – the cooperative-led municipal government of Barcelona, which I was also privileged to visit on my 2017 travels.[7]

Its genesis was the extraordinary community response to the 2008 economic crash, which hit Spain among the hardest in the world, partly thanks to drastic austerity policies. Millions took to the streets in protest, creating the Movement of the Squares, a mix of anti-government protest, mutual aid projects to help each other survive austerity, and community assemblies to discuss what to do next.

In some cities, the assemblies swiftly developed into an electoral project, Podemos, which has won some seats. But in Barcelona, they built a different approach by focussing primarily on practical, participatory projects from health cooperatives to squatters' support, childcare cooperatives to food-sharing networks, actively ensuring that everyone in the community had what they needed to survive when the government had abandoned them.

Only after that was well underway did people involved in those groups come together, with a municipal election approaching, and begin to craft a political strategy, seeing the government as a key obstacle. They democratically developed a code of political ethics they agreed to be bound by, nominated housing activist Ada Colau as their spokesperson, ran for election as Barcelona en Comú – and won! With Colau as mayor, they began to institutionalise the changes they were making on the ground, from legitimating squats to seizing back control of the water supply which had been privatised, to handing as many decisions as possible to the community. As one of their advisors, Francesca Bria, told me, 'sometimes it's better not to regulate, not to govern, but to enable autonomous self-government'.

It hasn't been easy. With key grassroots activists being elected or taking staff positions, and others stepping back from the movement thinking they had won, participation dropped, leaving fewer people working to keep government and community connected. And the Spanish and European Union governments have fought them every step. Despite that, Barcelona en Comú was re-elected for a second four-year term in 2019, and has formally joined the European Greens Federation as a grassroots party.

Rojava takes it a step further. They're actually creating a new nation by living democracy together!

These are all, in their ways, examples of anarchist or commons politics – the collective development of rules, with no rulers, and no coercion. They're dissolving top-down dominating power by growing shared power from the grassroots.

Let's look at a few brilliant Australian projects that put participation at the heart of democracy.

The first is the amazing participatory conversations that my friend Dr Amanda Cahill leads, through her organisation,

The Next Economy, in communities in transition out of fossil fuels. Only ever going where she is invited, Cahill helps communities work out what they can do for themselves. By guiding communities to sit down together and think about their strengths and what they can bring to the table, and by telling stories of what other communities in similar circumstances are doing, Cahill helps people to find – and activate – their own hope.

In one community torn asunder by controversy over gas extraction, Cahill's gentle, participatory approach brought together two men who hadn't spoken to each other for years, having found themselves on opposite sides of the divide, to jointly start a community-owned renewable energy company! She has effectively midwifed the birth of projects from catering cooperatives for unemployed young people to arts and tourism initiatives. And she shows government representatives that transition out of fossil fuels doesn't have to be scary – it can be creative and fun.

For Cahill, the key is bringing democratic conversations into people's everyday lives, rather than leaving it to the abstractions and tribalisms of politics. As she told me, 'The more you can narrow it down into time and place, the more real and useful and practical a conversation you're going to have. The further away you get from that, the more people have to identify with a position without any context around it.'[8]

Cahill's work proves that the cynical belief of a lot of progressives that 'we can't trust people' enough to rely on democracy isn't reflective of reality. It demonstrates that, when people are invited to participate in decision-making, most of us genuinely want the same thing. Imagine if communities all around Australia were doing this. It would up-end our climate politics, turning it from a fight to the death into a constructive contest for a rapid, fair and fun transition.

A second Australian example is Voices for Indi, a participatory politics project which has seen community delegates elected to the federal parliament. The regional Victorian electorate of Indi, around the town of Wangaratta, had been represented for generations by conservatives, and for four terms by a hard-right member of parliament increasingly out of step with her constituents. A group of community members decided to hold a series of 'kitchen table conversations' to gather a set of agreed community values, as well as a political vision for the region.

When it came time to select a representative to run for parliament, the first candidate won not once but twice, and, when she chose to stand down, her successor was easily elected as well. This is thanks to ongoing community engagement, inviting community members to actively participate in setting the agenda for their member of parliament, work in her office, and help shape her decisions.[9] Voices for Indi is an extraordinary example of a member of parliament within our existing top-down system truly working as a bottom-up delegate of the community.

In the 2016 Brisbane City Council election, Jonathan Sri caused a minor earthquake by becoming the first Green elected to a historically conservative local government – and on a truly radical platform challenging speculative, profit-driven development. Central to his approach was participatory democracy. As he said at the time: 'My primary goal as an elected representative is to help reshape our local governance systems to be less centralised and less hierarchical. As much as possible, decisions should be made at the neighbourhood level, rather than top down from City Hall.'[10] After squeaking across the line, Sri set about running genuine community consultations, co-designing proposals to take to council, organising discussion sessions to help him decide his approach to issues, and trialling participatory budgeting. He was re-elected in 2020 with a massive 12.4 per cent swing.

My campaign for election in 2019 included a small participatory process to test the waters, to gain experience, and to see how it might work as a member of a party, albeit one committed to the principles of grassroots democracy. We ran four public meetings, asking people to discuss how they'd like to be involved in political decision-making, what kind of relationship they'd like with their MP, and how to formalise participation.

The process was the most joyous and fun-filled experience I've had in politics. But the most refreshing aspect was the clear message that community members were seeking agency, not control. People recognised that their voice was one among many. They weren't going to insist that their personal position won every time, but they wanted to trust that their voice was heard and taken into account. Reporting back on how a final decision was taken was crucial for building trust.

Our primary task, then, in living democracy, is to create as many spaces as we can collectively imagine for people to get involved in their own communities. We can all do this. Talk to your neighbours and set up a shared compost. Organise a phone tree for checking on neighbours during a heatwave. Start a local sharing group. Or establish a People's Assembly. It's all vital.

Although this needs to come from the community, government can sometimes enable it and nourish the seeds of its own replacement. Local government is supporting Participatory City, for example. And the tightrope that Barcelona en Comú and Jonno Sri are walking, governing in a way which enables the community to take agency, can be seen in city governments from Bologna to Seoul negotiating co-governance agreements with their communities, relinquishing aspects of their power and inviting the people to help set the agenda and deliver changes on the ground. Participatory budgeting projects across the world are building social cohesion and trust, increasing equity, and improving the quality of government funding decisions. The success of Citizens' Assemblies in East Belgium has led their government to establish a permanent Citizen Council to set the agenda for rolling issue-based assemblies to discuss.[11]

Governments won't voluntarily abdicate their power, but when they do make participation possible, we can use it to drive change, seeking out every opportunity and either turning it into a success or exposing it as a failure in order to demand better next time.

And, though it's insufficient, as we discussed in Part 1, we must also demand reforms to how government currently blocks participation. We must, for example, demand more open, transparent government, with donations and lobbyists' registers, open diaries, better Freedom of Information and more. Withholding information and punishing whistleblowers is central to how governments hold power. Similarly, the delegitimising and criminalising of protest is fundamentally anti-democratic and must be resisted – protest is a crucial part of democratic participation.

In all these cases and more, the only way we can ensure participation is to actively participate, and to bring people together with food, fun and things that matter in their lives. The journey is the destination.

## Deliberation: Changing the way we disagree

In a hall in the heart of Queensland 'coal country', Amanda Cahill asks a crowd of people to share what's good in their community. What are their strengths, and their special attributes? After this, she explains to them that they're not alone, telling stories of other communities she's visited who are facing similar challenges, asking similar questions. Only then does she ask people to start discussing what they want for the future, and she does so by allocating them to small groups with agreed rules for how to manage the conversation: listen to each other and respond; critique ideas not people; use 'and' instead of 'but' wherever possible.

That's how The Next Economy came out of consultations in Gladstone, Toowoomba and Rockhampton, with a report calling for a science-based rapid transition to renewable energy and community members excited about the next opportunity to get involved.[12]

I asked Cahill how it is that, working in communities who tell pollsters they don't believe in climate change, who consistently vote for parties who promise to protect the coal industry, who react angrily to climate activists, she can gather consensus support for transition out of coal.

Her advice: 'don't ask people to pick sides'.[13]

Participation doesn't guarantee a constructive process. I'm sure that, like me, you've been involved in poorly facilitated meetings that have degenerated into shouting matches with people backed into corners and the same old voices dominating.

Diversity needs interdependence to be meaningful. Likewise, in living democracy, we have to shift our decision-making away from winners versus losers towards coexistence, away from a simplistic battle towards an appreciation for complexity and ambiguity. This means moving from adversarialism, where competitors seek to dominate and destroy one another, to cooperative contestation, creativity, deliberation.

This isn't some naive vision of universal agreement – in fact, it relies on vigorous disagreement. But it means changing the way we disagree.

Adversarialism runs deep in our system of separation and domination. The structures of our parliaments, our political debates and our legal system are all designed on the model of a mediaeval tournament, opponents jousting for supremacy. This embeds a culture of domination, reduces diversity as 'enemies' are vanquished, erodes trust and erases complexity in decision-making. From this perspective, adversarialism and authoritarianism share some troubling attributes: you're either with us or against us, our party or theirs, a member of The Party or an enemy of the state. Divide and conquer is inherent to both, keeping opponents fighting among themselves.

The binary worldview makes political decision-making a linear zero-sum game, a tug-of-war instead of a web of ideas. Cooperation and negotiation become signs of weakness to be withstood. Witness the howls of derision at minority parliaments when they tend to be the most productive periods of government.

Linearity also creates the inanity of 'sensible centrism', which assumes that the best outcome will be found directly between two opposing teams. You don't get good policy by compromising between climate science and the profits of coal companies, or between billionaires and the billions without. And it leads to absurd political 'debates' where people, having picked a side, will brook no criticism of that side, such as with the abusive attacks on people raising reasonable critiques of the management of pandemic lockdowns. Adversarial politics hinders sophisticated political conversations where we can offer both support and constructive critique.

Deliberation – genuine discussion, listening to each other and seeking a way through – enables a radically different conversation. Avoiding 'us and them', it isn't about winning or even compromising – it's about creating something. Crucially, it allows participants to listen to expert advice with open minds. And it enables expert advisers to give frank advice without fearing retribution. Where adversarialism suppresses cooperation, trust, creativity and complexity, deliberation cultivates them. Where adversarialism entrenches dominating power, deliberation dissolves it.

Deliberation makes participation in decision-making processes more attractive, especially for marginalised voices. Adversarialism is unpleasant for everyone, and particularly for marginalised people. It turns people off politics, whether it's Question Time or aggressive community consultations. Where the non-solution of 'sensible centrism' pretends we can avoid unpleasant disagreement by meeting in the middle, deliberation cultivates pleasant disagreement. Well-facilitated creative conversations, constructive contests of ideas, are genuinely enjoyable. People leave them feeling uplifted and hopeful, having exercised their agency with everyone else, looking forward to the next opportunity to do so.

Elinor Ostrom beautifully articulated the crux of this in her Nobel lecture – shifting from a system that assumes the worst of us to one which brings out our best:

> Designing institutions to force (or nudge) entirely
> self-interested individuals to achieve better outcomes
> has been the major goal posited by policy analysts for
> governments to accomplish for much of the past half
> century. Extensive empirical research leads me to argue
> that instead, a core goal of public policy should be to
> facilitate the development of institutions that bring out
> the best in humans.[14]

Tyson Yunkaporta has explained yarning in very much these terms, as 'protocols of active listening, mutual respect and building on what others have said'.[15] And Frances Moore Lappé set out how 'solutions arise in relationships of mutuality – where all participants are both givers and receivers, and all are held accountable for ensuring rights and fulfilling responsibilities'.[16]

Disagreeing constructively means we need ways of making sure participants are held accountable to the aim of working together. This was Ostrom's life's work, and she highlighted the critical need for democratically developed and managed rules of behaviour, monitors who are accountable to the group, carefully graduated sanctions for breaches of the agreed rules, and accessible dispute resolution mechanisms.[17]

Importantly, while the aim is for everyone to participate, not everyone will always be willing to do so constructively. It's a reality that every participatory system includes provision to (temporarily or permanently) exclude people who refuse to abide by the agreed rules. As Yunkaporta wrote:

> The basic protocols of Aboriginal society, like most societies, include respecting and hearing all points of view in a yarn. Narcissists demand this right, then refuse to allow other points of view on the grounds that any other opinion somehow infringes their freedom of speech or is offensive. They destroy the basic social contracts of reciprocity.[18]

But when a conversation is set up and facilitated well, the results are amazing. It's incredible how you can get completely different conclusions from exactly the same people with a different approach.

Amanda Cahill's work in communities in transition is testament to this, and holds a vital lesson for us all – build common purpose, and don't ask people to pick sides.

This is central to reimagining the role of citizens around agency rather than power or control. Taking part in deliberative discussions as a participant with agency means being willing to change your mind, informed by trustworthy expert advice and the opinions of others; letting go of control, embracing your vital role.

A whole field of study exists around deliberative democracy, examining the ways in which people come together to consider and discuss ideas to reach consensus. Professor John Dryzek, a global leader in the field, has written with his colleague Jonathan Pickering of how deliberation 'depends on the quality of relationships among different parts of the system',[19] and the

Centre for Deliberative Democracy and Global Governance at the University of Canberra, which Dryzek established, studies ways in which those relationships can be cultivated well or badly. Their research shows that establishing and maintaining agreed ground-rules for constructive discussion, and doing so together so as to build group trust, actually changes the way we think.

The centre's co-founder, Professor Simon Niemeyer, has, with colleagues, undertaken a meta-analysis of deliberative processes, examining what happens in them to deliver results. The clearest signal is the quality of group-building. Most people tend to agree on issues but disagree on what to do about them; the process of well-facilitated deliberation brings them together, aligning issues and action by building shared understandings of each other and the world. The process of building group trust enables that alignment, whereas voting undermines it:

> What we've shown is how we as citizens can be primed
> to behave in particular ways depending on the political
> circumstances that we find ourselves in. In our case, group
> building is geared toward building trust and a shared sense
> of purpose where a group collectively seeks to understand,
> and solve, a common issue. Dramatically, we've shown that
> it changes the way in which we reason, compared to when
> either there is no work to build shared purpose or when
> we're set against each other.[20]

Democratic theorist, Chantal Mouffe, has a usefully different approach in her call to 'transform antagonism into agonism' – agonism simply meaning struggle, rather than struggle against.

Mouffe has emphasised that we need conflict in decision-making, but in ways which 'will not construct the opponent as an enemy but as an adversary'.[21] Her fear is that deliberation, by focussing on finding a consensus path, can 'eliminate passions from the sphere of the public', passions which we need to harness if we're to deal with the huge challenges we face. While my experience is that deliberation does not necessarily 'eliminate passions' – in fact it can be immensely passionate – the distinction is a reminder that non-adversarial decision-making can and should involve vociferous disagreement.

With this in mind, one of the most crucial tasks in cultivating living democracy is to train large numbers of facilitators who can give people positive experiences of well-run participatory democracy. Many organisations like the Greens, Friends of the Earth and School Strike for Climate, as well as community organisations and cooperatives, already operate on consensus, and good facilitation is the difference between them working and failing. Those of us with this experience can and should help others, offering guidance, and leading by example in conversations on social media and in the community, in the way we behave in parliaments, and in the way we campaign. Bearing Mouffe in mind, we should absolutely not be afraid of contestation, of championing our ideas and critiquing others'. But we should do it in a way which seeks to find a path through, rather than seeking to destroy opponents.

This is an incredibly difficult task from within a political system designed around adversarialism. But it's not impossible. Indeed, given how sick people are of the pointless gladiatorial theatre of politics, it is likely to be popular, if also done with ambition. And, by leading the way from the grassroots, we can cultivate deliberative democracy throughout the system, reversing the way adversarialism has worked its way into everyday life. That can only make life better for us all.

## Integration: Complex democracy in a complex world

In Rojava, local assemblies of a few hundred people are responsible for day-to-day governing. With new communities seeing that the model works and wanting to join, there are now astonishingly some 4000 local assemblies, encompassing a multi-ethnic population of two million!

Lots of things need coordination across the region, so the assemblies send delegates to confederal councils. There are confederal councils for every seven to 10 assemblies, and then an over-arching confederal council for the whole nation. Each council operates through consensus the same way each assembly does, all of them facilitated by co-chairs, at least one of whom must be a woman. The councils coordinate and share ideas, and actual decision-making returns to the assemblies.

In this way, amid the wreckage of the semi-failed states of Syria and Iraq, threatened by Russia, Turkey, Iran and ISIS, Rojava survives and grows.

Clearly, they are doing something right.

Some people argue that a large and complex society requires strong, centralised government, and participatory democracy can only ever be a dinky little space at the edges. For others, because true democracy can only ever work through direct participation, large-scale government of any kind is inherently dominating and centralising.

Both perspectives reveal anti-ecological thinking.

Ecological systems operate at and across every scale. Each cell, each atom, is a transferable part of 'individual' animals, people or plants, which, interconnected, make up the meso scale of flocks of birds, cities, catchments or bioregions, which themselves combine and recombine at the continental and global scale. Seeing one scale as separate from or more important than others, is nonsense. They are interconnected, interdependent and integrated.

Living democracy is people acting together, at every scale, interdependently. Attempting to control this through top-down power and coercion is both anti-democratic and anti-ecological. Equally, however, uncoordinated, disconnected localism is also both anti-democratic and anti-ecological. Neither fragmented ecosystems nor monocultures are ecologically resilient. So living democracy needs regional and global democratic systems based on integration, not centralisation.

Can we have nations that aren't states? Can we have internationalism without nationalism? Ostrom, Bookchin, Öcalan, Colau and others say we can.

This tension is the core of Murray Bookchin's philosophy. He warned that 'notions of decentralism that emphasize localist isolation'[22] create parochial communities with a tendency to fight among themselves. On the other hand, '[t]o create a state is to institutionalize power in the form of a machine that exists *apart* from the people ... [and] that, however weak or however well-intentioned it may be at first, eventually takes on a corruptive power of its own'.[23] His answer was municipal confederalism – the system that excited Abdullah Öcalan and that Rojava is building.

Making the basic governing unit small, directly demo-cratic assemblies avoids the threat of top-down statism, while coordination through confederal councils ensures interdependence and avoids fragmentation. Delegates are nominated by the assemblies to chair meetings, to attend meetings of the various confederal councils, and to take on specific roles – to lead but never to rule. Those delegates can be recalled at any time, and the confederal councils' role is primarily coordination, ideas-sharing and building common cause, while administration stays with the assemblies. The structure institutionalises mutualism, sharing responsibility among individuals and groups and across scales.

There's a close parallel here with Elinor Ostrom's concept of polycentrism. For Ostrom, while good governance requires grassroots participation, coordination is vital for management of scales such as bioregions, cities or the global climate. Polycentrism simply means that that coordination must be done in the same manner as local governance – through negotiation, based on agreed rules and practices.

Rather than bringing the management of an entire river system into one centralised, hierarchical organisation, for example, Ostrom's research shows that negotiated coordination between local commons management groups works far better.[24] What evolves is 'a *polycentric set* of limited-purpose governmental enterprises whose governance includes active participation [by a range of relevant groups] ... This system is neither centrally owned nor centrally regulated.'[25] Everybody benefits from transparent information flows; responsibility for everyone belongs to everyone; decision-making power is shared, among and between scales.

Anti-ecological culture insists that this kind of complex, mutual governance is inefficient. But the redundancies in the system, with multiple people and groups playing the same role instead of 'efficiently' streamlining them, are, in an ecological sense, what gives the system its resilience.[26] Ostrom detailed numerous examples of polycentrism working over large areas and extended periods of time.

The experiences of Barcelona en Comú highlight the difficulties of cultivating commons governance from within anti-ecological state structures. Everyone I spoke with there agreed the biggest challenge has been the reluctance of people to let go of control, both internally and externally. Municipal managers initially didn't want to implement government policies and citizens didn't feel welcome in the imposing town hall. At the other end of the spectrum, some proposals, such as de-privatising water and energy services and bringing them under community management, were blocked or delayed by Spanish and European Union state power. Only through tremendous commitment to decentralising and devolving decision-making has the transformation begun.

Barcelona en Comú and Rojava both present a different way of thinking about nationalism and internationalism – a bottom-up globalism based on mutualism and interdependence. Rojava identifies itself as a nation but not a state. Barcelona en Comú is a municipality within a state within the European Union. Both reach out to others seeking to do similar things around the planet. Colau has championed the idea of a Fearless Cities Network as a way for municipal governments to support each other in challenging and replacing the dominant power of states competing with one another. We'll explore the exciting geopolitical implications of this polycentric, mutualist internationalism in the chapter, 'Practising peace: From coercion to coexistence'.

Between Ostrom and Bookchin, from Barcelona to Gladstone, Wangaratta to Kurdistan, what's beginning to take shape is a network of projects with a multitude of models, all working towards a goal we can call living democracy.

There are crucial lessons for us here, as we co-develop our own projects. We need to resist the urge to pull everything together into single forms. We need to embrace complexity, ambiguity and redundancy as we reach out to work with others. We can have formal and informal democratic bodies; standing and temporary bodies; small and large – as long as they are interconnected. Whatever we build needs to have a clear, bounded identity, with permeable walls, allowing for overlapping spaces of democratic decision-making.

We can join with Barcelona en Comú, Rojava and others in cultivating a new polycentric ecological democracy from the grassroots up, with green shoots all over the world, and, bit by bit, weave them together in a global living democracy.


## Adaptation:
## Living democracy can't be fossilised

Thomas Jefferson, one of the Founding Fathers of the United States, wrote: 'I hold it that a little rebellion now and then is a good thing ... It is a medicine necessary for the sound health of government ... God forbid that we should ever be twenty years without such a rebellion.'[27] Constitutional 'originalists', who insist on trying to interpret documents as their crafters intended generations ago, and who abhor social and democratic change, might be surprised by this.

Thus far, through participation, deliberation and integration, we've applied the ecological principles of diversity and interdependence to democracy. The one principle we haven't looked at is impermanence. Nobody likes to talk about that. It reminds us of our own mortality. But it's vital that we grapple with it.

As Murray Bookchin said: 'The assumption that what currently exists must necessarily exist is the acid that corrodes all visionary thinking.'[28] And he reminds us that this doesn't apply only to now, to our desire to change the world as it is, but also to what we ourselves seek to build.

Ecologists Lance Gunderson and Buzz Holling, in their remarkable book *Panarchy*, explained this beautifully in ecological terms:

> Conserving the elements we have is not the goal for a search for what is enduring … The challenge, rather, is to conserve the ability to adapt to change, to be able to respond in a flexible way to uncertainty and surprises. And even to create the kind of surprises that open opportunity.[29]

In other words, creating a system and setting it in stone is both anti-democratic and anti-ecological. This has profound implications for both utopianism and constitutionalism.

Our democratic systems have to shift with changing circumstances. Australia and the USA, with our old national constitutions, are frequently grappling with how to apply rules from a different age to our own. More deeply, democracies are based on trust, and trust needs to be continually refreshed and cultivated. Outsourcing trust in each other to a constitution can only work for a short time before you need to revisit it. That's the point Jefferson was making, echoed by Bookchin two centuries later: that each generation could be advised to revisit the constitution.

This is not to say that we throw everything away and start again each generation. As Gunderson and Holling wrote, it's about adaptable systems. For Ostrom, it's about establishing processes that make renegotiation smooth.[30] Frances Moore Lappé reflected that this is, in fact, what democracy is all about: 'Living Democracy is … not a set system, finished and done, but a set of system values – with inclusion, fairness, and mutual accountability among them – that infuse all dimensions of our common life.'[31] Bookchin, too, reminded us that we have to keep our change within a framework of agreed values: 'We must learn to be flexible without allowing our basic principles to be replaced by a postmodernist quagmire of ad hoc, ever-changeable opinions.'[32]

In our anti-ecological culture, when we set something up or get involved with it, we like to imagine it will last forever. From an ecological perspective, that's neither desirable nor possible. As you take the examples here and go out into your community to chart your path, the aim should be for every project, each organising group, to reformulate, re-establish or be replaced as needed. Just like with moving from adversarialism to deliberation, we have to drop the ego and let go of control.

The wonderful thing is, as Ostrom found with her examples of centuries-old commons, if we do that, what we build can truly be long-lasting.

Our current system is hurtling us towards the precipice, so these ideas can't be tweaks at the margins, making it slightly less destructive; they need to be truly building the new systems. And, in working to grow such systems from our instinct for mutual aid, we need to be constantly aware that the instinct of the anti-ecological state is to take over, co-opt or suppress mutual aid as a threat to its power. We need an approach to governing that enables mutual aid to flourish and supports it without taking over.

In doing all this, we will put ourselves well on the path to surviving and thriving.

But cultivating democracy is not enough. We need to recognise that power is currently held not only through governing systems but through economic systems. The capitalist interference with democracy that has been a constant feature of the liberal democratic system has, in recent years, become corporate capture of the machinery of the state. Living democracy needs that to end. We must democratise the economy, and make it ecological. That's where we head next.

# EXERCISING ECONOMY

## From extraction to cultivation

Imagine you lived in one of the early city states in fertile Mesopotamia, a few centuries before the Great Pyramid of Giza was built.

Let's say you brought your Sumerian ruler a flagon of your new innovation – apricot nectar. This man who (as it turned out!) actually was an omnipotent god king, swooned in delight. In reward, he blessed you with eternal life and extraordinary wealth, magically bequeathing you the equivalent of $100 000 every single day, accumulating forever.

Scrooge-like, you haven't spent a cent, as you've watched your loved ones die, your home crumble into sand, empires rise and fall.

Five thousand years have passed, and the money has piled up, day by day.

You're still not as wealthy as Jeff Bezos.

Astonished to learn this mindboggling statistic, you travel

the world, trying to work out what on earth wealth and value actually mean.

You find yourself in Barking and Dagenham, a London borough with high unemployment, a large immigrant population, over a third of people living in social housing.[1] On a high street, next to a boarded-up window, you see a bright, cheery shopfront labelled Participatory City, and decide to pop in. The coordinator asks what you're interested in and, hearing about your love of stone fruit, phones a local retiree who helps manage a community garden nearby.

Minutes later, you find yourself in a flourishing oasis in the middle of the concrete and brick desert. There, by the south-facing wall of a block of council flats, behind the beans and blueberries, you see a row of apricot trees, groaning under the weight of ripe fruit!

Together with the English lady, a Bangladeshi teen, and a young Nigerian mum and her kids, you spend a delightful morning harvesting buckets of golden, sugary goodness, watching the children pop them in their mouths as much as in the buckets. When you're done, the teenager suggests you take them to the community kitchen down the road and make jam for the markets.

'I have a better idea', you say.

You chat as the fruit simmers, with some extra sugar and lemon juice. You hear how the knitting group makes clothes and blankets for people in need. You learn about the mural kids painted on a bare wall, livening up the neighbourhood, creating a sense of shared purpose, and giving them a thrill of pride every time they pass it. As a crowd gathers for an evening planning meeting, you're told about the parents' group that helped the young mum cope, and the repair cafe where they've learned new skills, shared old ones, and kept clothes and toys, bikes and even electrical appliances usable for longer.

When the nectar is ready, you pass cups around the buzzing room. Your heart soars as you hear contented sighs, as you watch eyes close, lips sipping the liquid sunlight, revealing the same delight as your god king, millennia ago.

From this harvest in this run-down neighbourhood, you realise, you've finally reaped real abundance.

'The cost of a thing is the amount of ... life which is required to be exchanged for it, immediately or in the long run.'[2]

So wrote Henry David Thoreau in his elegy to simplicity, *Walden*, published shortly before the first volume of Karl Marx's *Capital*, in those tumultuous mid 19th century years.

While Marx was rubbing shoulders with workers and radicals, and writing in the British Library, Thoreau was chopping wood by a pond in Massachusetts, tending his garden and, for a time, sitting in prison for refusing to pay taxes to fund America's expansionist wars.

Though utterly different people in dramatically different circumstances, both challenge us to consider how we value what we value. Where Marx argued, in the Labour Theory of Value, that value is created by work put in, and captured by the owners of capital rather than those who labour, Thoreau embedded it in life – life put in, life extracted. They're similar ideas, both insisting that value must be grounded in something tangible, something that truly matters, something real.

'The economy' isn't a thing that exists; it's a set of stories we tell ourselves about how we think it *should* exist, intertwining with structures of power that the stories reinforce. We've been convinced, as Yuval Noah Harari told us, that made up things like corporations and states are more important than real things like the land, trees and ourselves, to the extent that we're willing to destroy the land, trees and ourselves in the name of these 'imagined entities'. This mythology is why, in variously attributed famous words, 'it's easier to imagine the end of the world than the end of capitalism'.

It's these economic stories, the structures of material power they enforce, and their implications for how we live democracy, that we're going to explore now. We'll uncover ideas and inspiring examples for how we flip our economy from one which drives constant extraction of scarce value into one which cultivates shared, abundant value – a living economy intertwined with our living democracy.

Ecology and economy.

The words come from the same root – the Ancient Greek *oikos*, meaning home or dwelling place. Ecology combines it with *logos* to become the meaning or understanding of home, while economy adds *nomos*, becoming household management. I reckon the difference in practice, a difference that evolved with anti-ecological culture, is the question of control. And it starts with how we build the walls of our home.

In ecological thinking, the 'walls became the world all around', in Maurice Sendak's immortal phrase from *Where The Wild Things Are*. All boundaries are porous and overlapping. Walls are necessary, as Elinor Ostrom told us through the importance of setting agreed boundaries. But, like the walls of the cells in our bodies, they need to be permeable and changeable.

Hadrian's Wall. The Berlin Wall. Walls between Israel and Gaza, the USA and Mexico. The wall the lord built to keep peasants from 'poaching' – getting food from land that used to be commons. Anti-ecology builds walls to divide 'us' from 'them', to control what's inside, to enclose ever more, and to pretend that we could continue this forever.

The economic aspect of this is evocatively described by Naomi Klein, Mariana Mazzucato and others as 'extractivism'. Extractivism up-ends the Indigenous principle that 'country owns us', replacing it with the belief that everything is subject to ownership. The soil under our feet, the water we drink, the air we breathe, the animals and plants we share the land with, and we ourselves – our time, our bodies, our emotions – become resources to be bought, sold and stolen, and from which to extract value. This commodification underpins land clearing and industrial agriculture, and the subjugation of women, colonised peoples and the poor. Today we see extractivism in everything from sacrifice zones, where poor communities are forced to live in the most polluted areas, to coercive welfare systems, where people are punished for not being able to find jobs. We see it in wars for resources, and in whole farms and towns in regions from the Hunter Valley to Mongolia being swallowed by mines.

Through this lens, we get a revealing view of a central concept in economic theory: scarcity. Anti-ecological culture tells us that, like selfishness and competition, scarcity is a fact of life which modern economics was developed to manage. But enclosure abuses scarcity to maintain control. By making us feel we need ever more stuff, and by limiting our ability to be independent cultivators, anti-ecology doesn't manage scarcity – it intensifies it.

Now of course scarcity exists on a finite planet. But the self-organising living world generates abundance. Value (life, as Thoreau put it) constantly moves from one place or form to another, *increasing* mutual value as it's shared. Whether it's seeds being distributed by birds or farmers, or a carnivore eating another animal and excreting waste elsewhere, fertilising the soil, that constant redistribution is what creates the healthy, resilient interdependence that is ecology. Trees use the sun and nutrients in the soils, mobilised by fungi, to accumulate sugars in their wood, putting excess into fruits which animals eat, giving the animals concentrated energy and the trees mobility. In a sense, that's what life is: proteins and sugars and minerals gathered together in complex forms before being disaggregated and reaggregated somewhere else. The multi-stage accumulation and redistribution of interdependent life increases the value of the common pool available to all.

Indigenous economies, and more recently reinvented gift economies, are based on this idea. If the 'cost' of something is the amount of life we exchange for it, sharing and recirculation costs less life, or even creates life. Using currencies of gratitude and reciprocity, it creates abundance for all.

Enclosure deliberately prevents this. Remember Ester Boserup: the best way to control people is to deprive them of the capacity to be independent cultivators. The creation of scarcity starts with controlling land and the growth and distribution of food. It gains sophistication through royal grants of monopoly and the invention of intellectual property, laying the foundations for the industrial revolution and capitalism. It continues in online paywalls, enclosing the internet commons.

In each case, natural abundance is turned into scarcity so the powerful can exert control and extract value.

It goes without saying that capitalism is the clearest embodiment of extractivism. Its entire philosophical and structural basis is competition between individual entities seeking constant growth within the context of (manufactured) scarcity.

But extractivism is also visible in Soviet and Maoist communism and (to a lesser extent) Nordic and Latin American state socialism, all of which structure their economies on extraction of both natural and human 'resources', and which, through centralised control, manufacture scarcity. Marx recognised the perils of metabolic rift, but the political structures that followed him remained extractive.

Like adversarial democracy in our parliaments, extractivist economics has become embedded in our systems through institutional structures like corporations, labour and welfare. We've institutionalised our most damaging instincts, and built a self-destructive system that has brought us to the very edge of collapse.

What would it mean to rewrite our economic story based on our more creative instincts? What would cultivating an economy of interdependence instead of competitive individualism, an economy of abundance within limits rather than one of scarcity, look like? How do we live a living economy that will help us end the destruction and survive what's coming?

We'll start with reclaiming the commons, cultivating abundant, shared value in our communities. Then we'll take back our labour, challenging the enclosure and commodification of ourselves. We'll bring the commons into institutional structures by replacing that most extractive of ideas, the corporation, with democratic alternatives. And finally we'll ensure that the abundance we cultivate keeps circulating.

Through inspiring examples, we'll learn how we can replace extractivism with cultivation in our communities, culture and institutions, dissolving dominating economic power and growing a living economic system that can enable us all to survive and thrive together.

## When growth is good: Reclaiming the commons

Walking to the local shops recently, I spotted a kid wearing a jumper I recognised. I smiled and stopped to chat with the parents and, sure enough, they'd picked it up on the Buy Nothing group. We worked out it had probably been through at least two other families since my children had outgrown it. The family had recently moved into the area and already found a lovely community, partly through the group.

It was after leaving an incredibly busy job and taking on more parenting responsibilities again that I set up Canberra's first Buy Nothing group. One of my kids needed a white shirt for a concert, and I asked friends on Facebook if I could borrow one. A few days later, a friend asked to borrow my kayak. Surely we could formalise something like this, I thought, and, investigating, I came across this model.

Like Freecycle, Buy Nothing groups are online spaces where people can offer things they no longer want or need, ask for things they're after, or borrow and lend things. But what makes this model special is that groups are hyperlocal

WHERE ARE WE GOING?

and designed not just to swap stuff but to actively cultivate community. People are asked to tell stories about what they're offering or asking for, to move slowly with gifting so as to allow plenty of people to participate, to have polite exchanges instead of posting soulless demands, and to be friendly when exchanging items. A few volunteers provide administrative support to steward this commons, but it's everyone's responsibility to nurture relationships and negotiate shared space. I enjoy occasionally ribbing folks about how what we're doing is radical anti-capitalist organising, but in truth the greatest joys are the stories of friendships formed, of people being welcomed into the neighbourhood, of a loved item being loved by someone new.

I've seen people offer up everything from open packets of cereal to beautiful old furniture and even a piano! You get people asking for anything from urgent costume help for Book Week to a mattress for local public housing tenants. In our group, a suitcase of ever-changing clothing constantly circulates, and a communal lawnmower keeps the grass of dozens of homes at bay. I've found someone able to fix a broken bike headlight. And we've collected blankets and winter clothes for refugees and homeless people.

The group I set up initially covered a dozen suburbs. We had several hundred members within weeks, and within months other groups were forming across Canberra. With repeated 'sprouting' into smaller groups as each gets too large (usually around 1000 people) there are now almost 50 groups covering the whole city, with over 37 000 members – approaching 10 per cent of the city's population! Regional admins help resolve disputes, share advice, and occasionally offer items across the groups. It's such an easy, joyful practice of living well.

What we're doing is truly generating abundance, both by reducing waste and by increasing the value of what's being shared. That jumper given away still brings me warmth by warming others. And how much tastier is a meal made with ingredients from someone down the street who you had a lovely chat with?

Environmentalists have long pointed out that eternal extractivist growth on a finite planet is nonsensical.[3] But ecological thinking gives us a different perspective on this question, asking not 'should we grow?', but 'what should we grow?'

Let's explore this idea before we return to practical examples of abundance.

Economists like Kate Raworth argue that we should be more concerned about the shape of the economy than its size. Should we encourage production and consumption of everything, regardless of impact, because it increases Gross Domestic Product (GDP)? Clearly not. But we should absolutely continue to grow things like healthcare, housing and education, clean water, good food, great art, and a genuine say in our common future. Just as we love to see plants and birdlife flourishing thanks to bush regeneration, if we have a cultivationist economy rather than an extractivist one, and we measure what we contribute to the common pool, growth can be good.

As Bobby Kennedy famously said, GDP 'measures everything ... except that which makes life worthwhile',[4] so all sorts of alternatives are being developed across the world.

Raworth's *Doughnut Economics*,[5] for example, tracks progress towards decent standards of living (reaching the inside of the doughnut) against efforts to stay within ecological limits (the outside of the doughnut), measuring and guiding the shape of the economy rather than its size.

Shifting what gets measured and valued changes how we picture the economy.

Raworth, Ostrom and many feminist economists point out that modern political economy's binary division of the world into market and state erases the vital economic spaces of the commons and the household. These 'reproductive' spaces where value is grown rather than extracted aren't measured by GDP, so they don't exist in our economic picture. This gives us another insight into the growth question.

Where capitalists want to shrink government, to get it out of the way of their ability to make money, we can increase wellbeing by shrinking both the market economy and state control, supporting and enabling the commons and the household, the non-monetary economy, the spaces in the community where we grow, create, exchange and repair things, where we care for and support each other, and cultivate better lives together. The market–state dichotomy deliberately erases this beautiful world, precisely because it's hard to control, to tax, to extract value from.

Bob Brown, former leader of the Australian Greens, expressed this powerfully: 'The political debate of the 20th century was … about control of the economy in the narrow sense of material goods and money. A free market versus state control. Bitter experience tells us that the best outcome is neither, but some of both.'[6] Murray Bookchin similarly observed that, just like democracy, we need to understand the economy as an aspect of how we live together, and 'integrate the means of production into ... existential life'.[7]

In other words, just as we need to cultivate a government that is us making decisions together rather than a separate entity we call a state, we need to stop fetishising the economy as something separate from us, an all-powerful entity we have to sacrifice to. We need to start valuing instead things that really exist and matter.

Alongside this, we have to abandon the invention of *homo economicus* that we discussed in Part 1 – the mythology of a purely rational, entirely self-interested, utility-maximising human – and re-embrace a more complex understanding of who we are as competitive and cooperative creatures. Yes, self-interest exists, and we can design systems to temper it, rather than bolster it. And cooperation, collaboration and creativity are just as much part of who we are, and are actually better at creating value.[8]

The best way to shift the understanding of who we are is to live it.

It's no accident that one of my main examples of living democracy, Participatory City, is also how I started this living economy chapter. Gently helping people to improve their quality of life together, they create deep connections and build individual and collective agency, growing abundant value for everyone.

Community gardens and cooking groups, where people with skills help others learn, sharing the bounty with each other, turn a chore into a joy. Parent groups, gathering in friendly cafes or community spaces to swap stories and give each other a break, lighten the exhausting load of parenting for everyone. Community art projects, where folks come together to paint a mural to beautify a street, give the participants common purpose, shared experience and a joint sense of achievement that renews each time they pass it. Swap meets and upcycling sessions, where people can exchange clothes and learn how to mend them or adjust their size, keep goods circulating longer through a fun, shared process. Working bees to install draft-proofing make each other's homes more liveable while reducing environmental impact and cultivating community cohesion.

We don't always have to participate in either the market economy or government programs to get what we need in life. In fact, as Participatory City's research shows, by doing things ourselves, together, we take back our agency, we cultivate a sense of capability and mutuality, and we build trust.[9] Each activity creates flows of value in the community, value which grows with use and exchange instead of being extracted, generating abundance where before there was scarcity.

Central to the program's success is that it's friendly, open, welcoming, generous, with no expectation of payment. All ideas and impetus come from community members, supported by trained facilitators who help them navigate the path they've chosen. This participatory approach is a dramatic shift from traditional paternalistic programs to help the poor, telling people how to live their lives and usually failing.

Participatory City isn't unique. Countless communities all around the globe are doing similar things, whether it be Buy Nothing groups, repair cafes, little street libraries and pantries, or community kitchens. All these circumvent both the scarcity-based market economy and controlling, bureaucratic government, and generate abundance through interdependence.

I'm sure it's the deep connection between people that they cultivate that led so many Buy Nothing groups to pivot into mutual aid during the pandemic – a vital practice run for the years ahead. Already used to thinking about each other, members swiftly came together to letterbox neighbourhoods offering support, whether in collecting groceries, sharing toilet paper, or just having chats on the phone or Zoom to keep each other company. The currencies of gratitude and reciprocity came into their own.

Something I've noticed about these grassroots gift economies is how much they tend to revolve around food. I suspect this is because food gives us joy as well as sustenance, and is so grounded in the very basics of life. Food is also the most obvious space at the boundaries of the market and the commons – farmers' markets and food co-ops.

These are, of course, part of the market economy in that we buy and sell goods there, but they're far more participatory spaces than impersonal supermarkets, for example. By building personal relationships, and helping out where we can, we create more value for everyone involved. Giant supermarkets, on the other hand, extract value at every step – from producers, suppliers, employees and from us, through advertising, store design and, most blatantly, making us provide free labour by checking out our own groceries. Supermarkets, with their packed shelves and huge choice, are places of policed scarcity, where co-ops and farmers' markets are spaces of generative abundance.

Food co-ops are many people's main experience with the cooperative economy, alongside other 'reproductive' economic spaces like childcare and health. We'll explore cooperatives more later, but it's worth noting here that they are among the most powerful ways of reclaiming the commons in our communities. Sharing, repairing and creating don't always have to be done entirely outside the market economy. If you feel it's important to sell goods from the maker spaces or community gardens, for example, doing so as a cooperative is an excellent way to share abundance instead of extract value. Arts and craft co-ops, where participants share the costs and profits and jointly make decisions, are a great example, as are health and housing co-ops, where providers and users cooperatively manage vital services and see value retained, recirculated, and growing with reuse.

While we're in the space between commons and the market, I've mentioned currencies of gratitude and reciprocity a couple of times. What if we could actually use them as tender? That, in a sense, is what various communities are doing through local currencies; by keeping money circulating among local enterprises, they're building social cohesion and connecting the economy to participation.

One of my favourite ideas in this space is that currency can be designed to expire without use – you have to keep it circulating because that's where its value is. There are numerous examples to look at, from actual cash like the Bristol Pound through to more complex Local Energy Transfer Schemes, and how-to guides have even been developed.[10] While it's important to avoid monetising all interactions, this is something communities can do to complement the gift economy.

A final idea for reclaiming the commons, and one of my personal passions, is resisting the privatisation of public space by advertising. Outdoor advertising sends a powerful message to the community that public space is not ours – it belongs to private interests to profit from. It embeds the primacy of private profit over public interest into our lived environment, it continues the enclosure of the commons, and it drives the extractivist economy by convincing us to buy things we don't want or need.[11]

I'm sure one of the reasons Canberra is such a progressive city is that, thanks to having been purpose-built as a seat of government, it's always had strict limits on outdoor advertising. A recent proposal to loosen those limits met with vociferous opposition.[12] Other cities are realising the benefits of ad-free space. In 2006, the Brazilian city of São Paolo introduced its Clean City Law,[13] which has seen the removal of some 15 000 billboards across the city, and has proved very popular. Chennai, India, banned billboards in 2009,[14] and in 2014 the French city of Grenoble started rolling back street advertising.[15] Several US states, including Hawaii, Maine and Vermont, have banned billboards, and Paris has reduced advertising space across the city by 30 per cent.[16]

Meanwhile, passionate groups of citizens are directly reclaiming public space from advertising. One delightful project called CATS – the Citizens Advertising Takeover Service – has crowdfunded buying ad space in London Underground stations, replacing commercial messages with cute pictures of cats.[17] Others are engaging in civil disobedience to rid their streets and public transport of advertising.[18]

We can all work together in the community to reclaim the commons and, in doing so, loosen a linchpin in the extractivist economy.

But one of the biggest barriers to growing our abundance economies and reclaiming the commons is the way we ourselves have been enclosed and commodified, extracting our time, our energy, our imaginations. We need to reclaim ourselves. That's where we head next.

## Reclaiming our labour

'You don't have a choice. You belong to us.'

That's how a job service agent responded when Elisha Portelli told him she couldn't attend an in-person appointment.[19] Portelli was receiving income support to supplement her low wages from unpredictable shift work. She couldn't drive, and lived a long way from public transport. She had sometimes thought it was better to skip a shift than risk having her welfare suspended thanks to being marked 'non-compliant' by the private corporation running the government's job service. Portelli describes feeling 'degraded' and 'full of despair' in the face of a machine that was keeping her in poverty, making it harder to get on her feet.

But, in mid 2020, with Australia in pandemic lockdown, the government took the extraordinary step of both doubling the rate of income support and suspending the Orwellianly named 'Mutual Obligations'. People would no longer be required to attend appointments, apply for countless jobs, or go to parenting programs. They would be given payments unconditionally, as long as the lockdown lasted.

This move, which saw a dramatic reduction in mental illness, stress and poverty, has been described as a real-world experiment with Universal Basic Income (UBI).[20]

UBI treats income the way we currently treat universal health and education. Where our society agrees that every person should have access to basic levels of health care and education, UBI structurally eliminates poverty by setting the base level of income above the poverty line. Just as public hospitals and schools are open to all, and we pay for them collectively through a progressive tax system, the same goes for UBI. Everyone gets a regular, unconditional deposit, and those who have more pay more into the common pot.

While it wasn't universal, Australia's unconditional COVID supplement demonstrated how this approach changes lives. Portelli says of the suspension of 'Mutual Obligations': 'In the absence of their ever-present shadow I felt a sense of relief I hadn't felt in years. I felt more productive and worked meaningfully towards my employment goals.'

Extractivist economies need a supply of cheap and obedient labour. Governments ensure this supply by undermining the ability of workers to collectively bargain, by keeping us too busy and exhausted to self-provision, and by making unemployment intolerable.

In Australia, as elsewhere, we've seen punitive policies introduced to make those who cannot find work suffer. From work-for-the-dole and internship programs that leave people less employable and reduce the amount of available paid labour, to compulsory parenting classes that make parenting responsibilities harder, from pointless bureaucracy to needlessly humiliating drug testing,[21] not to speak of the horrific automated 'Robodebt' program that is thought to have contributed to some 2000 suicides,[22] the system is deliberately coercive. It's an approach designed not just to punish the currently unemployed, but to use their suffering as a warning to others: do not quit your job, no matter how unpleasant it is, no matter how badly you're treated.[23]

By reducing the value of human life to what we can sell our labour for, by entangling our ability to sell our labour with our capacity to survive, extractivism is turned on us. We are commodified.

In one of extractivism's greatest successes, it's become culturally ingrained that selling our labour is the only legitimate way of contributing to and participating in society (unless you're wealthy). It may have been coerced originally, as Boserup suggested, but it made a leap into culture with the Protestant work ethic in the 18th century, with industrialists insisting that leisure only gave the devil time to whisper in your ear. This is deeply patriarchal and colonialist, erasing the value of reproductive labour, of caring, sharing, non-market participation of all kinds, that have been depicted as women's work, or as 'uncivilised'.

The commodification of us is a linchpin of the extractivist system. The struggle to reclaim ourselves is central to any effort to replace it.

To be clear, this isn't an argument against work. There'll be a lot to do as we face up to the intersecting crises anti-ecological culture has wrought: as we transition to renewable energy, build energy-efficient homes and mass transit and cycleways, and create whole new industries of reuse and recycling; as we have to work harder to grow food; as we reprioritise care and education; and as we learn to govern our communities together. But it's crucial, in doing this, that we extract ourselves from extractivist labour: insisting on our rights to collectively bargain; taking direct agency in our labour through worker-owned cooperatives; shortening the working week; ending degrading and punitive conditionality on welfare; and using industrial policy to guide job creation. But overarching it all is Universal Basic Income.

UBI ends extractivist labour. It dramatically changes our relationships with government, and with each other. It opens up new ways of valuing participation. And it brings us together around a vision of an abundant, interdependent world.

UBI structurally ends the extractivist nature of labour by disentangling work from the capacity to survive. If you can leave a job which is unpleasant without the fear that you'll be abandoned, you're no longer a human resource, you're a human being, an innately valuable and valued member of our interdependent society.

UBI recasts the relationship between citizen and government. Instead of the Leviathan state surveilling, judging and punishing you, putting conditions on your right to survive, government becomes an enabler for every citizen to choose their own path. Crucially, it doesn't do that as atomised individuals; it does it through a universalist approach, applying the benefits to everyone, and requiring everyone to contribute to the extent of their abilities. Where conditional payments create an 'us and them' conflict between deserving and undeserving, universalist policies bring us together around the common good. Where surveillance-based welfare institutionalises distrust, UBI assumes the best of people, and by doing so, cultivates trust.

UBI enables broader participation. One of the most punishing aspects of extractivist labour is that it deliberately keeps us so busy and distracted that we become politically submissive. UBI gives us time in our lives to come together, to do democracy, to make change. Or just to live how we choose to live. This is one of the reasons why it's a fantastically intersectional policy. It's clearly a feminist and anti-colonialist policy, valuing caring, non-market participation, and other 'reproductive' work. And, by creating space in our lives, it helps every volunteer-run organisation that struggles to find people able to commit time. It also, frankly, will lead to better quality 'productive' work. The assumption that people will only work if forced is both wrong and repressive. In fact, people tend to work better if given the space and opportunity to find their own agency – if we cultivate them instead of extracting their value.

As a musician, I'm fascinated by the possibility of UBI to enable artists to survive without the necessity of commodifying our art. Living on royalties has always been impossible, and is becoming absurd as royalties decrease and cost of living increases. But it's also problematically anti-ecological, this idea that everything can and should be owned applying not just to land, water, air, labour ... but to art? Art has always borrowed and built on other people's art. Creativity isn't an individual pursuit. It only makes sense as part of the ecosystem of other art and ideas. UBI can enable artists to live while making art and not considering their creativity in extractivist terms.

Finally, I believe that unionists can come to embrace it, although many currently object to it as somehow 'giving up on work'. Though much of the labour movement has embraced the century-long shift from caring about the dignity of the working person to the dignity of work itself, there are still plenty who recall that unionism started as a fight to not allow work to be all-consuming, not allow it to control the lives of working people, to disentangle labour from the capacity to survive. It started with the fight to work less, the struggle for weekends and the eight-hour day, paid sick leave and holidays. UBI is simply the next logical step at this moment in history.

Why do so many left-wing people think a rallying cry of 'give us work' is either inspiring or transformative? It's a rallying cry which locks us into a supplicant position, begging the wealthy to let us help increase their wealth while being given scraps from the table. It abdicates our agency, demanding that powerful people give us something to do.

Is it paid labour we want? Or is it what we're told only paid labour can give us: the capacity to survive, and the sense that we're doing something valuable?

Let's shift the terms of our political economy entirely, demand the right simply to live, trust each other to choose our own way to participate and contribute, and transform labour from extractivism to cultivation.

And, as we do that, let's also topple the other pillar of our extractivist economic architecture: the corporation – the ultimate extractivist invention.

## Reclaiming corporations

In 1972, almost a decade late and plagued by controversy, what was to become one of the world's most iconic buildings, the Sydney Opera House, had been under construction for 15 years. It could have been a disaster when one of the construction workers was fired and the union called industrial action.

But the Builders Labourers Federation, the union behind the 'Green Bans' that saved heritage buildings in The Rocks and laid foundation stones for the Sydney Greens party, took an unexpected path. When the managers refused the union's demands and locked them out of the site, the workers returned with crowbars, marched through the gates, and locked the bosses out in a remarkable reverse picket. Gathering to democratically decide what to do, they choose to set up their own flat structure and get on with the job.[24]

Thanks to their cohesion and trust, strong information flows, and their shared stake in success, the work was done to high quality and in a shorter 35-hour week. It became clear that the workers' demands were reasonable, and before long they won their pay rise, rehiring, extra leave, and the right to choose their own foremen.

Ensuring that people can participate fully, sharing in decision-making, and in risk and reward, does the same thing in the economic space as in the democratic – it makes decisions in the common interest far more likely, and suppresses greed and self-interest.

Corporate governance does the opposite.

Just days after the Intergovernmental Panel on Climate Change released its 6th Assessment Report, global mining giant BHP announced that it was offloading its fossil fuel business to Woodside Petroleum. Alongside existing and planned fossil fuel operations, Woodside began working to open an array of new gas and oil reservoirs easily sufficient to tip the planet well beyond 2 degrees Celsius of heating, making it arguably among the world's most dangerous entities.

But Woodside is legally obliged to increase profits to its shareholders now. If that means burning our future, that's not

Woodside's problem. If it means pressuring governments not to legislate to make it harder for them to increase profits, that's what Woodside should do. And it does.

Woodside is often at the top of the list of Australian corporate political donors. In 2020, it 'donated' $198 750 to the governing Liberal and National parties, and $137 500 to the Labor opposition. It's handed them some $2 million over the last decade.

Woodside also has very close ties to members of parliament. Gary Gray, former Labor minister for resources and energy, was Woodside's director of corporate affairs immediately before entering parliament. His predecessor, Martin Ferguson, had a former Woodside employee as his policy advisor and chief of staff. Resources minister at time of writing, the Nationals' Keith Pitt, put out a press release welcoming Woodside's new CEO, and in 2020 gave it an $8.8 million grant to advise the government on how to clean up its own mess from abandoned infrastructure in the Timor Sea.

Speaking of the Timor Sea, it was on Woodside's behalf that John Howard's Liberal-National Government bugged Timor Leste's cabinet room to gain advantage in negotiations over access to gas fields, leading to diplomatic controversy and the prosecution of whistleblower Witness K and his lawyer, Bernard Collaery. In a remarkable coincidence, then Foreign Minister Alexander Downer found a position as a consultant to Woodside after leaving parliament.

Government of the fossil fuel industry, by the fossil fuel industry, for the fossil fuel industry. That's just one example.

The corporation is the ultimate extractivist invention: an entirely profit-driven machine, rewarding short-term selfishness, punishing sharing, dismissing stewardship, and demanding constant growth. Designed to enclose and extract value from the natural world, from 'consumers', from labour, and convert it to shareholder profit, the existence of this cancerous model effectively guarantees that it will come to dominate everything in its path. The fact that not every corporation follows this destructive path is more proof of basic human decency. But the model percolates into culture – if corporations are legal persons and their only obligation is to seek profit, the sociopathic idea seeps in that the only obligation of any person is to seek profit. Having made corporations persons, we're making all of us, including governments, into corporations.

Governments are particularly susceptible to hostile corporate takeover. As political analyst Matthew Yglesias has written, 'if lobbying to create bad laws is profitable for shareholders, corporate executives are required to do it'.[25] This is why banning corporate political donations is necessary but insufficient. The donations are just the tap on the shoulder, reminding politicians who's in control. Unless and until we fundamentally redesign corporations, they will continue to find ways to circumvent democracy to extract value, leading inexorably to the corporate capture of the state.

Can business cultivate shared, abundant value? It can if we shift from corporatism to cooperativism by democratising ownership and management, by redesigning enterprises on the polycentric model rather than the single, massive firm, and by replacing profit-only legal obligations with stewardship responsibilities.

First up, what do we mean by democratising? Remember

what Raworth and Ostrom told us about thinking beyond both market and state? That's what we have to do here again: think beyond privatisation and nationalisation.

The privatisation of public goods like water and energy utilities has been long resisted by large majorities. People instinctively see it as yet another enclosure of the commons – taking something that belongs to us all and selling it to a corporation to profit from. If anything, it's becoming more stark that operating services like aged care, education, incarceration, and health care for shareholder profit is morally repugnant. The pandemic certainly opened a lot of eyes to the fact that running aged care facilities as for-profit corporations which are incentivised to cut costs and corners wherever possible, and to lobby against regulation, is … kinda problematic.

But nationalisation, putting these bodies under centralised state control, is not the only or the best alternative. When government operates like a corporation, it doesn't necessarily fix anything. Bolivian activist, Pablo Solón, watched in horror as the state expropriated privately-owned resource extraction companies, and kept running them the same way, to the detriment of Indigenous people, workers and the environment. He warned that nationalisation 'does not in itself alter the productivist and extractivist essence of capital – it can even reinforce and aggravate it. The logic of capital can continue to govern even when the state has nationalized large-scale enterprises.'[26] Distant, hierarchical, centralised control, private or public, inevitably leads to extractivism and mismanagement.

Barcelona en Comú took a different path, 'remunicipalising' water under city ownership but polycentric, co-operative management. Local communities make the decisions, and communities of communities coordinate those decisions.

This cooperative, shared stewardship model does a better job of managing the service, and sees value added to the common pool instead of extracted from it.

Like we saw with the Sydney Opera House, cooperative organisation works. And Ostrom's research shows that it works precisely because it's cooperative. Because it involves everyone in collectively setting the rules they agree to be bound by, it builds cohesion and trust. Involving everyone in day-to-day decision-making, it gets the best possible information flows and analysis from a wide range of perspectives, and enables people to listen to each other and change their minds. Because everything is shared, it protects and enhances common resources for the long term.

Business regulation in Australia pushes us towards corporate models. But organisations like the Business Council of Co-operatives and Mutuals have been established to help people form co-ops and lobby to lower regulatory barriers so that, as in Scandinavian countries, they can become a normalised, even majority, part of business.[27] With their help, any community can do it. And many are.

Communities around the world are taking on shared responsibility for services through community-owned renewable energy, childcare and housing co-ops, for instance. Others are converting existing corporations into co-ops, sometimes when they collapse or when workers are locked out, like with the Opera House. Latin Americans pioneered this approach through the economic crashes of the late 20th century in a process they call 'recuperation', combining mutual aid for families who'd lost income with workers simply taking over shuttered businesses and restarting operations. They even managed whole supply chains through a 'horizontalist' approach, built on decision-making by each group, connecting on an equal level with other groups operating in the same manner.[28]

Some forward-thinking governments are driving the establishment of co-ops and mutualisation of businesses as a way of boosting flagging local economies. In Cleveland, Ohio, and Preston, UK, municipal governments are allocating lucrative government contracts – for cleaning, manufacturing, catering – to local businesses on the condition that they adopt cooperative management, and keep funds and employment in the city.[29]

This brings us back to the question of scale. 'Business is business, and business must grow,' said Dr Seuss's Once-ler. But is that true?

During and after the 2008 global financial crash, small community banks performed better than big global banks, losing less money and recovering faster.[30] When puzzling about why this happened, the business-friendly thinktank, The Brookings Institution, discovered that it had a lot to do with relationships and local knowledge, which big banks undervalued.

The corporate imperative to grow at all costs leads inexorably towards monopoly and monoculture, as corporations eliminate or swallow their competitors. Monopoly is fundamentally anti-ecological. It's also anti-democratic. An entity which is 'too big to fail' is, in ecological terms, doomed to collapse. A company which is 'too big to fail' is too big to be democratically regulated, too big to be democratically governed, too big to be responsive to the community.

A healthy economy, like a healthy ecology, is diverse, with countless interdependent elements constantly interacting.

And, once again, Elinor Ostrom points the way. Her polycentric model, with democratically organised groups closest to the action having responsibility for decision-making, and coordinating across groups on the same democratic basis, provides a far better model for business than a massive, anonymising, bureaucratic, hierarchical agglomeration, whether private or public. This is the opposite of a franchise, where a corporation with centralised control rents out the right to wear their uniforms and sell their products. Polycentrism devolves decision-making to the local level, understanding that that's where the information is, and where trusting relationships enable good decision-making. Scale comes through coordination, not hierarchical control.

The imperative to grow must end. We should break up the behemoths that are more powerful than governments, and support polycentric models that cultivate interdependence instead of domination.

Ostrom's research on the commons, as well as Simon Niemeyer's on deliberation, shows that once we devolve decision-making, once people find their agency and groups their cohesion, the decisions made will naturally tend towards longer term thinking, stewardship and mutuality. Cultivation will come to trump extraction because that's how we think in well-facilitated democratic spaces. But we do nevertheless have to update corporate governance to require stewardship instead of just profit.

The B Corp is an alternative structure that embeds social and environmental obligations in a corporation's constitution and governance.[31] Similarly, US Senator Elizabeth Warren proposed legislation to require all corporations over a certain size to 'obtain a federal charter of corporate citizenship ...

[obliging] company directors to consider the interests of all relevant stakeholders – shareholders, but also customers, employees, and the communities in which the company operates – when making decisions'.[32] That would go some way to shifting corporate governance from extractivism to cultivation.

Warren's bill also sought to bring cooperative elements into corporate governance by requiring worker representation on boards. The simple presence of employees in the boardroom can change corporate culture, requiring directors to consider responsibilities other than profit. Around the same time as Warren announced her bill, then shadow chancellor of the UK, John McDonnell, announced a policy to require all corporations that employ more than 250 people to gradually transfer 10 per cent of their shares into an 'inclusive ownership fund', managed by employees cooperatively. This would effectively make all large corporations 10 per cent cooperative, giving workers dividends for their work, and making employee groups effectively institutional shareholders able to drive change in governance in the companies they work for.[33]

These are both welcome proposals to dissolve economic power. But we can't wait for governments, especially since, as Warren and McDonnell found, there are enormous barriers in the way of being elected when proposing such policies in our corporate-dominated electoral system. If we want a polycentric model of cooperatively owned and run enterprises to be the ecological future of business, we need to follow the examples from the Opera House to Barcelona, and start building it.

Instead of seeing corporations extract value from us all, this model of interdependence will see us cultivating value together to create shared abundance.

## Sharing the abundance

In our apricot nectar story, your wealth was magicked into existence. But Jeff Bezos's was extracted. He amassed his fortune by extracting value from the public utility of the internet and from delivery on public roads, from other booksellers and retailers he undercut, from customers, from underpaid and un-unionised employees, from financial markets, from the Earth itself.

And while amassing this fortune, he contributed virtually nothing back to the common pot, paying 'a true tax rate of 0.98 per cent as his wealth grew by a staggering $99 billion between 2014 and 2018'.[34]

Bezos isn't Robinson Crusoe. In Australia, around a third of listed corporations pay zero tax, even on sizable profits. It's particularly common in corporations which make their profits by extracting wealth from the ground and dumping the waste in the atmosphere. In the 2019/20 financial year, Shell Energy made over $5 billion and paid zero tax. Whitehaven Coal made $2 billion and paid zero tax. Yancoal paid no tax on its $5 billion income.[35]

Meanwhile, one in eight Australians lives in poverty.[36] Over 3 million people are having to skip meals, avoid filling prescriptions or getting new glasses, struggling to keep a roof over their heads and feed their children, while billionaires get richer.

The dragon on its hoard. The king in his counting house counting out his money. Jeff Bezos. Accumulation for the sake of accumulation is ugly and unpleasant. It's also anti-ecological. It's the disaster of metabolic rift, extracting value from one place and storing it elsewhere, disrupting the flows that are crucial to life. Eventually it triggers nature's revenge, whether it's collapse of crops, suffocating smog or social upheaval.

It's also, as economist Yanis Varoufakis has pointed out,[37] unproductive, even on capitalist terms. This is capitalism's logical conclusion and its fundamental flaw: it institutionalises disruptive accumulation. The 'trickle down' mythology had to be invented to pretend that resources keep circulating but, between tax avoidance, wage suppression, resource extraction and more, the wealth gushes upwards and out of circulation.

In order to cultivate an abundant, ecological economic system, we have to get those flows of value moving again, through redistribution of wealth.

Redistribution is crucial for institutionalising inter-dependence, but it doesn't mean that everyone has to have the same. An appreciation for diversity means we recognise that people have different desires and interests, and express them in a range of ways. But we have to end the cultural and institutional drive to accumulate inordinate wealth, and we have to establish systems of justice and equal access so that people's different desires and interests aren't circumscribed by an accident of birth.

While we're abolishing poverty through a UBI, let's also abolish extreme wealth through a maximum wage and maximum wealth. It's been flippantly suggested that, once you hit a certain point, you get a little trophy declaring that you 'won capitalism' and anything more gets taxed at 100 per cent.[38] I'm not sure about the trophy, frankly. That wealth was extracted from the rest of us. Why should you get a prize?

Trees actively share nutrients. Those growing faster pass carbon through roots and mycorrhiza to others struggling nearby, helping the whole forest thrive.[39] So should we. In an ecological economy, as people and corporations get richer, more should get directed back into the common pool it was extracted from, and used to support abundance across the community through universal public health, education and services, UBI, social housing, and more. If we had a sliding progressive scale that actually reached 100 per cent, the law of diminishing returns would make the drive to extract more pointless, and we could focus instead on generating mutual abundance.

The flipside of wealth is debt. The brilliant David Graeber explained debt as a fundamentally extractive practice. Separating society into debtors and creditors is a means of enforcing subservience.[40] Bankruptcy laws and corporate bail-outs that enable the wealthy to avoid the perils of debt, while people who have been accidentally 'overpaid' income support are hounded to suicide, expose the fact that debt enforcement is about power, not fairness. Debts can be, and often are, cancelled, improving debtors' lives while making no noticeable difference to creditors' wealth.

Graeber, an activist and academic, was heavily involved in advising debt cancellation campaigns that have dramatically changed people's lives and the political landscape. Thousands of Americans have had their student and health debt cancelled, and the idea of cancelling these debts for everyone is now part of the mainstream political conversation.[41] This is a vital campaign we can run and win, improving lives, shifting economic power, and removing one of the bricks in the extractivist wall.

A final point on redistribution relates to the way colonial

societies have extracted value from the colonised peoples on whose land we live and from whose land we profit.

There hasn't been a serious conversation in Australia about reparations, but we should be discussing it, because it's the right thing to do and because it's an important form of redistribution, helping to reverse intergenerational trauma and inequity. If we're to cultivate an interdependent democracy on this continent, justice must be at its heart, and paying reparations will be vital. Many of us with privilege can start to do this ourselves, paying the rent by donating to, buying from, and hiring Indigenous-led organisations.

This whirlwind tour of economic ideas leaves out far more than it includes. But hopefully it begins to paint a picture of how we can reclaim our right and capacity to be interdependent, independent cultivators, creating shared abundance together. It's my fervent hope that, through everything we've discussed – through grassroots gift economies, cooperative enterprises, UBI and redistribution; through reclaiming the commons, our labour and corporations, and sharing the abundance we create – we can finally recognise that seeking to own and control and extract value from everything was a foolish path, and that the land, in reality, owns us.

Combined with the participatory and deliberative approaches to decision-making discussed in the previous chapter, our model of living democracy is starting to take shape. But we still face the tremendous challenge of replacing systems of coercive power with respectful coexistence.

# PRACTISING PEACE

## From coercion to coexistence

You'd enlisted because, hey, there weren't many options.

You knew that the fancy recruitment ads were nothing like reality, but never thought you'd actually have to go to war. And, with the industry your dad worked in all his life dying, housing costs through the roof, and stuff-all other jobs around, what choice did you really have?

Afghanistan was worse than you'd imagined. It wasn't only that you can never unsee people being blown apart beside you. It was the way human life was deliberately stripped of meaning. It was how you were forced to learn to treat other people as ... less. As expendable. To be feared and hated. Otherwise, how could you shoot them?

Coming home was worse. At least over there, you were part of something bigger. Back home, you had nothing to hold onto. One by one, your mates fell into depression and drink. Nobody was surprised by the bloke who got called into the war crimes investigations, but the group splintered between those defending him and those condemning. Another, who'd landed a job in a special operations police team that used the same training as the army, was caught on camera flashing a white power hand-sign after clobbering a climate protester.

You'd taken a job in the mines, as it happened. But the explosions triggered your post-traumatic stress disorder. And after you quit that, well, that's when the downward spiral really started.

You hated yourself for hitting her. She was the best thing that ever happened to you. But sometimes the anger inside just exploded.

Her aunties had warned her about you. 'He's no good,' they'd said. 'And what happens when he starts hitting you? Who are the cops going to believe – you or the whitefella?' But love doesn't bend to reason, and she'd stayed with you, even though you both knew the aunties were right. You'd seen how the cops had given your white fly-in-fly-out mining mates a caution when they were stopped with drugs, while her Aboriginal cousins ended up behind bars. And the gaol time just made everything worse.

One day the world came apart. Her sister's boyfriend bashed her sister and, when her sibling swore at the cops, they arrested her too. She died on the floor of the lock-up because they never thought to get her medical attention. They saw her as less. As expendable.

After the initial grief had subsided a little, she sat you down one morning when you were sober. 'We know how this story ends,' she said. 'Unless we change it. So what are we going to do?' In that conversation a new world opened up.

Some of her cousins were involved in a community

patrol on country in the Northern Territory, checking in on families, making sure everyone was okay, taking people to a dry house to sober up, helping women and children into safe houses away from violence if needed. Respected elders call people to account in front of everyone for their actions and the community supports them to change their ways, instead of seeing them taken into custody. And one of your old mates from Afghanistan was starting a professionally guided support group to help work through trauma and anger management. Those two projects were the place to start.

And, over time, much more grew. With neighbours, relatives and friends, you started community activities giving people meaning and agency in their lives, learning language and culture and skills. You got early intervention projects and violence interruption models going, to redirect people off a destructive path onto a more constructive one. You cultivated networks of compassionate connection helping people feel more human, more valuable, to themselves, to each other, and to society.

By creating these deep and broad connections, by learning how to live together better, you healed yourselves and your community. And you made the cops redundant.

## Violence and power

Mao Zedong said 'Political power grows out of the barrel of a gun.'

Hannah Arendt disagreed. 'Out of the barrel of a gun,' the great moral philosopher said, 'grows the most effective command, resulting in the most instant and perfect obedience.

What can never grow out of it is power ... Power springs up whenever people get together and act in concert.'[1]

You can guess which one I reckon is a more ecological view of power.

Violence exists in nature. Of course. You can't spend time in nature, or even watch a nature documentary, without being aware of a lion devouring a wildebeest, a dog killing a backyard chook, or a magpie catching a skink. Plants are nourished with the blood and bone of dead animals. Trees grow in the rotting bodies of their elders. All life depends on death.

But it depends *more* on other life.

A colony of bees abuzz with activity contains countless creatures collectively providing food and shelter for the group. Guiding each other using complicated dance moves, they gather provisions for their own community, and in doing so distribute pollen and fertilise plants. The bees and the plants need each other alive and well in order to survive; their existence is coexistence.

We see the same coexistence inside us. Billions of non-human organisms living in our guts help us digest our food, enabling us to eat a wider diet and get more nutrients, even playing a role in balancing our moods, while we provide them with a home and a steady supply of food. Healthy forests clean the air we breathe and filter the water we drink. Fertile soils are home to countless creatures coexisting, from microscopic to marsupials, turning the soil over, distributing nutrients and minerals. The greater the interdependence and diversity, the healthier and more resilient the system.

In examining democracy and economy, we discussed how competition and self-interest absolutely exist, and the problem is that instead of acknowledging their existence and working to limit the damage, we normalised and institutionalised them as the only legitimate way of being. We erased the idea of cooperation, calling it 'enlightened self-interest' when we want to praise the behaviour and 'virtue signalling' when we don't.

Well, we've done the same with violence. Instead of acknowledging violence and working out ways to suppress it, anti-ecological culture institutionalised and normalised violent relationships of separation and domination, developing them into coercive systems of supremacy.

When we decided that we were separate from nature, that we could dominate nature, we chose to believe that the rules of interdependence didn't apply to us. We declared our species to stand at the pinnacle of a food chain – an idea we invented to replace complex, multi-directional relationships with a simple hierarchy. And we constructed hierarchies within our species, placing man above woman, coloniser above colonised, white above black and brown, rich above poor.

It began, as you'll recall from Part 1, with building walls, dominating those within the walls, and keeping them compliant by convincing them that those outside are barbarians worthy of contempt. The violence used to seize and maintain control over others came, over time, to be exercised primarily through culture, but physical violence remains, with its coercive consequences permeating the entire system, as we saw in our opening story linking war, policing, poverty, racism, and family violence.

If the ultimate mechanism of extractivism is the corporation, the ultimate mechanism of coercion is the state.

Yikes, some of you will be saying. Really? Yes, really, but hold on: recall here the distinction we made between the state and democratic government, the state and the nation.

Where a democratically-governed nation is the people collectively codetermining our common future, the state is Hobbes' Leviathan to which all are subservient. It's what Bookchin defined as 'institutionalize[d] power ... that exists *apart* from the people'.[2] Most relevantly for us here, it's what social theorist Max Weber defined at the close of World War I as 'the rule of men over men based on the means of legitimate, that is allegedly legitimate, violence'.[3] The 'allegedly' is doing a lot of work here. Weber's point is that the state's monopoly on violence is made legitimate by translating physical domination by those in power into cultural norms through which they manufacture the consent of the masses.

The state is congealed coercion. It is institutionalised and normalised violent control of people instead of respectful coexistence. And, just as the constant competitive self-interest of the corporation trickles down into all other behaviour, just as the adversarialism of our politics infects the rest of society, so too does the violence of the state. There's a clear connection between the state's external violence through war, its internal violence through policing and suppression of dissent, and the interpersonal violence seen in racism, sexism, ableism and general aggression.

The majority of us consent to the state's monopoly on violence because we don't feel it ourselves. It's primarily exercised against a minority who can easily be 'othered': Indigenous people, refugees, people of colour, 'dole bludgers', 'ratbag protesters'. The process of 'othering', indeed the violence itself, can often be outsourced by the state to its citizens; think about how white workers on American plantations were kept from rising up against the owners by encouraging them to punch down on the slaves who were so much worse off. This enables most of us to continue in the genteel pretence that our society isn't violent. Tyson Yunkaporta painfully punctured this pretence:

> If you live a life without violence you are living an illusion, outsourcing your conflict to unseen powers and detonating it in areas beyond your living space ... Your peace-medallion bling is sparkling with blood diamonds. You carry pillaged metals in your phone from devastated African lands and communities.[4]

Ursula Le Guin turned this into a perfect parable, *The Ones Who Walk Away From Omelas*, which I encourage you to read in order to deeply understand this idea. It tells of a beautiful and happy city that owes its happiness to the abject misery, the torture, of one small child. Most people are content to live with that knowledge buried deep inside them. Some walk away.[5] Institutionalised violence is the pretence of a world without consequences, where we can live contentedly in Omelas because the violence of the state is comfortably compartmentalised elsewhere.

We must not turn away from the consequences of violence, because they echo through everything. Martin Luther King Jr expressed this perfectly:

> Violence never brings permanent peace. It solves no social problem: it merely creates new and more complicated ones. Violence is impractical because it is a descending spiral ending in destruction for all. It is immoral because it seeks to humiliate the opponent rather than win his understanding: it seeks to annihilate rather than convert.

Violence is immoral because it thrives on hatred
rather than love. It destroys community and makes
brotherhood impossible. It leaves society in monologue
rather than dialogue. Violence ends up in defeating itself.
It creates bitterness in the survivors and brutality in the
destroyers.[6]

The institutionalised violence of the state, both internal towards its own citizens and external towards its inevitable enemies, is what makes human extinction such a real possibility. As climate and environmental crises trigger water and food shortages, fires, floods and other 'natural' disasters, and displace millions of people, we can expect states to resort to ever more violent means to control populations. What will nuclear-armed states do to protect their borders and trade routes? I dread to think.

Communities, however, have an extraordinary instinct and capacity to come together to help each other at times of emergency, creating self-organising systems of mutual aid. In the same way that we can cultivate participatory and deliberative decision-making to replace adversarialism, and can cultivate shared abundance to replace extractivism, we can replace the systems of coercion that got us into this mess and could well lead to our demise with systems of nonviolent coexistence.

It may sound like I'm a dreamer but, as John Lennon sang, 'it's easy if you try'. We're now going to examine how violence is the opposite of living democracy, digging into the insights of David Graeber and Hannah Arendt about connection, power and violence, before drawing out the links between the violence of the state and the violence of our society, thanks to the clarity of thought of Angela Davis and Petra Kelly. Then we'll map out how the vision of coexistence can be – and is being – made real.

### *The opposite of violence is connection*

In Afghanistan, you learned to erase people's humanity so you could aim your gun at them. The police did the same to your sister-in-law. To turn things around, you cultivated networks of support, of connection and communication. Your response to violence was living democracy.

There's a reason why institutions of violence, be they armies, police forces, gangs or authoritarian regimes, dehumanise those they target: we humans don't actually like hurting each other. Rutger Bregman, in his book *Human Kind*, detailed tremendous evidence that soldiers in the heat of battle often try not to hurt each other, aiming over each other's heads or not firing at all.[7] Dehumanising rhetoric, from calling prisoners by numbers to racist propaganda, puts sufficient distance between us and our target to do what we would otherwise resist.

In one of his many startling insights, David Graeber wrote that violence:

> is perhaps the only form of human action that holds
> out even the possibility of having social effects *without*
> being communicative. To be more precise, violence may
> be the only way it is possible for one human being to do
> something which will have relatively predictable effects
> on the actions of a person about whom they understand
> nothing. In pretty much any other way in which you
> might try to influence another's actions, you must at least
> have some idea about who you think they are, who they
> think you are, what they might want out of the situation,

their aversions and proclivities, and so forth. Hit them over the head hard enough, and all of this becomes irrelevant.[8]

Violence is fundamentally anti-democratic in that it shuts off consideration of others' views. Violence severs connection. It requires us to disconnect from each other in order to commit it, then feeds off that disconnection.

Conversely, nonviolence is about interdependence. It's an ecological philosophy and practice that values the whole and the parts, and the connections between them. As philosopher Judith Butler wrote, 'an ethics of nonviolence cannot be predicated on individualism, and it must take the lead in waging a critique of individualism as the basis of ethics and politics alike'.[9]

Tyson Yunkaporta explained how, in his Indigenous culture, the reality of violence is drawn into rituals of reciprocity: when people fight each other, for each time one fighter has cut their opponent, they have to also cut themself.[10] In this way, interdependent coexistence is made painfully concrete.

Coexistence means we need to get comfortable with difference. And getting comfortable with difference means, somewhat counter-intuitively, that we need to be comfortable with ourselves, confident in our own identity. Prejudice is often closely related to the fear of losing what makes us special, and coercive systems of supremacy explicitly play to that fear. Hence fears of being 'swamped by Asians', and chants of 'Jews will not replace us'. As Rutger Bregman said, 'We need to realise it's okay that we're all different – there's nothing wrong with that. We can build strong houses for our identities, with sturdy foundations. Then we can throw open the doors.'[11]

We're beginning to see now, I hope, that where violence is the opposite of connection, living democracy is the opposite of the state with a monopoly on violence.

The idea that really brought this home for me is Hannah Arendt's insight that violence can never create genuine power. Power needs legitimacy, and that, Arendt said, comes from a process of connection and communication: 'Power springs up whenever people get together and act in concert, but it derives its legitimacy from the initial getting together rather than from any action that may follow.'[12]

This dovetails with Graeber's insight that, in any form of human interaction other than violence, we need to make an effort to understand each other if we want to influence others' behaviour. Violence might work to assert control, but turning that control into power requires a coming together, even if it's uniting against others. What grows from that contradictory process, however, will always be a fragile power, with every act of violence undermining power by driving people apart. There's a constant tension in such a system between the construction of power through connection and its destruction through violence – a tension that runs through history, as we learned in Part 1.

Power through people coming together and acting in concert needs to be constantly renewed through the next process of coming together. Which is a reasonably concise definition of living democracy.

### Violence ricochets through systems

You returned from military service and committed unforgivable acts of domestic violence. Others who've been subjected to the violence of the state at home do the same. It's no surprise.

We touched on the idea that, because we humans are actually, mostly, not very good at violence, we need to dehumanise those we're fighting in order to attack them. That severing of our mutual humanity has devastating implications. Violence by states, whether through war, policing or any other form of coercion, cannot but create the conditions for interpersonal violence.

This is not widely understood in our anti-ecological society. In fact, as Professor Richard Jackson, director of New Zealand's National Centre for Peace and Conflict Studies, has pointed out, there is an 'unquestioned assumption that violence can be employed neutrally as a rational tool of policy – a tool which can simply be put back into the toolbox once its purpose has been achieved'.[13] Not so, he argued:

> [I]t is impossible for any human actor, including states, to simply pick up and use violence as a doctor would a scalpel and then put it down and remain unaffected. Instead, employing violence has a number of effects on the user. At the very least, it dulls their sensitivity to the suffering of others and makes using violence in the future easier.[14]

This is what African American political activist and philosopher, Professor Angela Davis, meant by 'the connections between public violence and private or privatized violence'.[15] 'Intimate violence,' she has said, 'is not unconnected to state violence. Where do perpetrators of intimate violence learn how to engage in the practices of violence? Who teaches them that violence is okay?'[16] Referencing the feminist adage 'the personal is political', Davis argued that it runs in both directions. 'There is a deep relationality that links struggles against institutions and struggles to reinvent our personal lives, and recraft ourselves. We know, for example, that we replicate the structures of retributive justice oftentimes in our own emotional responses.'[17] As Australian Indigenous activists have also long pointed out, if a marginalised community, excluded from much mainstream participation, is heavily policed, over-incarcerated, and faces constant state violence, can we be in any way surprised that members of that community act violently to one another and to others? Can we judge them for it?

Where anti-ecology disconnects, compartmentalises, and imagines a world without consequences, in our inextricably interwoven reality, actions in one part of a system flow through to others. As Dr King said: 'Injustice anywhere is a threat to justice everywhere. We are caught in an inescapable network of mutuality, tied in a single garment of destiny. Whatever affects one directly, affects all indirectly.'[18]

Petra Kelly, a co-founder of the German Greens and one of the key figures in the development of environmental politics, drew together state violence, violence against women and violence against the natural world in her analysis. 'Feminism, ecology and nonviolence belong together and are interrelated,' she said, in:

> the big and the little war waged against us as individuals, against smaller countries, against the planetary environment, every single day. Resistance to war ... is impossible without resistance to sexism, to racism, to imperialism, and to violence as an everyday pervasive reality. There is a very profound relationship between the fact that many women and children are commonly

attacked, beaten up, and raped, and that a nuclear war as well as a nuclear catastrophe threatens this entire planet Earth, which has no emergency exit.[19]

Kelly's vision of ecological democracy puts nonviolence to each other, between nations, and to the Earth at its core. 'We must find a way to demilitarise society itself,'[20] she said. Deeply aware of both the feminist axiom that 'the personal is political', as well as of the powerful cultural impact of violence, she wrote, 'We call upon people everywhere never to accustom themselves, never to allow themselves to become accustomed, to the idea of war and the preparation for war ... We call upon people to build and develop communities of peace everywhere.'[21]

Institutionalised violence has been with us a lot longer than our current political or economic systems, so we have to work harder to understand it before we can imagine ways to evolve past it. But now we can turn to building those 'communities of peace'.

Very often, any talk of peace is shut down by ridiculing the idea that we just want people to hold hands, sing, and get along. But through understanding violence as the opposite of connection, we can see that cultivating systems of connection and coexistence is a pragmatic, realistic path to peace. It's not about always agreeing or being the same; it's about developing better ways of disagreeing and being different.

Let's have a look at how we do that.

## Cultivating coexistence

A hot wind is blowing across the desert in Tennant Creek as the Julalikari Council convenes. A young man faces the elders, with other members of the community observing. Last night, the community patrol had intervened after he'd staggered home drunk and threatened his girlfriend, whom he'd previously injured. The patrol had taken him to a dry house overnight, and this morning he is being called to account.

The group shares stories of the damage family violence and alcohol abuse are doing to them all. They mourn together those lost to both, and those dead in custody when the police intervened instead of the community. The young man is given the chance to make commitments to the group about how he'll work to change his behaviour, and the group commits to him that they'll support him in his efforts.

As Aboriginal anthropologist and activist, Professor Marcia Langton, has written, this 'calling of offenders to account before ... the community' has been shown to be a 'much more effective way of dealing with minor law and order problems than the rotation of intoxicated people through the ... police cells and courts'.[22]

A world away, in South Sudan, amid civil war, Nonviolent Peaceforce members are walking with women as they collect water and firewood. They're simply walking alongside them, unarmed, talking among themselves.

They say truth is the first casualty of war, but sexual violence follows on its heels, and these women had been repeatedly attacked by soldiers. Horrifically, there are as many as 20 rapes a month. The Peaceforce works with women to ensure that they move in larger groups, accompanied by foreign observers where possible, or by trustworthy local men. The attacks stop.[23]

It's mid-winter in Serbia and a massive crowd packs into Republic Square. Protests aren't allowed under the dictator, Slobodan Milosevic, who is getting more brutal as his grip on power slides. But these young people are here for a rock concert. The nonviolent resistance group, Otpor!, has announced that the Red Hot Chili Peppers, at the height of their global fame, will be performing at midnight this New Year's Eve and tens of thousands of people show up.

Otpor! has a reputation for madcap stunts poking fun at Milosevic and his cronies – things like stencilling his face onto metal drums and encouraging passers-by to hit it with a baseball bat. This time they really do put on a rocking gig, featuring a line-up of local bands. But, at midnight, instead of the Chili Peppers, they project a slideshow showing the evils of the regime, and an opposition leader takes the stage calling on the audience to 'make the coming year count!' The crowd gets the point loud and clear, and leaves in high spirits.

By the end of the year, Milosevic is ousted.[24]

In different ways, in various contexts, each of these projects works to help people understand each other, appreciate their common humanity, and work in concert.

They are all building coexistence.

Communities all around the globe are doing this work. They're cultivating social cohesion to build new forms of power, whether it's through grassroots community-building, via nonviolent direct action for political change, by implementing alternatives to policing and punitive justice, or by growing a mutualist geopolitics from the grassroots up. Let's dig into some more examples.

## *Cohesive communities: Building Arendtian power*

Can we head back to London's Participatory City again?

You might recall that one of the reasons they set up their community-led commoning project in Barking and Dagenham was that the combination of poverty and a very ethnically diverse community had seen a deeply troubling increase in hate crimes and support for extreme right political parties. They already report positive trends in this space,[25] and it's relatively obvious why when you think about it.

By bringing people together in constructive ways for mutual benefit, through gardens and murals, maker spaces and cooking groups, they create the conditions for coexistence. The approach gives people solid foundations, helping them feel confident they won't be replaced or left behind, because it gives them agency, both as individuals and collectively.

To create power, Hannah Arendt told us, we need people to come together, to act in concert. David Graeber added that violence is the only form of human interaction that can work without seeking to understand each other, so cultivating mutual understanding helps us build a society which is less violent.

So these practices we've been exploring – citizens' assemblies, Buy Nothing groups, urban farms, food co-ops – are genuine sources of Arendtian power, and the first steps towards a nonviolent, living democracy.

Of course, acting in concert is more than just coming together. If we're to stay together we have to learn how to disagree constructively. That's where we need those deliberative and agonistic processes we discussed earlier that are all about working through with others 'who you think they are, who they think you are, what they might want out of the situation, their aversions and proclivities', as Graeber put it.

Amanda Cahill's advice that if you want constructive conversations, 'don't ask people to pick sides', echoes in my ears. In communities in transition out of fossil fuels, where people can come to blows over their differences, Cahill brings people together across wide divides of opinion by focussing on what they have in common and what they can actually do together. It's proof that nonviolent, non-adversarial problem-solving and decision-making works in fraught circumstances.

This reminds us that adversarial politics is part of the problem. The theatre of conflict is terrible for reaching good outcomes, and it embeds an aggressive, combative culture. There'll always be an element of adversarialism in decision-making; as Chantal Mouffe told us, conflict can be constructive. But making it synonymous with democracy is disastrous. We need nonviolent communications and dispute resolution, well-facilitated consensus processes, and appropriately managed spaces wherever we come together if we're to build what Petra Kelly called 'communities of peace'.[26]

We'll all benefit from learning to disagree better, but it's particularly crucial for ensuring every voice is heard. Our hyper-aggressive political spaces, as we're tragically frequently reminded, are not safe for women, for people of colour, for LGBTQIA+ people, for disabled people, pretty much for anyone who isn't an alpha male. All our spaces of living democracy, from community groups to parliaments, workplaces to marketplaces, must be made truly welcoming for all.

In this context, we'd better talk about calling out and calling in. African American feminist scholar, Professor

Loretta J Ross, has set out the difference: 'Calling out assumes the worst. Calling in involves conversation, compassion and context. It doesn't mean a person should ignore harm', but it seeks a path through. 'It's a call-out done with love', she explained, suggesting options like private conversations instead of public shaming, encouraging the other to be open to change rather than backing them into a corner where they're only likely to fight back harder. She also highlights the difference between punching up, calling out those in power in order to hold them to account, and punching down, puffing ourselves up by calling out those already in a weaker position.[27]

Calling in is tremendously important, but it has limits, of course. As we discussed earlier, any participatory process needs to be able to exclude people who refuse to follow agreed rules. Mutual trust is crucial and, as Ostrom showed, communities need the capacity to exclude those who breach trust, either temporarily or sometimes permanently. Bookchin and Öcalan's model put that into practice by providing for delegates to confederal councils to be recalled at any time, to be asked to explain their actions, to discuss them, or to be removed if that's what the whole group decides.

Bringing people together, learning how to disagree better, developing agreed rules of mutual respect – this is how we act in concert and make the ground fertile for coexistence. Hate and violence need the disconnection of less fertile ground. When the ground is more fertile, some of those we otherwise might exclude can be called in. As we cultivate connection, interdependence and mutualism, we leave less space for hate.

## *Nonviolent direct action for political change*

When the 2004 Boxing Day tsunami caused devastation around the Indian Ocean, the idyllic island nation of the Maldives was living under the dictatorship of Mamoon Abdul Gayoom, who learned brutal tricks from his friend Saddam Hussein. Global aid was made conditional on Gayoom holding elections. But how were opposition candidates to build support when mass gatherings were illegal?

One group hit on an ingenious solution. They set up trestle tables on a city beach and put on a massive feast of rice pudding – a Maldivian favourite. Huge crowds gathered and saw the dissident leaders serving up free food. Conversations bubbled up, and a sense of connection and shared humanity started to form. The police response, breaking up a free feed, looked ludicrous.

Providing people with basic needs, building political momentum, circumventing authority, and cultivating common cause: this is a tactic that drew on one of the world's most famous civil disobedience campaigns – Mahatma Gandhi's salt marches. In 1930, the colonial British rulers introduced a tax on salt, a staple in India as elsewhere. So Gandhi led peaceful marches to the coast, where the people gathered their own salt, challenging the authorities by circumventing the tax, and building opposition by self-provisioning and acting in concert.

The salt marches were only a start. And it took a lot more to bring down Gayoom, too. But the rice pudding feasts, replicated around the country, were a tasty beginning![28]

'The distinction between violent and non-violent action,' Hannah Arendt said, 'is that the former is exclusively bent upon the destruction of the old, and the latter is chiefly concerned with the establishment of something new.'[29]

While some claim that the ends justify any means, an ecological understanding of actions and consequences tells us that we simply cannot separate the two. If our goal is simply to dismantle destructive systems, violence can be effective; but if we aim to cultivate a better system, it can't help us. As Professor Jackson put it, 'violent means cannot produce peaceful ends'.[30]

What's really stark, though, is that, regardless of the philosophical debate, nonviolence is actually more effective than violence at delivering deep change. The oldest part of anti-ecological culture makes it hard for us to acknowledge that this could be true, but it is. Harvard Professor Erica Chenoweth and Maria Stephan's analysis of 323 conflicts between 1900 and 2006 showed that nonviolent resistance achieves its aims twice as frequently as violent resistance and seven to eight times as frequently as terrorist campaigns.[31] An update in 2016 showed that the effectiveness of both violent and nonviolent resistance had reduced, but the gap between them had increased: 30 per cent of nonviolent campaigns succeeded while only 12 per cent of violent ones had.[32]

Tellingly, as Arendt would have predicted, nonviolent campaigns are more likely to see their success maintained. And Chenoweth and Stephan attributed the success and longevity to the way nonviolent campaigns build power – coming together and acting in concert. Whether it's through food, concerts, fun stunts, silent gatherings to read in public squares, or even mass kiss-ins,[33] nonviolence encourages active and repeated participation by large numbers of people while violence drives potentially sympathetic people away. Nonviolence builds the legitimacy of the cause in the public mind while violence undermines it.

Philosophy and evidence also align around what happens at the turning point of conflicts. Arendt noted that, as a state realises it's beginning to lose power, 'rule by sheer violence comes into play'.[34] State violence gets more intense the more threatened the state is, and that undermines its power. And if dissidents stick to nonviolence, goading security forces to break up feasts, chase after thousands of ping pong balls, or gather up tiny speakers broadcasting opposition slogans hidden in piles of dog poo, violent repression is far more likely to backfire and cause the state to lose even more legitimacy. Central to this is that nonviolent campaigns encourage loyalty shifts by key people. As Arendt observed, the 'superiority [of the violent state] lasts only so long as the power structure of the government remains intact – that is so long as commands are obeyed and the army or police forces are prepared to use their weapons'.[35] Security forces often resist orders to open fire on peaceful protesters. Once that happens, a regime's collapse is imminent.

Some argue that only privileged people can truly commit to nonviolence. While evidence from around the globe of a wide range of marginalised and oppressed peoples successfully using nonviolence gainsays this, it's vital that we have compassion for those who use violence against oppressors. Angela Davis explained why those who've been targets of state violence for so long might be violent with one another; how much more understandable might it be that they would use it against the state? The fact that history shows nonviolence to be more successful only makes it that much more important that those of us with privilege use it to shield those without.

### *From coercive state to nonviolent nation*

In the Julalikari Aboriginal Council, and the community patrols working with it to divert people from the police and justice systems, we've seen a living illustration of an alternative to the state as congealed coercion.

Looking back, we've discussed what it might look like for a nation to build systems of governance around nonviolent coexistence. Rojava and Barcelona en Comú are shining examples, as is the idea of replacing coercive welfare with UBI. Instead of subservience to a dominating state, they help us understand government as us, working together towards our common future. As Hannah Arendt said, 'It is only after one eliminates this disastrous reduction of public affairs to the business of dominion, that the original data in the realm of human affairs will appear ... in their authentic diversity.'[36] This is the nation as a mutual project, the nation as living democracy.

As we cultivate this nation, let's now look deeper at the ways in which the state most obviously exercises violence in controlling the people: policing, incarceration and the justice system.

This is how Derecka Purnell, an African American human rights lawyer and activist who grew up in poverty, articulated her experience that, instead of actually helping people, police 'manage inequality' and exclusion:

> Police couldn't do what we really needed. They could not heal relationships or provide jobs. We were afraid every time we called. When the cops arrived, I was silenced,

threatened with detention, or removed from my home. Fifteen years later, my old neighborhood still lacks quality food, employment, schools, health care, and air – all of which increases the risk of violence and the reliance on police.[37]

This experience is mirrored in Indigenous, poor and otherwise marginalised communities the world over. The state has ensured that police are often the only place to turn in situations which would be better served by mental health professionals, counsellors, medical professionals, or simply properly resourced and supported communities. And, where those under-funded alternatives are designed to defuse problems before they get worse, over-funded police respond with force after the fact, too frequently creating more problems. As Graeber said:

> Most of [policing] has to do with the ... application of
> physical force, or the threat of physical force, to aid in
> the resolution of administrative problems ... [W]hat
> police mostly do is ... bring the threat of force to bear
> on situations that would otherwise have nothing to do
> with it.[38]

And they do so unequally. Remember how, in our story at the start of this chapter, your fly-in fly-out mining mates were given cautions for drug use? Alcohol and drugs that are treated as recreational for wealthy white people are violently policed for Aboriginal people (as well as for many poorer settler colonials, immigrants and refugees), being a leading cause of arrest, incarceration and horrifically frequently death for Indigenous people, as for African Americans.

The violent metaphor of the War on Drugs encapsulates so many aspects of the violence of the state. It involves often violent domestic policing, which Angela Davis reminded us increases violence in the policed community, as well as global military exercises from Colombia to Afghanistan. The same companies provide the same weapons and training to soldiers around the world and police at home. And often the same people are at the end of the gun. Sociologist Dr Stuart Schrader has explained this from an American historical perspective:

> US soldiers and marines ... ended up training police
> officers in occupied zones after the [1898] Spanish-
> American War, from the Philippines to Haiti to
> Nicaragua, sometimes acting as commanding officers for
> 'native' constabulary regiments. In turn, many of these
> US military men joined domestic police agencies after
> returning home, bringing with them colonial ideologies
> that treated racial difference as sufficient grounds for
> suspicion.[39]

The same process occurred in Australia, where police forces emerged from the origins of the state as both a penal colony and a genocidal project.

Simply decriminalising drug use and public drunkenness and treating them as medical and social issues would have tremendous implications for reducing state violence, particularly against Indigenous people. But the problems with policing go deeper, involving housing, driving, access to public space, opportunities for participation, and so much more in daily life.

When we think about alternatives to policing, then, a lot of it has to do with taking mutual agency in our communities, funding the things communities need, and building systems that bring out the best in us. For Purnell, defunding the police is primarily about 'eliminating the reasons people think they need cops and prisons in the first place'.[40]

Increasingly bloated budgets for increasingly militarised policing should be redirected towards the increasingly starved budgets of health and education, decent housing, public transport, childcare and social work, and towards creating local opportunities in employment or volunteering. And communities can set up their own local programs to prevent, interrupt and respond to problematic, violent, and potentially violent situations, to protect those in harm's way, and to support individual and collective agency in the community. Properly funded community housing programs, drop-in centres and well-resourced social workers create safe and peaceful neighbourhoods far more effectively than policing homeless people.[41] Successful 'violence interruption models', in streets and in homes, see trusted and trained community figures calm down situations before they get out of hand. Governments from Los Angeles[42] to Canberra[43] are introducing diversion programs where, in certain circumstances, health and mental health professionals and social workers respond to emergency calls rather than armed police. There's a lot further to go, but even some police departments already recognise that they're the wrong people for many of the jobs they're given.

Julalikari is far from the only Australian Aboriginal community taking agency in their own security, resisting and replacing colonial policing. Harry Blagg and Giulietta Valuri have documented well over 100 different models of Night Patrols, Barefoot Patrols, community buses and suchlike, run by and for Indigenous communities, pre-empting policing. Instead of identifying people to target and criminalise them, they identify people at risk and support them to manage potentially problematic behaviour and find constructive paths that reduce encounters with policing and the justice system. They might involve traditional activities on country, support through social work or job training, or just keeping a close eye on them. 'Underpinning these diverse initiatives is a commitment to working through consensus and intervening in a culturally appropriate way to divert Indigenous people from a diversity of potential hazards and conflicts.'[44] Programs based in local cultural knowledge, and driven and accepted by the local community, have demonstrated success in decreasing drug and alcohol use, reducing violence, and building trust and cohesion both in the community and between the community and state authorities. There are complications and controversies when they're seen as an outsourcing of criminal justice to the Indigenous community. But when started and effectively led by community for their own benefit, they can be a remarkable way of devolving and dissolving state power.

The logical conclusion for many here is the abolition of prisons which, other than capital punishment, are the starkest example of state violence against citizens. Now, as discussed, exclusion is sometimes necessary; every form of community organising structure from Ostrom's commons to deliberative democracy to Indigenous government includes the option to exclude those who breach trust. But let's think about the difference between this and modern prisons.

Commons exclude people, usually temporarily, in order

to support them to improve their behaviour and return to the group. The modern state uses prisons to discipline and punish people and manage surplus population. Exclusion in the commons tends to be a last resort mechanism to avoid violence and promote rehabilitation. As Davis pointed out, on the other hand, 'in prison [people] find themselves within a violent institution that reproduces violence. In many ways you can say that the institution feeds on that violence and reproduces it so that when the person is released he or she is probably worse.'[45]

Living democracy needs dramatically reduced and dramatically different use of exclusion, but this is a long-term goal. I echo Angela Davis again: 'I do think that a society without prisons is a realistic future possibility, but in a transformed society, one in which people's needs, not profits, constitute the driving force.'[46] Which is precisely what we're trying to build through living democracy.

The central piece of this puzzle is the justice system, and again there are many remarkable innovations around the world seeking to transform a deeply coercive and punitive system into one closer to living democracy's bottom-up, mutualist system of coexistence. Justice Reinvestment, the idea that funds planned for building new prisons should instead be invested in community programs to help people stay out of prison, is now mainstream, as are diversionary courts such as drug courts and mental health courts that focus on referring people to treatment or counselling services rather than prison. Some programs devolve criminal justice processes to the community in the same way that participatory and deliberative democracy does with political decision-making. Restorative justice, an over-arching term for this approach, is defined as 'a process whereby all the parties with a stake in a particular offence come together to resolve collectively how to deal with the aftermath of the offence and its implications for the future.[47]

Some Indigenous communities have adopted 'circle sentencing', drawing on their deep history of yarning circles. The idea of restorative justice is that it makes offenders aware of the consequences of their actions, it gives victims and the community a sense of agency, and it tasks everyone with finding a constructive way through together, like we saw in Julalikari. Central to it is the idea of reintegrative shaming – calling people to account for their actions, and bringing them back into the fold. It's the institutionalisation of coexistence in criminal justice.

A step further, compassionate and therapeutic jurisprudence seeks to reinvent the law as a therapeutic tool rather than a coercive or retributive one. This encompasses a wide array of programs from diversion out of courts to innovative modes of sentencing, seeking literally or effectively to replace judicial officers with social workers, supporting and encouraging those who come before them. In all of these approaches, however, including restorative justice and circle sentencing, everyone involved understands that it has the weight of the state behind it, and the option of incarceration hangs over it with constant coercive power.

These ideas are contested and imperfect, but they point to a different way of doing justice, and they teach us vital broader lessons for nonviolent coexistence. Be patient, supportive and forgiving. We all make mistakes. Sometimes because we're struggling or stressed, marginalised or oppressed. Sometimes because we don't know enough yet. Sometimes just because we're fallible creatures. The path to living democracy is through compassion and forgiveness, accountability when appropriate, exclusion where necessary. But always leading us back to coexistence.

### *Mutualist internationalism*

In June 2017, Mayor Ada Colau welcomed delegates from all around the world to Barcelona for the first Fearless Cities Summit.

Over three days, people from communities and governments with similar municipalist approaches to Barcelona en Comú shared ideas, learned from each other, and built active partnerships. Ideas like a network of Sanctuary Cities were developed to help city governments wanting to welcome refugees replicate each other's work around housing, participation in civic life and democracy, social inclusion, and working to drive national and international policy change. City climate partnerships are seeing city governments take the lead from national governments that are delaying and denying, moving ahead with action on renewable energy grids, electric transport, urban design and more.

Through these partnerships, and the informal connections building around them, Colau sees 'municipalism ... weaving its own international web of solidarity':

> The phrase 'globalizing municipalism' may sound
> slightly contradictory, but it is not. It is simply a way of
> overcoming the divisions between 'above and below', 'us
> and the others' in order to create an international network
> of cities that defend human rights, that fight together
> against climate change and misogyny and against all the
> policies that only benefit a few and condemn the rest to
> uncertainty and fear.[48]

The amazing, participatory politics of local governments like Barcelona en Comú is now forming the modular building blocks of a new polycentric globalism that's all about coexistence rather than confrontation.

Our current geopolitical system essentially guarantees war: wars over resources, wars of expansion, or even wars of intervention, seeking to protect citizens from their own governments. There's genuinely little alternative while we operate in the current system of sovereign states, known as the Westphalian system, which essentially brings the separation and domination of anti-ecology into the international space.

This is what Prussian general, Carl von Clausewitz, was describing when he declared war to be 'the continuation of politics with other means',[49] and 'an act of violence to compel the opponent to do as we wish'.[50] I don't think anyone who's got this far in this book will think of either domestic or international politics as fields where we should use 'violence to compel' our opponents to do anything, but that is still, with some fragile and largely unenforceable limitations, the international order we operate in, 200 years after Clausewitz died. This applies just as clearly to internal armed conflicts, and the difficulties the international community has in responding to them, as it does to wars between states.

War, at its core, is a failure of democracy, a failure of connection, interdependence, coexistence. War tears us apart, it depends on dehumanising the enemy and, with modern weaponry, it often involves being as far away from our enemy as possible in order to kill them. It's the ultimate disconnection, the ultimate domination. And, ricocheting through the system, the constant preparation for war makes nonviolent government of nations far harder.

Living democracy seeks peaceful ways to resolve disagreements and rejects war as shutting off that possibility. In order to cultivate living democracy, we need a geopolitics of coexistence. We need to learn how to manage conflict nonviolently and develop a new geopolitical system that makes war as unlikely as possible, rather than inevitable.

Remember the foreign observers walking with women in South Sudan? It doesn't make for as good TV as buildings obliterated by bombs, so most of us know nothing about it, but examples around the world of similar Unarmed Civilian Protection abound. In Colombia, Peace Brigades International accompany locals when travelling between towns, enabling them to pass through paramilitary roadblocks just by being there as foreigners with phones and cameras. The presence of Nonviolent Peaceforce volunteers in Mindanao in the Philippines has increased the capacity and legitimacy of ceasefire monitoring and enhanced trust in the community.[51] And there are many more examples of highly successful nonviolent interventions to protect civilians during conflict, de-escalate conflict, and work towards lasting peace between combatants.

In all these cases, what's going on is that people are cultivating connection, listening to each other, empowering local communities to take agency, and encouraging people to recognise their common humanity. There's a key element of bearing witness, which can sometimes involve reintegrative shaming, as well as interposing bodies with privilege in front of those without, all of which challenges those acting violently to pause and consider their actions. As Chenoweth and Arendt noted, nonviolence calls into question the legitimacy of violence. And, as they also both discussed, relationality is crucial, as violence is far harder when we connect to each other. This approach is not just about ending conflict, but about building peace, helping people see the option of nonviolent resolution, and creating the capacity for coexistence.

And that's what we have to do at a grand scale, too. We need to embrace our multiscale interdependence and cultivate a geopolitics of mutualism and cooperation. True geopolitical coexistence can't be based on relying on sovereign nation states to act in their 'enlightened self-interest'. Arendt pointed out during World War II that sovereign nation states are fundamentally at odds with universal values and human rights, which are unenforceable in a global order of hard borders and dominating power. We need an international, polycentric, living democracy where, at every scale, we see ourselves as different but interdependent. As peace scholar Sara Koopman has put it, we need a geopolitics that 'does not work to keep "us" safe by keeping "them" out, but rather works to keep a larger us safe by building connections with former thems'.[52]

And yes, as we learned with the Fearless Cities Summit in Barcelona, this too is being done! Grassroots communities around the world are connecting and cross-fertilising, piecing together a polycentric globalism.

Think about how Rojava, the autonomous nation in north-east Syria, is doing this, too. It's crucial to acknowledge that Rojava is not entirely nonviolent – it has armed forces, for defence against Syrian, Turkish and Islamist attack. But one of its remarkable achievements is how, having started as a revolutionary independence project of Kurdish nationalists, it has grown into a multi-ethnic nation encompassing two million people, not through conquest but through communities voluntarily joining the confederation. The beauty of the municipal confederal model is that it's modular – as long as communities agree to abide by the principles, they can take part.

And then there's Progressive International, a global network of activists, academics and communicators, working to support the growth of a mutualist internationalism as a 'strategy for survival' through building networks, sharing information, and driving public debate. Their ethos is an ecological one, seeking 'unity not conformity ... aim[ing] to build a broad coalition, while making space for creative contention inside of it', based on mutual power and pluralism, and against all forms of domination.[53]

For all these new globalist projects, it's early days, and yet to be seen what they can achieve. But there is real momentum growing towards global living democracy.

Community cohesion programs that are reducing hate crimes; deliberative democratic forums that bring together divided communities with constructive, collective projects; nonviolent movements for change being far more successful at delivering deep and lasting change than violent ones; community-led alternatives that are reducing engagement with and harm from policing, the justice system, and even war; and the building blocks of a new, mutualist globalism. So many people and communities are doing amazing work cultivating coexistence, connection, at every level, while creating new democratic and economic models.

Let's finally bring it back to nature as we turn to the fourth pillar of living democracy – connection between us and the more-than-human world.

# KNOWING NATURE

## From disconnection
## to interdependence

After another morning staring at my computer screen, piecing ideas together, I swapped my ugg boots for hiking boots, and went for a walk. Climbing the side of Black Mountain, I plonked myself down on a rock and stared out across the Brindabellas, the mountains ringing Canberra's south and west, watching as a spring cold front rolled in across the suburbs. The wind rustled through the stringy barks and scribbly gums, the bushpeas, wattles and grasses. Lilies and orchids showed off their bright yellows and purples, vying for attention with the crimson rosellas and eastern rosellas flitting around me, and the tiny bright blue head of a superb fairy-wren. A magpie hopped up, eyeing me off. I said hello, and it nodded to me. As they do.

I breathed. I decompressed. I relaxed. Feeling the stress leaving me, I wandered back down the hill, past the log where I've seen an echidna snuffling around, by the patch of leaf litter where I'd recently watched two bearded dragons tussling, and under the trees where I've spotted a glorious family of yellow-tailed black cockatoos. Coming home, I was able to write with greater clarity about what I was saying and why.

Throughout life, I've found immersing myself in nature to be reinvigorating. And almost everyone I know finds the same, whether they think of it as such or prefer to talk about surfing, bushwalking, gardening, or lying on the beach.

It shouldn't be a surprise, then, that an increasing array of evidence shows that we humans, having evolved as part of the web of life, need connection to nature for our wellbeing. Late last century, ideas such as Edward O Wilson's 'biophilia',[1] Theodore Roszak's 'ecopsychology',[2] and Richard Louv's 'nature deficit disorder',[3] variously seeking to explain a range of ills through the lens of disconnection from nature, emerged. While some of these ideas remain controversial, evidence is piling up that exposure to the natural world is associated with better physical and mental health across a range of factors from hypertension and diabetes to depression and attention deficit, and even recovery from surgery and cancers.[4] It's also demonstrably good for learning and working. Professor Tonia Gray, a Greens councillor and researcher in outdoor education from Western Sydney University, has cited research that 'contact with nature can enhance creativity, bolster mood, lower stress, improve mental acuity, well-being and productivity, cultivate social connectedness, and promote physical activity'.[5]

With his term 'nature deficit disorder', Louv asks what happens if we bring up children without regular contact with nature, living in concrete jungles, not knowing where their food comes from, rarely seeing animals other than pigeons and cockroaches. In positing an anti-ecological culture, I ask what happens when we construct social norms and institutions around separating ourselves from nature, shifting from living interdependent with it to enclosing and seeking to control it. Having translated that disconnection and domination into exclusion and adversarialism in politics, extractivism in economics, and supremacy in institutionalised violence, it's time to bring it back home. How much better would our lives, our communities, our democracies and economies be if we re-embraced their inextricable interdependence with the natural world?

The ecological crises we find ourselves facing are the entirely predictable outcome of a system built on the mythology that we humans are separate from and superior to the natural world. Tightly entangled with other relationships of domination (of women, workers, colonised peoples), anti-ecology establishes a relationship of conflict between humans (and our jobs, industry and economy) and the environment, with the environment always coming off second best.

It's possible, if you think about it in these terms, to be an anti-ecological environmentalist. Indeed, most of us have been, at least at times. When we think in the short term; when our goals are contained to protecting a particular patch; when we are willing to set aside justice or democracy in favour of environmental outcomes because we haven't put in the effort to consider how to bring them together; when we choose to use tools and tactics which emphasise disconnection and domination instead of seeking ways to reconnect and to dissolve dominating power, we are anti-ecological environmentalists.

But time has run out. With intersecting crises bearing down on us, we can no longer tinker around the edges of the system, tiptoeing around structures of power and the cultural ideas that hold them up. As the great Czech freedom fighter and playwright, Vaclav Havel, said, 'we have little chance of averting an environmental catastrophe unless we recognise that we are not the masters of Being, but only a part of Being'.[6] From within the anti-ecological system, we cannot protect nature.

Richard Louv reminded us to reconnect with nature. Living democracy makes that reconnection systemic, cultivating interdependence with the natural world at every level. We're going to look at how an ecological approach would firstly, reverse the way we separate nature from the spaces in which we live and work; secondly, draw together democratic decision-making and scientific guidance in planning processes which prioritise protecting and restoring nature and embrace complexity; and thirdly, embed interdependence with nature into our economic and democratic systems. By building encounters with nature into our everyday lives, and institutionalising the interconnection in our systems, we will make our lives – all our lives, human and non-human – immeasurably better.

We will finally begin to live by my favourite ecological slogan: 'we are not protecting nature, we are nature protecting itself'.


## Living with nature

I'm lucky enough to live somewhere where, on the spur of the moment, I can take a reinvigorating walk through the bush, and also be a short bike ride from cinemas and theatres, universities and libraries, business and government offices, cafes and music venues, and even the national parliament. My garden is home to chooks, blue-tongue lizards, possums, bugs and bees, and I've watched kookaburras, honey-eaters, crows, magpies, sparrows, gorgeous tiny spotted pardalotes, and at least seven species of parrot. While my family is not exactly skilled in the garden, a group of young urban farmers have recently converted a sizable portion of our yard into a veggie patch, growing food for the neighbourhood. Across the road, under the gum trees and next to the bike path, I set up a little library and a neighbour added a community pantry, where locals share and swap things, and gather to chat.

Canberra is a remarkable city. Designed in the early 20th century by the transcendentalists, passionate democrats, and nature-lovers Marion Mahony and Walter Burley Griffin, interconnection with the natural world is embedded in the urban plan.[7] Tongues of bush stretch right into the centre of town, and trees line the streets. Or at least they do in the older area where I'm privileged to live.

And that's the thing – even lovely Canberra isn't a utopia. From the beginning, houses were bizarrely built with no consideration of the alpine climate's 45-degree Celsius temperature range. As the city sprawled, that situation worsened, with outer suburbs treeless expanses of asphalt and black roofs, an extraordinary 7 degrees Celsius hotter than the suburbs with trees, lakes and red-tiled roofs.[8] Too much of the urban infill is of poor quality. With inner-city gentrification driving those with less wealth into homes which cost more to heat and cool, we see how environmental planning and equity go hand in hand.

If this is the case even in Canberra, it is far worse in many larger and less progressive cities which now make up a majority of the world. According to the United Nations, 55 per cent of humanity already lives in cities, and that's projected to grow to 68 per cent by 2050.[9] In Australia, already 71 per cent of us live in cities of 100 000 or more.[10]

But do we have to follow the anti-ecological culture of binaries, and see urban areas as spaces which automatically exclude nature? We're trained to think of nature as that which isn't human development, but when we think ecologically we can recognise cities as ecological niche construction in the same vein as termites' nests and wombats' burrows. That niche can be destructive of other interdependent parts of the ecosystem, in which case it will inevitably undermine its own resilience, as termites and wombats can bring down trees and erode hillsides, or it can embrace the interdependence and become regenerative.

City living can alienate us from each other and from the natural world, driving unhealthy and unsustainable consumption and destruction of land. And it can also reduce our encroachment on green fields areas, lessen time and fuel spent commuting, and bring people together in cohesive local communities, experiencing greater diversity of views and backgrounds and lifestyles which make us more open to coexistence. Like Canberra's nature parks, verge gardens and green-walled apartment blocks, urban environments can also become wildlife sanctuaries and agricultural spaces, cultivating abundance and interdependence.

Earlier we discussed how participation needs to start with things directly relevant to people's lives, and that will often be related to 'place-making' – local planning issues and doing things in the community where we live. This literal 'grounding' is the core of ecological politics, and has been central to the efforts of those resisting anti-ecological culture. For Indigenous governance, 'country owns us', and we must act as stewards for it. For Gerrard Winstanley and the Diggers in the English Revolution, and for the Paris Communards, communal stewardship and management of the land was a crucial first step in cultivating a better world. For Elinor Ostrom and Murray Bookchin, participatory management of local spaces and local communities is key to valuing and institutionalising mutualism. For all of them, interdependence with the natural world is the beating heart.

That's where we have to start in our task of reconnecting with the natural world. Place-making projects that embrace interdependence, blurring the boundaries between city, nature and agriculture, recognising that everything can be multi-purpose, showing that this leads to better quality of life and more resilient, more equitable, communities – this is a crucial step in cultivating our living democracy. And around the world, there are people doing exactly this, in wonderful examples of collective, DIY community action, dragging governments and urban planning policy along on their coat tails.

### Urban agriculture

Karina and Mikey set to it with shovels and pitchforks, digging up the lawn with gusto. Soon other volunteers join in, and by the end of the day the patch of land by the side of the road is tilled and planted into rows, with broadbeans, snowpeas and sugar snaps set to grow on the suburban street.

Canberra's Patchwork Urban Farm grows veggies for sale through a Community Supported Agriculture scheme, where people subscribe to get a box each week. But Patchwork is about far more than growing food. People come together for working bees, and meet up each week to collect the veggies, cultivating social cohesion. All workers, volunteers and customers are respected as valuable, contributing community members. Ecological farming techniques are being used to build healthy soils instead of extracting nutrients from the land. It's also deliberately being visible, to engage neighbours and passers-by in conversation.

You see the same approach in community gardens, allotments and city farms from Brisbane to San Francisco. You see it in apartment buildings, where communal composting groups are popping up as people seek ways of connecting with food, nature and each other. Even with people's private veggie patches and backyard chooks, tended by one person or family, the community connections inherent in cultivating food emerge when proud cultivators delight in sharing the fruit of their labours with as many friends, family and neighbours as they can.

The urban agriculture movement is flourishing around the globe as people seek ways of connecting with the land, building food security and cultivating social cohesion. A direct descendant of the Diggers, the Paris Communards, and so many others throughout history, it demonstrates the flipside of Ester Boserup's warning: reclaiming the right to be independent cultivators is one of the best ways to dissolve dominating power.

One of the most thoroughly thought-through projects in this space that I have come across is the Lyneham Commons, also in the 'lentil belt' of inner Canberra. This project arose when a few keen gardeners dreamed up the idea of a true, old-style commons in Canberra – a communally-tended, open, un-owned food forest on public land. The government tried to offer a form of leasehold over the land the group was after, but the Commoners insisted it was to be truly public land or nothing. Eventually, they negotiated an agreement around insurance and got it off the ground, in a fantastic spot on a bike path between two schools.

All these models are wonderful examples of participatory democracy, place-making, commons economies, and connection to the natural world in the heart of a city.

### *Rewilding the city*

Growing food is an incredibly deep way of connecting with nature, but there are also, of course, many projects that are simply about bringing flora and fauna into the urban environment in what's becoming known as 'rewilding' the city. Bush regeneration and park care have long been popular and excellent ways to see and hear more birds and frogs, to cool the streets, and to improve quality of life.

Ambitious communities have remediated filthy creeks and storm-water drains in cities like Sydney and Melbourne, turning them back into wetlands and havens for frogs and birds. Nature playgrounds are being built in suburbs, replacing (or supplementing) geometrical metal and plastic swings and slides with more creative, often asymmetrical wooden and stone structures that children (and adults) find more stimulating and that feel more part of the ecosystem. These tend to be installed when schools or community groups, planning collectively, decide they want one and work together to make it happen.

Some of the best ideas are where people have an off-the-wall thought about fun activities that carry a serious, important message. Here are two of the absolute best. The

PARK(ing) movement started when members of the Rebar design collective in San Francisco decided to temporarily turn an inner city parking spot into a mini park, complete with 'turf, a tree, a bench and signs inviting passers-by to sit and relax'.[11] People loved it so much that they developed a how-to guide, and PARK(ing) day evolved, with people taking part all over the world. On one level, it's a bit of absurdist theatre, but it gets people thinking about reclaiming what should be common space in our cities for us to reconnect with the natural world, and it's inspiring communities and urban planners to make more permanent changes.

And then there's guerrilla plant labelling! This is a viral movement of 'rebel botanists armed with chalk'[12] who graffiti labels for plants growing in urban environments, whether they're weeds sprouting through the cracks in pavements or flowers and trees that have been deliberately planted. The idea is to draw attention to the wild in the city, as well as to address the loss of our vocabulary of nature, teaching us the words we've lost.

More formal ways of learning about nature also still exist in our cities, like guided tours by ecologists or Indigenous people (or Indigenous ecologists), or wild food foragers, pointing out and identifying flora and fauna. By reconnecting with nature in our cities, we can inspire people to help it flourish.

Architecture is vital here, too. Green roofs and walls are beautiful and practical. They capture and distribute water far better than concrete, and they cool the city. Replacing the mirror walls of skyscrapers which are death traps for birds, focus the sun's heat, and channel wind through bare tunnels, with vertical gardens which clean, calm and cool the air, welcome wildlife, and can even grow food, will make life better for us and for the animals we share the urban environment with. We should work to change planning regulations to encourage, enable or even require them to be implemented wherever possible.

### *Blurring boundaries*

Newcastle's Carrington Bowling Club was struggling financially, like so many similar community clubs around the country. Its energy bills were through the roof, despite sitting a stone's throw from the largest coal port in the world and being told that coal keeps electricity cheap.

In 2017, this working class community came together with a local environment group, raised funds from members, locals and supporters across the country, and put a bank of solar panels on its roof, saving money, emissions and the club itself.[13] A couple of years later, the Croatian Wickham Sports Club nearby followed suit, halving its energy bills and slashing its climate impact in the heart of 'coal country'.

Urban renewable energy, whether on people's homes, on schools or parking lots or shopping centres, is a great way of blurring the boundaries between domestic and industrial and environmental. It directly challenges the environment versus economy and environment versus community worldview, showing that ecological thinking finds co-benefits by making things multi-purpose. Why can't a home also be a farm, a power station, and a community hub? Even better, as many communities are finding, these projects can be done very successfully as community-owned cooperatives, giving people a common stake and sharing the benefits.

The Newcastle example, led by working class and immigrant communities, highlights another vital point: it's crucial that these projects aren't just wealthy, suburban phenomena. They have to be done in a way that cultivates equity and justice rather than entrenching the ecological injustices that see poorer and marginalised communities relegated to sacrifice zones. Sometimes this means demonstrating success where it's easy to start and then replicating it elsewhere. But those of us with more time and resources need to make sure we don't just spend them in our own communities.

Like the community commoning projects led by Participatory City in east London, communities of colour in cities like Atlanta and Chicago are explicitly using urban greening projects to address entrenched inequity. Getting marginalised communities involved in caring for parks and remediating riverbanks, paying people decently to make their own neighbourhood more liveable for everyone, brings incredible co-benefits. It reduces over-policing, gives people agency that keeps them safer, creates a shared sense of achievement and pride in the community, and much more.[14]

The flipside of bringing nature into urban environments is that we also need to end the separation of humans from nature in agriculture and wilderness protection, and there's already plenty of progress in both. Regenerative farming and other ecological agricultural practices are getting a foothold as farmers increasingly recognise that they bring tremendous benefits. Many farmers are also finding that using their land for renewable energy generation as well as agriculture is a great way to build resilience.

At the same time, managers of national parks are moving beyond the old idea of 'locking up' wilderness and seeing it as better off without us. Increasingly, we're learning from Indigenous custodians that humans have actively managed country for our entire existence. Well-resourced Indigenous stewardship, from fire use to species management, will be crucial in making our land and communities more resilient.

And, given how much we humans have already changed the face of the planet, with land clearing, pests and climate change wreaking havoc, we have no choice now but to seek to actively engage with the land, increasing diversity and interconnection in the bush, on farms and in cities, to give ecosystems and species the best possible chance of survival as the planet heats.

Building interaction with the natural world into our everyday lives helps us appreciate our interdependence. In a very real way, seeing more trees and birds, putting our hands in the soil, and eating carrots grown next door, can contribute to making more ecologically sound decisions about major infrastructure developments as we recognise that everything is connected.

## An ecology of environmental planning

We've all seen it happen. Many of us have been caught up in it.

A developer announces a proposal – it might be a knock-down-rebuild next door, a new stretch of highway bulldozing critically endangered habitat or sacred trees, or another coal mine. The government goes through the motions of proper process, with assessments and consultation, but everyone knows it's a foregone conclusion. Both the developer and government are banking on our cynicism, hoping we won't bother to even try to stand in the way of their profit-making, using failed opposition to disempower us further.

Every now and then, something remarkable happens.

In the New South Wales Northern Rivers in 2010, locals learned about plans to frack their green, rolling hills for gas. They went about building a broad coalition to stop it, bringing together farmers and tree-changers, scientists and Indigenous people, working hard to create a shared purpose despite different worldviews. They participated in formal consultations and used legal processes to delay the development. They lobbied local councils, locked farm gates, and finally set up a massive blockade – a joyful, festive, musical, democratic celebration of direct action.

By mid-2014, after four years of campaigning and organising, the government had given in and suspended the fracking licence, and the whole region was declared gas free. The Bentley Blockade had won.[15]

So much can and must start with the community simply acting together and dragging the government along.

In some cases, like the Bentley Blockade, our collective power can be enough to make the government listen. In others, the refusal of governments to do what is clearly necessary in the face of concerted campaigns can expose the failure of the system and help motivate and stimulate change. But we can no more organise mass actions to save everything that needs to be saved than we can rely on the government and developers to choose to do the right thing. We need to change the system.

By and large, from local council development regulation to national-scale laws about major infrastructure, environmental planning regimes can best be described as systems of managed destruction. Having evolved within anti-ecological culture, they're designed in a way that presumes that extraction of value from the land and the community is the end goal, excludes people from decision-making, makes planning processes adversarial battles that those with the most dominant power are mostly guaranteed to win, and treats the short-term profits of a small group of humans as supreme.

We have to flip this whole approach. But most high-level campaigns to change environmental planning laws do so from within this anti-ecological framework. They ask for tweaks to make it a little less destructive, a little more participatory, more responsive to science. Our living world desperately needs a living democracy. We need environmental planning systems anchored in deliberative, participatory, polycentric community leadership, informed by frank and fearless expert advice; a presumption of protection and restoration; and systemic thinking.

### *Participatory, polycentric planning*

With honourable exceptions, scope for participation in environmental planning decisions is a sick joke. Developers put forward a proposal which the state sees as its role to facilitate, after asking for a bit of feedback which it knows it can ignore. A successful process is one where enough tweaks are made to the proposal for planning departments and developers to be able to plausibly claim the community was heard, but the development goes ahead largely in its original form. Democratically developed planning guidelines, such as they exist, are frequently stretched or ignored, and monitoring and compliance are almost non-existent.

The people with the most at stake and the most inform-ation – the community and scientists – are most excluded.

Scientific advice is shockingly suppressed. A recent study found an appalling half to three quarters of environmental scientists saying their advice had been silenced, censored or ignored, or they had self-censored for fear of retribution in the form of research funding applications being knocked back.[16] Scientists tasked with developing management plans for threatened species are shamefully underfunded.[17] Public 'consultation' sessions too often descend into acrimonious shouting matches, or piles of submissions are patronisingly acknowledged and ignored.

Remember Amanda Cahill, working with communities in places like Gladstone and the Hunter Valley, and coming out with consensus reports calling for faster transition, and all sorts of plans being put into action by the community themselves? She comes into incredibly divided spaces, with old friends not talking to each other, with governments and corporations creating immense pressure, and, instead of telling people to pick a side, she helps them come together around a common vision they develop themselves.

Imagine if our environmental and urban planning processes could work like that. Imagine if younger people wanting more affordable housing could sit down with older people wanting to protect the character of the neighbourhood, alongside members of the local frog watch group, the school community, and the managers and staff of local shops. Most people, of course, will wear several of those hats, and, talking together, they can find creative ways through.

We've learned from Elinor Ostrom and John Dryzek how these processes, when well facilitated, work to satisfy people and steward shared resources for the long term. We've seen them in action from Rockhampton to Rojava. These models exist. We need to implement them. We need to put environmental management decision-making into the hands of the community, supporting groups to democratically and deliberatively develop the rules they agree to be bound by, and link them together into a polycentric network of communities so they can understand each other's concerns and situations and cooperatively plan across larger areas. Communities need access to well-funded scientific advice to help them make their decisions. And they should be developing proactive plans for what they want to see happen, not be simply responding to someone else's proposal, always being on the back foot. That's the path to better outcomes for people and nature; to building trust and social cohesion; to long-lasting but adaptable plans that everyone can rely on; and to more justice and equity.

While we're not likely to leap straight from where we are to this polycentric, grassroots system, there's plenty we can do along the way. We can gather our own communities together to make proactive plans, as many community associations are already doing, and challenge governments and developers to accept them. We can, like Amanda Cahill, offer facilitation services that demonstrate how deliberative conversations change both the process and the outcome.

Importantly, we can reach out to marginalised communities and make sure they have a voice they feel able to use in community conversations. This is particularly vital with First Nations communities. Free, prior, and informed consent, a minimum standard that is too often perverted by deliberately splitting traditional owner groups, needs to be deepened into a system that truly puts self-determination and agency into the hands of the people the country owns.

## *Presumption of protection*

Given how fragile our depleted ecosystems already are, and given that ecosystem collapse is non-linear and very difficult to reverse, it is vital and urgent that we institute in our environmental planning a presumption of protection.

Instead of the existing system of managed destruction, the presumption should be that, in the absence of overwhelming countervailing factors, proposals which will cause or risk damage to our remaining healthy ecosystems, or which, taken cumulatively with other projects will together cause or risk such damage, should not be approved.

Requiring developers to properly address environmental impacts will stimulate creative thinking that can come up with plans that will contribute to the common pool instead of extracting from it: buildings that generate more clean energy than they use, that incorporate habitat for other species, that enable communities to come together. With the right incentives and requirements, this is totally possible, and a presumption of protection is one part of the picture.

## *Systemic thinking*

Commons management gets us thinking systemically. By bringing every voice and perspective to the table, it helps us embrace complexity instead of attempting to enforce simplicity.

One vital piece of this puzzle is to ensure that the cumulative impacts of projects are accounted for in assessment, instead of processing each individual proposal separately, pretending it exists in a vacuum. The absence of cumulative impact assessment enables a death by a thousand cuts, chipping away at diversity, redundancy and connectivity. It makes a mockery of the approvals system and demonstrates either a complete misunderstanding of how ecologies work or a deliberate attempt to avoid scrutiny.

Similarly, we need to bring proactive restoration and resilience into environmental management. Resilience in ecosystems refers to both 'their ability to absorb change and persist while maintaining core structural and functional attributes' as well as 'the speed at which ... [they can return] to an equilibrium state following a temporary disturbance'.[18] Managing for resilience requires ensuring diversity and redundancy in ecosystems, fostering connectivity, increasing understanding about how complex adaptive systems work, broadening participation, and establishing more polycentric systems of governance rather than centralised, top-down management.

Thinking systemically also means dropping the obsession with one-size-fits-all solutions to complex problems. The prime example of this is the persistent idea that climate change could be fixed by simply putting a price on carbon. In reality, such a complex problem always needed multi-pronged, systemic approaches, including regulation, industrial policy, trade policy, economic levers and much more.

Former leader of the Australian Greens, Christine Milne, struggled hard to bring this idea into Australian politics. Her great success was the innovation of the Multi-Party Climate Change Committee, established on her advice after the 2010 federal election. This brilliant deliberative political process brought together politicians from across the spectrum, as long as they were interested in achieving a positive result, along with expert advisers. Embedded in the committee's goals was the idea that the negotiated final package would include a range of measures, not simply a carbon price. Of course, adversarial politics destroyed much of the package that was negotiated after only two years, but it stands as a shining example of how a parliament can move beyond adversarialism and embrace complexity.

If this deliberative approach seeking sophisticated solutions could be followed in communities across the country, it could move us towards the change we need. But we still need to step a level deeper into the system.

## Institutionalising interdependence

North-west of Wellington, the capital city of New Zealand, flowing down from volcanic mountains through rolling hills recognisable from the Lord of the Rings films, the Whanganui River burbles and rushes.

In 2017, the New Zealand parliament officially granted the Whanganui legal personhood. The act was guided by the local Maori iwi's understanding of the river as a member of their family, and they represent and speak for the river in legal affairs.

Personhood hasn't fixed the problems the river faces, from agricultural run-off and silt to the threat of mining in its headwaters. But it has changed the conversation. It has put the river at the centre, asking not what we can get from it, but what it needs, what we can do for it. It requires the legal system and all those who work through it to take the river seriously as a stakeholder in its own right. It requires all of us to reconsider our relationship with it – with that river, and with the rest of the natural world.

It's a stark contrast to how many of our politicians see the world.

'It's important to have a balance in your emissions reductions policies,' said Prime Minister Scott Morrison. 'Our Government will take, and is taking, meaningful, practical, sensible, responsible action on climate change without damaging our economy or your family budget.'[19]

It's amazing how often you hear ministers, business-people and commentators wanting to balance environmental outcomes with economic ones. Interestingly enough, you never hear it the other way around. Have you ever heard a politician say, 'It's important to have balance in your economic policies. Our government will take sensible action on corporate profits without damaging our environment or your family's clean air and water'? No? I thought not. Because it's not really about balance at all.

From an ecological perspective, the idea of balancing the economy and the environment is nonsensical. It's like balancing your bank account and your brain. The rhetoric is a factor of the imagined separation of humanity from nature and the relationship of dominance that's established in anti-ecological culture, seeing us devalue nature as nothing more than resources for us to extract value from. Damage to the natural world in this view is an 'externality', not even counted among the things that matter.

When we try to count it on those terms, to internalise the externalities, we make it abstract, fungible, a product for sale, with bizarre consequences. The Great Barrier Reef, according to Deloitte analysis, is 'worth' $56 billion.[20] In this view, if we can extract more than $56 billion in profits by destroying the reef, it's worth doing. When ecosystems are valued because they provide 'services', if we can replace those services more efficiently and cheaply in some other way, the ecosystems can be – no, *should be* – destroyed. As John Locke told us back in Part 1, unused nature is 'waste', and it's wasteful not to use it.

This view of the world has to end before it kills us. Separation and domination must be replaced with true, respectful interdependence. As we seek to change government and power, we have to embed ecological culture into the heart of our new structures.

The bizarre balancing of environmental outcomes with economic ones is actually written into law, in a predictably one-sided manner. Australia's national environment protection act includes the clause 'decision-making processes should effectively integrate both long-term and short-term economic, environmental, social and equitable considerations',[21] while no economic or social legislation requires the integration of environmental considerations. I've often thought it'd be fun to try to do that – amend every business-friendly act to add an objective to ensure it doesn't damage the environment. Jokes aside, various jurisdictions with Human Rights Acts have introduced a practice of assessing every piece of legislation on the basis of its compliance with that act. The introduction of ecological impact assessment for all legislation might be a valuable idea. And the clearest way to embed it would be through legal rights for nature.

The concept of legally instituted Rights of Nature was first introduced into modern legal thought through a 1972 article by Professor Christopher Stone called 'Should trees have standing?'[22] The paper challenged the idea that the natural world, that trees, should be treated as objects only in the eyes of the law – as property. Doesn't the environment, Stone asked, consist not just of 'natural resources' for human use, but of living entities which themselves have a right to exist and to be respected by our legal systems? Policy, theory and jurisprudence around Rights of Nature have grown dramatically in the intervening half century, often drawing on and based around Indigenous worldviews and political movements.[23]

The most famous examples of existing legal rights for nature include New Zealand's Whanganui River, and Bolivia and Ecuador's constitutional 'Rights of Mother Earth'. But there are numerous examples around the globe of legal recognition that the natural world, specific natural phenomena, and certain ecosystems, have inherent legal rights. Former Western Australian Greens member of the legislative council, Diane Evers, introduced The Rights of Nature and Future Generations Bill 2019 into the Western Australian parliament, seeking to enshrine the legal right for the natural world and its constituent ecosystems to exist, require government to act to protect it, and introduce stiff penalties for breach.[24] And the Blue Mountains City Council has announced plans to integrate Rights of Nature into their planning and operations.[25]

There are plenty of questions about how Rights of Nature would work in practice, but they are increasingly being nutted out. At a minimum, the laws are requiring governments and corporations to give more thought to how their actions impact on the natural world.

Parallel approaches are investigating introducing a global crime of ecocide, or the right to live in a healthy environment. In slightly different ways, these seek to ensure that we embed into the way we govern the fact that we are but one part of an interdependent ecosystem, and our health as individual humans and as a species is inseparable from the health of the natural world.

If we bring nature back into our world, building encounters with it into our everyday lives, and if we institutionalise the interconnection in our systems, we will be well down the path to living democracy.

But how can all these small, discrete ideas actually change the whole world?

That, finally, is where we head now.

# PART 3

# HOW DO WE GET THERE?

# MAKING THE
# IMPOSSIBLE INEVITABLE

It was a rainy spring day when Richard Dowling and Cormac Gollogly got married in the Irish town of Clonmel, county Tipperary.[1] They got engaged while on holidays in Spain, despite knowing they couldn't legally marry in their home country – a country where same-sex relationships were illegal until 1993, the year they turned 12. But, on 17 November 2015, Richard and Cormac became the first same-sex couple to be legally married in the Republic of Ireland. In less than a generation, equal marriage went from inconceivable to inevitable before becoming reality. It's a truly remarkable (and unfinished) story of social change around the world, and perhaps nowhere as swift as in Ireland.

It's easy for this change to be painted as the result of natural shifts in social norms, but it's no accident. It's one aspect of a long struggle for equal rights for LGBTQIA+ people, and it happened thanks to courageous advocacy and campaigning in Ireland and around the world for generations. The shifts in social norms are the result of deliberate, often dangerous, sometimes illegal work to normalise the diversity of sexuality and gender, including vital campaigns to protect people from violence, to destigmatise AIDS, to support positive representation in popular culture, and to change laws.

Crucially, alongside this sits the collapse of the immense institutional power of the Catholic Church in Irish society and politics. After a slow decay, the final crash followed the publicisation of terrible breaches of trust such as sexual abuse of children and forced adoptions.

The concurrence of that institutional collapse and the cultivation of new social norms through advocacy and campaigning created the space for transformational change. At that moment of opportunity, a popular movement built to demand and expect change pushed politicians to act. The government called a Citizens' Assembly which, after extensive deliberation, proposed amendments to the constitution that were put to the people in a referendum, passing with the support of 62 per cent of the population.

The impossible was made inevitable. Slowly; painfully slowly at first. And then very suddenly indeed.

Like so many who've spent decades working for change, through the ecstasy at small wins and the tears at big losses, the most infuriating thing of all for me is not outright opposition; it's being told over and over again to lower our ambition, to ask for far less than what is necessary, because 'politics is the art of the possible'. That quip from 19th century German statesman Otto von Bismarck is the bane of our lives. It's constantly used to silence and sideline anyone working for transformational change.

But the inconvenient thing I've come to realise about Bismarck's line is that it's true – we just need to reinterpret it.

It's obvious that politics can only deliver what's possible, constrained by the people in power and by the systems of power that they're operating within. It's equally obvious, though, that if we accept the limits of what is currently possible – and too many environmental and social activists do, limiting their advocacy and campaigning to fit within their assumptions of fixed reality – we will never successfully confront the deep challenges we face. We'll keep spiralling towards extinction.

But neither can we just baldly declare that we're going to do the impossible. Bashing our head against that brick wall is why so many of us have headaches so much of the time. That leaves only one alternative.

We have to change what's possible.

This is what Bismarck and friends carefully ignore – that what is possible changes. And can be deliberately changed.

What is possible is essentially a question of power. In some ways it's the most fundamental question of power; if you control the institutions that exercise coercive power, as well as the cultural norms that determine how power can and should be exercised, you control what's possible. Change those institutions and norms, and you change what's possible. The problem with the Bismarckian view is not so much that it tells us that change is impossible, but that it insists it's wrong to even try.

Changing what's possible is hard to do, but it happens all the time, at various scales. In fact, it's amazing how quickly the impossible can become inevitable, as Richard and Cormac found.

Of course, what we're trying to do with living democracy

is far bigger than marriage equality, important though that is. We're seeking to address a climate and ecological crisis of terrifying scale, interwoven with economic inequality spinning out of control, ongoing racial and gender oppressions, hard-won democratic norms and institutions being eroded or outright attacked, and much more. And we have to address them together, because they are all aspects of deeply entrenched systems of power. We can't, for example, just replace coal with renewables run by world-spanning corporations exploiting workers, destroying ecosystems, steamrolling vulnerable communities, and ignoring the will of the people. That may work in a few places and cases, but it simply cannot deliver transformational change to a system where fossil fuels are so entwined with power. Each contradictory step undermines the entire project for change. Steamroll over one community to build a wind farm or a mine for the metals in your batteries and the next will resist. Close one coal-fired power station without putting in place a just transition plan and the next will resist. The only way to succeed is to shift the systems of power, the cultures and norms and institutions that created these crises in the first place.

That's big. But here's the thing: they're in crisis.

As we discussed towards the end of Part 1, right now is an extraordinary moment of flux. We're seeing a dramatic collapse in trust in institutions of power, from politics to police, business to media, church to state. Simultaneously, the stories we've been told about how the world works – that corporations and states are more important than trees and rivers, that we're all entirely selfish individuals, that violent coercion is a fact of life, that we're separate from nature – are losing their sway.

There's a real danger that the vacuum this leaves behind

could be filled by authoritarians, stripping the planet bare on the headlong rush towards extinction. Or it could create the space for us to quite literally change everything. If we use this moment to model new norms, tell new culture-defining stories, and build new democratic institutions that embody these norms and stories, we can move change from impossible to inevitable at the grandest scale of all – not just changing who holds power and what they do with it, but changing the essence of power, and cultivating living democracy. If we choose that path, we won't just survive the difficult years ahead; we will thrive.

As we come to the end of the book, we're going to look at how we take all these ideas we've been discussing and bring them together into a project of transformation. We're going to dig into examples and theories of transformation, in ecology and in politics, thinking deeply about the nature of power. We'll ground ourselves at this moment of flux, asking what it is that's collapsing around us. And we'll consider what we need to do to cultivate living democracy amidst the collapse.

At its core, it's once again about learning to be ecological.

If we think of our social, economic and political system as a machine, we get solutions that are mechanistic – fix this cog here, append a new widget there, add an anti-corruption commission or a citizens' jury, take away corporate donations, give it a kick, and it should work fine. It doesn't. If we think of the system as a hierarchy of power, we get supplicant politics, where change can only come through begging or demanding it of those in power, or by replacing the people in power.

But if it's a living ecosystem, we have a very different approach. We need to seed a whole array of new alternatives, new norms and institutions, to replace the problematic ones that are beginning to collapse, and we need to cultivate the fertile ground and hospitable climate for the alternatives to flourish. We need to do this in a way that accelerates the collapse of the old system by withdrawing consent from its norms and institutions, and builds trust in new ones. It'll be slow at first. Then it'll reach a threshold, and what was impossible will suddenly be inevitable.

We can never know in advance when the tipping point will come. But we can push it along. And we must be ready when it arrives.

# CYCLES OF CHANGE, COLLAPSE AND RENEWAL

They would come in their billions, in clouds so huge they darkened the sky.

Each spring, huge swarms of bogong moths would fly up to the cooler alpine plains. They'd migrate as far as 1000 kilometres, along the mountain spine that European invaders would label the Great Dividing Range (despite it actually being a great connector across the continent). On a hill the shape of a moth not far from the range's highest peaks, the Ngunnawal, Ngambri, Wiradjuri and Ngarigo people would gather to feast on this delicacy, full of fat and protein. They'd yarn, sharing information, teaching younger generations, collectively making decisions, and rehearsing the songlines whose knowledge held their society together for millennia.[1]

In the 1980s, over the strenuous objections of the Traditional Custodians, that hill was excavated to build the new Australian Parliament House. But the moths kept coming. Each spring, millions would cover windows and block vents. The people who gathered on the hill now – parliamentarians and their staff, lobbyists, and journalists – found them amusing or annoying. Some hated them, and you'd hear people in corridors exclaiming 'can't someone do something about them!?'

It went oddly unremarked when their numbers declined over a few seasons. Then, very suddenly, in 2017 and 2018, they crashed.[2] For several years now, essentially no moths have arrived at all. Not at parliament, nor in the surrounding hills, nor up into the Snowy Mountains. Scientists believe a combination of rising temperatures and reduced water, thanks to both drought and over-extraction, has led to the collapse. For the denizens of Parliament House that's quite convenient. For the Indigenous people it's another aspect of genocide, wiping out a crucial part of their culture, a branch of their family. For the alpine ecosystem it could trigger a wave of extinctions.

Because the local people weren't the only ones eating this amazingly rich food. One of Australia's cutest animals, the tiny mountain pygmy possum, or *Burramys parvus*, would emerge from hibernation as the clouds of bogong moths arrived. For a creature all of 11 centimetres long (if you don't count its 14-centimetre tail), a moth is a fabulous feast, and perfect to help you put on enough fat to raise a family. But for some 20 years already, the *Burramys* has been listed as critically endangered. Its habitat has been progressively cleared for logging, grazing, and ski resorts, cut into smaller and smaller pieces, invaded by predators like cats and foxes, and trampled by feral horses. The balance of species was changed first by the replacement of the millennia-long Indigenous land management with European-style agriculture, and then again by rising heat and catastrophic bushfires.

One or two of these threats might have been manageable for the *Burramys*. Indeed, painstaking work by scientists and local ecological stewards was seeing tiny populations stabilise. But, when the moths didn't arrive, it spelt disaster. Devastated researchers started to find emaciated mothers with their young dead in their pouches. Extinction in the wild looms for this critically endangered species. And the disappearance of the bogong moths is bad news for many other species of marsupial, bird and reptile that feast on it.

At the same time, the combination of higher temperatures, less water, terrible fires, and a borer beetle whose population has exploded in the warmer weather, is contributing to a devastating die-off of *Eucalyptus pauciflora*, the magnificent, multicoloured snow gums that are so emblematic of the high country and provide homes for numerous creatures.[3] And repeated high temperature fires roaring through areas which previously didn't often burn threaten the alpine ash, *Eucalyptus delegatensis*. If fires come too frequently, burning saplings and mature trees, it simply can't recover.[4]

It's a perfect storm for the Snowies. Cycles of change as small as the life of individual moths and possums are overlaid with cycles at the scale of the lives of trees, which are nested within epochal shifts in ambient temperature, the availability of water, and the frequency of fire. The resilience of diverse and interconnected systems that used to spread across the wide high country has crumbled as the ecosystems have been divided into shrinking, disconnected, impoverished fragments. Discrete instabilities here and there that could previously be counterbalanced elsewhere snowball into system-wide collapse.

What happens next depends on what's growing in the spaces left behind, and what the conditions for growth are. They could end up a mountainous desert. Or new trees, bushes and grasses might grow to replace the ash and snow gum forests, bringing new mammals, birds and insects with them, and, over time, a new diverse ecosystem could emerge. Over time.

In one part of the high country, at Severn Park, about halfway between parliament and the snow fields, that timeframe has been compressed. In only 20 years, fifth generation farmer, Charles Massy, has taken land that his own traditional western farming had left barren and regenerated it into a beautiful, biodiverse, and highly productive oasis. As he detailed in his beautiful book, *Call of the Reed Warbler*,[5] Massy had thought he was doing the right thing by the land which he loved, using modern pesticides, fertilisers, irrigation and stocking techniques. He tells of confidently ploughing fields before a storm, expecting the water to permeate the soil, and instead watching what he now estimates to be 1000 years' worth of topsoil wash away. The ecological collapse was reflected in economic and emotional collapse for Massy – he became deeply depressed and nearly sold the farm. But the shock triggered a dramatic change in direction as he adopted regenerative farming techniques, learning to work with the land instead of against it.

He began to use worm castings and compost instead of chemical fertilisers, changed the way he irrigated, reduced stocking and let trees, bushes and native grasses return, and planted a diverse range of trees for shade, for birds, and for fixing the soil. Each action on its own would have been swamped by others pushing in the opposite direction, but together they changed everything.

There's far less need for pesticides now, as the birds and the nematodes in the healthy soil control pests like grasshoppers, eating eggs before they hatch and keeping mature insect numbers down. The healthy soils retain water, meaning the salt pans that had appeared are no longer a problem. The land is far more productive than it's been for generations, and wildlife, such as the reed warbler, has returned. With Massy's help, the self-organising magic of the natural world has created a virtuous cycle and swiftly rebuilt its interdependent diversity.

Change is the only constant – in nature, in society, in politics. We live among cycles of creation and destruction and recreation, from each of the cells in our body to all the stars in the sky. As our cells divide, disperse and die, in some cases within days, they metabolise minerals built of elements born in dying stars billions of years ago. Cycles within cycles create the magnificent diversity of life, give it stability, and occasionally line up to trigger transformational change.

In some ways, managing change is one of the starkest failures of our anti-ecological systems. The exclusive and adversarial politics, the extractive economy, the coercion, and the separation from nature all undermine our capacity to manage change by reducing diversity and cutting off vital feedbacks, creating brittle systems prone to breakage.

As natural systems teach us, trying to hold back change, or pretending it isn't happening, eventually ends in disaster. Ironically, if we try too hard to determine exactly what happens next, that usually fails, too. Our best bet is to cultivate adaptable systems, to seed the things we want to grow and nurture them carefully, to stop doing the things that are causing destruction, and to establish the conditions under which what we want to happen can emerge. And we can seek to line up the cycles of change in order to enable transformation.

To work out what to do, we need to look more deeply at how transformational change happens, in ecology and politics. To do that, we're going to explore two important ideas: panarchy and hegemony.

## Transformation in nature: Don't panic, embrace panarchy

Around the turn of the millennium, a group of ecologists led by Lance Gunderson and CS Holling proposed a new way of thinking about change in complex systems. After many years of studying ecosystems, bioregions, and social and institutional systems, they stepped back to look at the whole picture. They brought together a group of colleagues to workshop their ideas, and a remarkable framework revealed itself.

They called it 'panarchy'.

Panarchy understands the world as a complex system of complex systems, all going through cycles of change. These systems operate at various scales – some microscopic, some planetary; some over days, some over millennia – and change, impetus, direction can come from any of the levels and flow through to any or many of the others. This is what gives it the name panarchy (*pan-* meaning 'all', *-archy* being 'rule'), distinguishing it from top-down hierarchy and implying control by all parts. It's also a nod to the unpredictable nature god, Pan.

It's in their analysis of interconnected cycles of change that the really useful insights emerge. Gunderson, Holling and colleagues identified that every system goes through the same four-stage cycle of change: growth, conservation, release and reorganisation. Whether it's a cell, an animal or plant, an ecological community, a species, a bioregion, a company or a political system, the same cycle applies. And the cycles all interact with each other: small and fast cycles influence the make-up of the larger, slower ones; and larger, slower cycles influence the conditions under which the smaller and faster ones emerge and grow. And here's the crux: the feedbacks can create stability or they can generate transformation.

Growth, conservation, release and reorganisation.

You're born and grow to adulthood. You live your life. You die and your constituent parts return to the earth, ashes to ashes, dust to dust. If you had children, your DNA continues in another form, and the nutrients in your body feed the soil and are reorganised as new life grows.

Each cell in your body goes through the same cycle. Usually, it happens smoothly. Sometimes, however, a cancer cell appears. Its growth can disrupt the cycle of your whole body, possibly causing its sudden arrival at the release phase. But you were born into a larger cycle – perhaps that cycle was a community that organised itself in such a way that it developed sophisticated medical procedures that could treat the cancer, allowing your conservation phase to continue a while longer.

In the complex interaction between countless cycles, extraordinary things happen. It's how complexity develops from simplicity.

A cycle at one scale triggers a cycle at another scale to speed up or slow down, sometimes creating a positive feedback loop, sometimes a counterbalancing one. The interacting cycles can stabilise each other, or they can destabilise each other. As Gunderson and Holling put it, 'Those interactions are not only non-linear; they generate alternating stable states ... Variability in ecosystems is not merely an inconvenient characteristic of these productive, dynamic systems. It is essential for their maintenance.'[6]

It's the balance between stability and instability that gives us healthy, generative, evolving, adaptive systems. 'On the one hand, destabilizing forces are important in maintaining diversity, resilience and opportunity. On the other hand, stabilizing forces are important in maintaining productivity.'[7]

Your body needs a certain amount of stability to maintain its growth and conservation phases, but that stability depends on diversity – on other people and social structures, on food sources, clean air and water, healthy soils – and diversity only emerges through cycles of life and death and reorganisation smaller and larger than you. Just as you get stiff if you sit still for too long, too much stability – too long in the conservation stage – makes a system too rigid, which leads to release, often when an interlinked cycle changes. The mountain pygmy possum evolved over millennia to eat bogong moths in spring. As its habitat became poorer and more disconnected, that became a risky dependence. Moth goes; possum goes. Mr Peabody set up a company to mine coal. As the market shifted, the company failed to diversify. The coal market starts to collapse; Peabody Coal goes bankrupt.

In collapse is the space for renewal. Release flows directly into 'rapid phases of reorganization where, for transient moments, novelty can emerge'.[8] All of a sudden, there is scope for whatever else is growing to claim space. In a biodiverse environment, the removal of one species or destruction of one local ecological community will see a burst of growth of others, rapidly filling the gap. This can restabilise the larger cycles, although often with different characteristics that emerged through the localised collapse and renewal. Or the reorganisation can be far more dramatic.

In the complex interplay of cycles, there are thresholds and tipping points when gradual change within equilibrium suddenly tips a system into a new equilibrium. It's hard to predict when it will happen and what happens next, but it's clear that, especially in systems where there's less diversity, or less interconnection, forests can rapidly become grasslands, grasslands deserts, coral reefs wastelands. Equally, eroded farms can become biodiverse and productive havens, and reintroducing apex predators can bring back birdlife and restore riverbanks. The greater the diversity, the more interdependence, the more swiftly a new healthy balance can emerge.

The lesson from panarchy is clear: transformative change happens. It happens in every system at different scales all the time. It happens when systems become less diverse, more disconnected, less able to adjust to shocks. And the more cycles, small and large, fast and slow, line up when moving from release to reorganisation, the greater the scope for transformation.

All ideas and frameworks of ideas emerge from those that came before. Panarchy developed out of the way our understanding of evolution changed in the late 20th century. It evolved beyond ideas of survival of the fittest individuals towards an appreciation of cooperation, complexity, and group dynamics.

In the 1970s, evolutionary biologist Lynn Margulis began publishing on symbiosis, detailing organisms cooperating so closely that they literally became single organisms. This, she believed, is what led to the evolution of increasingly complex lifeforms and ecosystems. In this view, the evolution of diverse species is about the interaction between cooperation and competition, of everyone doing things differently together. Margulis' thinking, building on the work of the 19th century Russian anarchist scientist Piotr Kropotkin, contributed to the development of the evolutionary science of group selection, whereby evolution isn't just an individual process but one in which whole groups – communities, species, ecosystems – evolve together through the interaction between cooperation and competition, cycles within cycles. As one scientist puts it, 'evolution is not a weapons race, but a peace treaty among interdependent nations'.[9]

The idea that evolution is an individual competitive process is now outdated. And this shift in understanding is one of the large-scale cycles that shapes what happens in the smaller, faster cycles within it.

It's time to evolve our understanding of social and political change to match this shift in the understanding of evolution. It's time to see our social, economic and political systems as panarchy.

## Transformation in politics:
## No hedging about hegemony

In 2010, I was privileged to be part of the team advising Christine Milne and her Greens colleagues as they negotiated climate action with the minority Labor government and Independent members of parliament.[10] Introducing a carbon price and multi-billion dollar packages for renewable energy, agricultural innovation and energy efficiency, what was at the time a world-leading suite of reforms was legislated in 2011 and saw Australia's greenhouse emissions begin to drop almost immediately.

But in July 2014 I was among a group of citizens bearing witness to the next government's repeal of many of the reforms. As then environment minister, Greg Hunt, got to his feet in the House of Representatives to introduce the repeal bill, one by one some 20 of us in the public gallery stood up to implore him not to do it. We delayed the repeal, and made sure it didn't pass unmarked. But we couldn't stop it.

We couldn't stop it because, although we'd managed to get legislation through the parliament a few years earlier, we hadn't changed what was possible.

Remember what happened with equal marriage in Ireland: a long process of shifting social norms, alongside the collapse of the institutional power of the major opponent, the Catholic Church. Climate campaigning in Australia has successfully built strong movements demanding action, backed by clear majorities of the population. But political action has been and remains the target of immensely powerful opposition – opposition which reached fever pitch during the negotiation of the reforms and after their introduction. With control of much of the media, control of politicians and parties, and control of the political common sense, the power of the fossil fuel industry in Australia remained hegemonic.

Few words in political science seem to scare people more than 'hegemony'. It might be partly because there's no universally agreed way of pronouncing it. I say 'hedge-EM-ony' but plenty of people say 'HEDGE-emony'. Tomayto, tomahto, let's call the whole thing off.

Seriously, though. Let's call it off. Hegemony means

dominating power by one group over others, making it effectively the definition of anti-ecology – separation and domination embodied. More than that, it's power that is maintained through a combination of coercion and common sense, of institutions and culture, a combination which makes it seemingly impossible to challenge. But, as we told Bismarck, it's not impossible – it's just hard.

For that understanding of hegemony's dual nature – and for insight into how to counter it – we have Antonio Gramsci to thank. Gramsci was an Italian linguist, Marxist philosopher and politician who, imprisoned by Benito Mussolini's fascist regime, spent the final decade before his tragically early death behind bars writing copious notebooks about political theory. His notebooks were informed by diverse experiences: building power from the grassroots up with worker cooperatives and councils in Turin; publishing newspapers to discuss and spread ideas; visiting the Soviet Union to observe what was happening in the years following revolution; being elected to parliament; being gaoled and effectively slowly executed by his country's government. Through those experiences he began to tease out sophisticated ideas of how power buttresses itself and how it can be most effectively challenged.

At the time, the dominant view in Marxist politics was one of historical determinism (that capitalism would inevitably lead to communism); that capitalist structures were maintained by physical and economic coercion (police, labour, class); and that awakening sufficient working class solidarity would trigger revolution to overthrow that coercive power. This is a simplification, but not a huge one. And really, it's not that different from so many other simplistic ideas of power and change.

Consider the argument from many today that, if we just

introduced an anti-corruption commission and banned corporate political donations (reformed some institutions), we could fix the climate crisis. Or the famous line from neoliberal economist Milton Friedman that, in a crisis, whoever has the best idea lying around (influencing culture) wins. Each identifies important aspects of power and change, but ignores the complexity of how it works. Do all ideas in a crisis hold equal weight, or do some people have their fingers on the scales? Is it the corporate donations that determine outcomes, or are they just the tap on the shoulder, reminding politicians who owns them?

Gramsci's key insight is that hegemonic power is not held primarily through coercion, but through culture, through the creation of a 'common sense' of how the world is. That common sense develops enmeshed with the institutions of power in self-reinforcing cycles. Actual coercion only needs to be used at the margins if most people can be convinced to consent to how things are through cultural norms.

Policing evolves with the norm of obedience to authority; coercive labour with the Protestant work ethic; state power with nationalism; corporate power with brand loyalty; permanent extractive economic growth with disconnection from nature; the inevitability of domination with white supremacy, economic class, and 'traditional' gender roles. Hegemony in this way can be seen as a confidence trick, dependent on people's faith in its permanence.

If those who hold the reins of institutional power begin to lose control of the world-shaping narratives, if the people stop believing the common sense and obeying the norms, forcing those in power to resort to more blatant coercion, the whole edifice can come tumbling down.

Remind you of anything?

When I first read about panarchy, my mind came straight here. Gramsci understood power as a complex system of complex systems, either reinforcing each other or occasionally tending towards collapse and transformation. One system might seem stable, but if another interrelated one reaches release, it can suddenly tip both over the edge. Transformation happens when multiple scales and cycles (institutions and norms) release, creating space for reorganisation. What seemed impossible suddenly becomes inevitable.

Gramsci called this moment, when the old world is dying and the new is struggling to be born, the 'interregnum', and he warned that it is full of both opportunity and danger. In order to seize the opportunity, we need to rapidly construct new institutions based on a different common sense – participatory assemblies, co-ops, community protection, urban agriculture – and use them to withdraw consent from existing common sense and demonstrate a different way of being. If we do this well enough, existing institutions of power will either be transformed, or they will collapse.

The danger exists if we haven't begun to build our better alternative institutions and norms when collapse arrives, leaving the space open for dominating power structures to reassert themselves, often in a more authoritarian way.

Gramsci was imprisoned not long after Lenin died and Stalin began consolidating power in the USSR, on his way to becoming one of history's most terrible dictators barely a decade after the revolution which was supposed to bring democracy to the Russian people.

Seeing power as a complex system of complex systems, interwoven cycles of change that stabilise or destabilise each other, gives us a new perspective on that age-old dispute in political change: revolution versus reform. It helps us understand why revolution can replace or exacerbate inequities, swapping one oppressive power with another and creating terrible destruction on the way, while reform can effectively keep existing oppressive systems of power in place by making them marginally less bad. Both are stuck in hierarchical understandings of power, when it's actually a panarchy. This is why there's such a tendency, as we saw in Part 1, for ideas for change to be co-opted into existing structures of power instead of creating structural change.

People often get uncomfortable when I suggest that seeking reform, while necessary, can also be problematic. The thing is, working within a system of centralised, dominating, adversarial power, those seeking social change have to organise as supplicants, to try to influence those in power, to beg or demand change, or occasionally to seek to change the people in the seats. The effect of this supplicant politics is, ironically, to stabilise existing hierarchical power.

What are we doing when we organise to write letters to ministers asking them to do something? Or when we mobilise to protest against the actions of a government, calling on them to change direction? We're telling them, and ourselves, that we consent to their power over us. We're abdicating our own power by seeking change from others, and we're emphasising the dominance-based power system instead of building a new one based on cooperation and co-creation. Most of the time, we know full well that our actions are futile. And when tens of thousands of people march for a cause and governments dismiss it out of hand, it can be incredibly disempowering. And, on the rare occasions when it works, it's like letting off steam to temporarily reduce the pressure in the system. Supporting one wind farm can provide cover for approving several new coal mines.

Seeking reform is a crucial entry point to activism. It brings people into a relationship with power. And, when it works, it improves the world. We need to do these things – organise protests and letter writing and more. But we have to learn how to do them in ways that cultivate new forms of power and challenge rather than buttress the old power.

If I'm sceptical of reformism, I'm even more sceptical of revolution. We need fertile earth in which to grow what we want to come next, and revolution creates scorched earth. Gramsci tells us that, if we seek to change institutions without changing culture, we are likely to end up with different forms of dominating power – possibly worse ones. And panarchy tells us that the more destruction that occurs at release, the longer reorganisation tends to take. By setting people intractably against each other, revolution undermines social cohesion, the positive feedback loops that are vital to building trust and cultivating the new, better system. By reinforcing the centrality of coercion, it ensures that that is what will grow after it.

This takes us back to what we learned from Hannah Arendt: violence cannot create power, only destroy it. Power springs up from people coming together. That's why revolution tends to replicate existing domination in different hands – a replacement hegemony.

Hegemony is the problem. It's a model of power based on domination by one group over others, presenting that power as permanent and unchallengeable. And panarchy tells us that that is, ironically, a fragile model, doomed to collapse when circumstances change. As Gunderson and Holling put it: 'New policies and development usually succeed initially, but they lead to agencies that gradually become rigid and myopic, economic sectors that become slavishly dependent, ecosystems that are more fragile, and a public that loses trust in governance.'[11] This is effectively identical to Arendt's point that 'All political institutions are manifestations and materializations of power; they petrify and decay as soon as the living power of the people ceases to uphold them'.[12]

Hegemony is calcifying. By repeatedly suppressing destabilising cycles and favouring stabilising ones in order to buttress its power, it creates a brittle system prone to crisis. Living power, in a living democracy, would establish a mix of feedback mechanisms, challenging domination and hierarchy, balancing stabilisation with destabilisation, creating a complex system of complex systems with the flexibility to help us survive and thrive together.

It's incredibly difficult to think about different forms of power. Anti-ecological common sense insists that power is always about domination and coercion. But there have always been other ideas. Beyond 'power over' others, we've always understood the 'power to' achieve something by exercising 'power with' others. I love the expression in the Tao Te Ching, used by Chinese democracy activists, that water can be stronger than stone. What they are trying to do – and what we must also – is dissolve dominating stone power and distribute the power to achieve things as widely as water.

If that's the power we want to build, that's the power we need to use to grow it. We can't think in terms of reform or revolution operating within hierarchical power. In order to cultivate living democracy, we need to think in terms of panarchy and work towards the reorganisation that follows release.

That means seeding a multitude of diverse and inter-connected alternatives and cultivating the conditions for them to grow. It means withdrawing our consent, refusing to be bound by the common sense, refusing to accept the limits of the current institutions. It means building trust through repeated cycles, creating positive feedback loops, the same way we might cultivate healthy soils.

We'll come back to how we do that very shortly. First we need to clarify something: remember what Gramsci said about the old world dying and the new struggling to be born? Remember how he called that moment – the moment that corresponds with panarchy's release – the interregnum? Well, I reckon there's a strong argument to be made that we're there.

Welcome to the interregnum.

# IT'S THE END OF
# THE WORLD AS WE KNOW IT
# AND I FEEL FINE

A police station burns in downtown Minneapolis. Armoured military vehicles enforce a curfew following yet another murder by police caught on camera. Refrigerated trucks supplement overflowing morgues in New York City as the pandemic runs rampant. Teargas is used inside the US Capitol building as a mob attempts to disrupt the peaceful transfer of power after Presidential elections.

The years 2020 and early 2021 in the United States of America carried strong 'end of empire' vibes.

Watching the US convulsions with queasy fascination, I imagined myself into the shoes of someone in Britain a millennium and a half ago, witnessing the collapse of the Imperial Roman occupation. A force that had brought roads and repression, prosperity and powerlessness, cash and crucifixions, that was an unchallengeable fact of life for a dozen generations, suddenly was no longer there. What would happen? What might be lost? What could be gained?

My imaginings were a funny mix of childhood pop culture: Asterix and Obelix (indomitable insurgents against incompetent imperialists), Monty Python ('What have the Romans ever done for us? Apart from aqueducts ...'), and Rosemary Sutcliff (boys' own adventures happen regardless of who's in charge). They were also informed by James C Scott's research, which we discussed early on.

Scott, as you hopefully recall, looked into why early city states and empires were short-lived, and their rulers overwhelmingly concerned with stopping people from running away. He found strong evidence that life for most people inside was less pleasant – it was crowded and smelly, food was worse, diseases rampant, and you lost agency in your life. Indeed, when these early states collapsed, though it may in some senses have felt like the end of the world, life became healthier, easier, and likely happier.

There is no evidence for greater brutality or violence – indeed there's evidence of less.

As the statue of Ozymandias ('look on my works, ye mighty, and despair') crumbled into the sand, centralised control and oppression dissolved too. Populations, power and culture dispersed and democratised. The idea that these were 'dark ages' is invented by hegemonic powers, claiming that the absence of monument-building or written records means no 'civilisation' existed. In fact, complex cultures thrived in those periods. The *Iliad* and the *Odyssey*, for example, were composed in the 400-year period between the collapse of the Greek city states and the rise of classical Greece.[1]

Watching the legions march away, I imagine that Celt might have felt a mixture of trepidation and emancipation, a sense of expanded possibility.

This is a crucial lesson for us right now: just because it's the end of the world as we know it, doesn't mean it has to be the end of the world!

What happens next depends on what's collapsing, what is growing to take its place, and how successfully we cultivate what we want.

## The Wizard of Oz exposed

The obvious convulsions of collapse in the USA might have quieted somewhat under President Joe Biden, but the underlying 'morbid symptoms', as Gramsci described them, are still present. And not only in the USA. A clear case can be made that we are in the interregnum. The hegemony of capitalist liberal democracy is over as old certainties disintegrate and institutions crumble. Panarchic release is underway.

Central to the release is that the promise of capitalism – the promise of progress, that things will always get better – has evaporated for the vast majority. In the face of mass unemployment, of people working several jobs and still stuck in poverty while billionaires get ever more obscenely wealthy, the mythology that working hard will get you ahead and that a rising tide will lift all boats has collapsed. From rusting industrial zones to dusty inner cities, rural regions to sprawling suburbia, more and more people see that reality doesn't accord with the story.

A 2021 ABC Australia Talks survey found solid majorities of Australians up to the age of 49, and pluralities all the way up to 74, agreed with the sentiment that 'capitalism as it exists today does more harm than good'.[2] The global Edelman Trust

Barometer asked the same question in 2020 and found 56 per cent agreed.[3] This isn't a minority of highly educated post-materialist elites – it's a widespread view, across demographics and across the political spectrum.

Such was the hegemony of triumphalist capitalism since the end of the Cold War that it's hard to imagine this question even being asked, let alone finding majority support, until a dozen years ago.

A dozen years because the immediate trigger was the 2008 financial crisis, and the responses to it by governments, corporations, researchers and communities. Blame for the subprime mortgage crisis was sheeted home to the greed and myopia of unregulated capitalism, with the wealthy literally trading on the precarity of the poor. And, while people were being made unemployed and homeless, the banks were bailed out by governments across Europe and America, including by the newly elected 'yes we can' president, Barack Obama. Popular movements of the left such as Occupy sprang up, creating political space for Bernie Sanders, Jeremy Corbyn and others to normalise an explicit critique of capitalism. Meanwhile, right-wing populists critiqued free trade and other tenets of the capitalist credo as part of their attack on elites.

Not unrelatedly, governments are simultaneously facing a crisis of legitimacy. If the promise of capitalism is ever-increasing prosperity, the promise of the state is that it will keep us safe – from barbarians at the gates and from predators within. It's been suggested that the horror of September 11 shook the foundations of this promise, with aftershocks from Bali to Paris exposing the seeming inability of world powers to protect their citizens. Differently politically-motivated mass killings from Norway to New Zealand, the horrific parade of US school shootings, and the sickening rate of murder of African Americans and Indigenous Australians by police (by the state itself) bring this reality painfully home. When governments protected the interests of banks over their citizens' lives in 2008, confidence was shaken further.

Ironically, when governments took the opposite approach in response to the COVID economic crash, temporarily increasing support to citizens dramatically, they undermined trust even more by showing that austerity was never necessary – it was always a political choice.

Poll after poll, in Australia and around the world, show confidence and trust in government and democratic systems crashing. The repeated episodes of panic buying in response to pandemic outbreaks and bushfires reveal that people's confidence in the capacity and willingness of governments to keep us safe is paper thin. The phenomena of Barcelona en Comú and Brexit, Voices for Indi and Trumpism, show the very idea of government being challenged – pulled in opposing directions, between open and closed, between internationalism and nationalism, between tearing down and building anew. And cynicism about democracy is rife, thanks to the impunity with which governments indulge in cronyism and outright corruption, and the dramatic difference between the expressed views of the people in polling and the decisions of government.

Indeed, a comprehensive analysis by two senior scholars at Princeton and Northwestern universities, Martin Gilens and Benjamin Page, found that the views of citizens had 'little or no ... influence' on US government policy. The real influence comes from 'economic elites and organized groups representing business interests'.[4] Historian and democracy advocate, Anne

Applebaum, has taken this further, detailing a global network of mainstream corporations, democratic governments, and autocrats, from McKinsey to Putin, Google to Trump to Xi Jinping, keeping each other in power with no regard for a rules-based order, domestically or internationally.[5]

This is the crux of it. Governments and corporations, working hand in glove, have effectively, and increasingly blatantly, undermined the integrity of both the state and the market. Witness how governments have underfunded public institutions, giving themselves a reason to privatise them on the basis that they're not delivering, then washed their hands of responsibility when they provide terrible services, undermining public confidence in both government and business.

See how governments let corporations co-design international trade agreements, including clauses that allow them to sue governments for decisions that harm their profits, when citizens have no such right, damaging trust in the whole system. Watch as, when the 'free market' fails to deliver for their favoured industries, like fossil fuels, governments intervene to fund them.

Like the Wizard of Oz coming out from behind the curtain, if governments and corporations effectively acknowledge that the invisible hand of the market was a lie, that it was always directed by and for those in power, why should the people believe them anymore? The confidence trick is exposed. The edifice starts to collapse. And once it starts, it develops an unstoppable momentum.

As cultural enforcement fails, explicit coercion becomes more necessary. And remember what Hannah Arendt and Erica Chenoweth warned: when states resort to violent coercion to suppress the reasonable demands of the people, they undermine the real power that comes from bringing people together, and they trigger stronger resistance. The internet and streaming video make it harder to hide this coercion. Whistleblowers like Chelsea Manning and Witness K, and activists like the Movement for Black Lives, spread evidence of the misuse of power by governments for all to see, feeding disaffection. And, as governments get used to using coercion, they care less about the views of the people – as evidenced by Chenoweth's analysis that all forms of protest are working less often now than last century. The downward spiral continues as both cultural and institutional power wane.

And in the 21st century, to Gramsci's intertwined institutions and culture we can add a third layer of power – the natural world itself. Butting up against ecological limits making themselves felt through fires, floods and plagues, weakened cultural and institutional powers, without the capacity and willingness to adapt, don't stand a chance.

As the environmental legal scholar, Jedediah Britton-Purdy, has written, 'The new coronavirus makes vivid the logic of a world that combines a material reality of intense interdependence with moral and political systems that leave people to look out for themselves.'[6] Climate chaos and the collapse of ecosystems do the same. Everything's connected, but you're on your own.

In this world, confidence in the capacity of the state to keep us safe, or even supplied with toilet paper, will increasingly fail. And the story of capitalism – that the market will take care of things if we all follow our own self-interest; that eternal growth on a finite planet is possible; that we are separate from and superior to the natural world – is exposed as the nonsense it always was.

The Wizard can't go back behind the curtain now. What happens next?

## Mad Max or mutual aid

Marauding bands in souped-up vehicles, all tattoos, crossbows, and surprisingly intricate hairstyles, hurtle across the desert. Frightened families pick a path down empty roads, searching for canned food, senses primed, muscles tensed, ready to run from the cannibals with chiselled cheekbones.

We're drawn to imaginings of apocalypse informed by *Mad Max*, *The 100* or *The Road*. These types of titillating tales draw on a rich vein of mythology running through our cultural memory. But do we ever stop to wonder why it's easier to imagine the end of the world than the end of capitalism or the end of the state? Perhaps now, as the veil is drawn back and we see a system designed to maintain its own power, we can let our imaginations lead us somewhere better. Perhaps we could keep the hairstyles and the cheekbones, but with kindness and care instead of spears and starvation.

The thing is, at times of crisis, we humans tend to reach out to each other in support. While the instinct of those in power is to raise the drawbridge, slam the gates, and try to set us against each other, the community tends to just get on with the important business of mutual aid.

In fact, as the historian and activist Rebecca Solnit has detailed, the mythology of widespread looting and marauding after disasters like Hurricane Katrina (2005) is part of the strategy of turning ordinary people against each other.[7] In reality, it's the rich and powerful who use these moments to embezzle, steal and cement their power while ordinary people sandbag each other's homes as floodwaters rise, prepare meals for those out fighting fires, donate clothes and even open our homes to those in need, letterbox our neighbours to offer help with groceries.

Now I'm not saying that everything's peachy. The decades ahead are going to bring tremendous hardships and tragedies as the globe heats, seas rise, rivers dry, and ecosystems collapse. Worse, as ecological crises bite, political certainties weaken, and economic mythologies evaporate, the siren song of authoritarian leaders promising protection from a scary world will get louder.

We have to sing a better song. If, as Hannah Arendt and others have told us, totalitarianism only thrives amid disconnection and alienation, the response must be to connect to each other like our lives depend on it! Our task is to bring people together in that spirit of mutual aid to cultivate the living democracy that is the only alternative now to authoritarianism, and the only thing that can hold it back.

And the crucial first step here is to believe this ourselves – to believe in each other. Far too many of us are willing to accept that all is lost, to expect dystopia, because we've accepted the story of original sin, of humanity's irredeemable selfishness. For many, this draws them to supplicant politics, if not authoritarianism, because they find it easier to trust the state than their neighbours. At a time when so much is in flux, this is not just underplaying our hand, it's potentially hugely dangerous. Helping the current system to hold on that little bit longer, without building what we want to come next, will make collapse more drastic when it eventually arrives, and we won't be ready.

Collapse leads to regeneration. What comes next depends on what is collapsing and what is growing. And here's the thing: we have a say in what collapses and what grows.

When faced with the idea of collapse, the mythology of the status quo tells us that it's cities and modern medicine, food supplies and schools, safety and decent behaviour that will disappear. But what if what is collapsing is the culture and institutions of anti-ecology, of domination being the only real form of power, of the credo of selfish individualism? What if it's extractive corporations that disintegrate? What if exclusive, adversarial governments cease to exist? What if violent and coercive policing disappears? What if the separation between cities and nature, human habitat and non-human world, dissolves?

The end of states could just as easily be a global network of interdependent participatory democracies as it could *Mad Max*. The end of capitalism could just as easily be shared abundance as it could deprivation. For Indigenous people, refugees, people of colour, people in poverty, LGBTQIA+ people, women, the end of this system could be a tremendous liberation if we work together to make it so.

Nothing is going to happen by itself. We can't just sit back and wait for the system's demise. Its hegemony depends on our participation, our consent, and the perception of permanence. By withdrawing our consent and building the alternatives, we hasten its demise, we cultivate the conditions for a better world to grow, and we make what was impossible inevitable.

Let's now finally turn to understanding how, by living democracy, we bring living democracy into being.

# THE JOURNEY IS
# THE DESTINATION

With unemployment ballooning to over 25 per cent, and as high as 50 per cent for young people, and food prices and housing costs soaring, life in Spain in the years following the 2008 global financial crash was extraordinarily hard. As things got dire, millions gathered in squares around the country to protest the government's austerity policies and discuss what could be done. Amid the rallies and protests, sit-ins and assemblies, new political movements were born.

In Barcelona, something particularly remarkable happened. You've heard this story, but it bears repeating, knowing what we now know about transformative change. Urban farmers, community gardeners and restaurateurs came together to make sure people had the food they needed. If you or your children were sick and you couldn't afford care, you could get help from free community-supported medical co-ops. Rent strikers and squatters groups mobilised, supporting each other to hold strong in the face of the housing crisis. Each group kept finding themselves blocked – or insufficiently supported – by government and business.

So, with elections coming up, they brought together a loose coalition around common values and goals that they developed democratically at a series of public meetings, and contested the elections under the banner Barcelona en Comú. Describing themselves as a 'citizen platform' rather than a party, they have now been governing Spain's second largest city since 2015, doing things they were told were impossible like municipalising the water supply, and supporting similar projects around the world through the Fearless Cities network.

As a political project, Barcelona en Comú emerged from community projects helping people in their day-to-day lives. It's a movement of solidarity between those projects, but it's far bigger than that. From its very beginning, it has framed itself as supporting and enabling local responses to global issues – the climate crisis and capitalism, racism and war. It's a systemic approach embedded in people's lives. As the housing-activist-turned-mayor, Ada Colau, put it, 'Globalization has brought us together, has made everyone realize that we are all connected, but it has also made us feel more alone, and more insignificant, than ever.'[1] Her response is to actively bring people together, build trust and social cohesion, and genuinely give people agency in their lives so they can see themselves individually and collectively addressing issues that matter to us all.

It starts with creating alternative ways of being – cooperatives and urban agriculture, access to housing and healthcare. It cultivates the conditions for these alternatives to flourish – building cooperation between projects, seeking the political capacity to support and enable them, and weaving them into new cultural norms. It withdraws consent from the existing systems – explicitly naming and contesting the power of capital and coercive government that are obviously failing people, and demonstrating a better way. And it reinforces confidence in the new system through creating cycles of trust – continuing to ensure that decision-making power rests with the community wherever possible, prioritising access for all, creating institutional structures that guarantee common control.

Seeding diverse alternatives; cultivating healthy conditions for them to thrive; weeding the ground by withdrawing consent from an old system in crisis; and reinforcing the new alternatives through cycles of trust and structures of support. This is panarchic transformation – destabilising the things we'd like to replace and creating virtuous cycles for those we'd like to grow. It's overthrowing hegemony – challenging old institutions, creating new ones, and rewriting the common sense. It's living democracy.

For Barcelona en Comú, the journey is the destination. And it's working.

A world away, in regional Victoria, something quite different but nonetheless recognisable emerged at the same time. In 2012, a group of citizens distressed by the state of politics and concerned that their local member of parliament wasn't representing the views of her electorate, decided to run a series of kitchen table conversations to find out what really mattered to people.[2]

Starting in the small city of Wangaratta (population 20 000), and spreading across the towns and regions of the electorate of Indi, they brought together people in small groups and large, genuinely seeking their opinions and ideas. It was the way the group, which became Voices for Indi, honestly and openly sought out everyone's views and fed them back to the community that created trust in the project. And it's what saw people in what was long assumed to be a conservative electorate produce an extraordinarily progressive platform featuring climate action and integrity in politics.

Like Barcelona en Comú, Voices for Indi never intended to be an electoral project. Their original goal was to take the ideas of the people to their representative, Sophie Mirabella, and ask her to consider them. But Mirabella's response was so dismissive that some of the participants immediately felt they should try to remove her. It took a lengthy process of discussion and deliberation across the community, however, to build consensus around the proposal to run an independent candidate. Some original members left; others rallied to the cause. Another lengthy process led to one of the organisers, Cathy McGowan, being nominated as their candidate.

The election campaign itself was an exercise in what they describe as 'radical trust' – extraordinarily decentralised, supporting locals to run their own campaign hubs, even produce their own materials, as long as they stuck by the democratically-developed principles and platform, and the ground rules of respect. And, having won elections, McGowan and her successor Helen Haines continue to cultivate trust, seeking people's views, input and participation through summits and community roundtables and rotating placements in the parliamentary offices. Power remains with the community, not the representative, to generate ideas and solutions, working with the member of parliament to deliver them. As Haines told me, '[it's not] about me fixing [the problems people raise]. [It's] about how do we work on this together? How are you going to go about solving these problems, with my advocacy [in parliament]?'[3]

Crucially, this is designed as an iterative process, deliberately working to create a virtuous cycle that cultivates trust in a new way of doing democracy that can spread well beyond Indi. Voices for Indi runs training programs across the country, helping people replicate what they are doing, develop citizenship skills, and shift cultural norms about politics. As one of their key organisers, Denis Ginnivan, told me, part of the process is people simply 'being nicer to each other', and there is anecdotal evidence that that's happening in the towns of Indi. With friendliness, mutual respect and social cohesion growing, trust builds more, and confidence in this new way of being can flourish. As Ginnivan said, 'If people feel positive about being a citizen, the system begins to change itself.'[4]

As in Barcelona, in Indi we see people seeding alternative ways of being, through participatory and deliberative democracy as well as the creative ideas and solutions they generate. We see them cultivating the conditions for these alternatives to thrive, by getting someone elected who can help deliver outcomes and build understanding of how this model can work. We see them withdrawing consent from the existing system, by working to unseat a sitting member of parliament through a radical, trust-based campaign, and refusing to be bound by old expectations of how representative democracy should operate. And we see them building trust through virtuous cycles, institutionalising processes that ensure that power remains with the people, giving them every opportunity to participate, develop skills, and find their own agency.

The same thing is going on with Participatory City in London. The same is happening with the Patchwork Urban Farm in Canberra, street violence interruption programs in

American cities, and Night Patrols in Aboriginal communities. The same at the Bentley Blockade, in Buy Nothing groups, and in Amanda Cahill's Next Economy sessions.

Each of these has a different focus and emphasis, not always covering all four aspects equally. For example, the urban farm is mainly about seeding (literally) an alternative, as well as withdrawing consent from the mainstream food economy. While it certainly builds community trust, it doesn't necessarily directly cultivate conditions for growth. On the other hand, Participatory City is primarily focussed on cultivating the conditions for people to seed their own alternatives through its high street drop-in centres and staff paid to help people navigate the challenges they face. It builds trust wonderfully, but I'm not sure that it withdraws consent from the existing system. Crucially, however, it doesn't encourage consenting to the system. Neither does the urban farm work against cultivating conditions for growth.

Now that we're here, looking back on key examples from Part 2 through this lens of how change happens, you may recall that, in each case, with democracy, economy, peace, and nature, we started from the community with things we can do ourselves for ourselves, and moved progressively towards systemic change.

Changing the impossible into the inevitable starts with us, with what we can do and create together, growing to fill the space as we challenge and replace the systems of power that bring out the worst in us with new systems that bring out our best. Simple when you think of it like that. But we have to get it right.

## Practice makes (im)perfect

There's an old musicians' joke about a lost tourist in New York trying to find his way to the famous Carnegie Hall for a concert. He sees a violinist busking by the side of the road and, interrupting the fiddler's flow, asks 'Hey, how do you get to Carnegie Hall?' To which the busker narkily replies, 'Practice, practice, practice!'

I wrote earlier about how my musical education taught me how the whole can be greater than the sum of its parts, and gave me amazing experiences of transcendence. It also taught me discipline. I had to learn not just *to* practise, but *how to* practise. In some ways the most important lesson my viola teacher taught me was that, when you make a mistake while practising, you don't just work until you get it right and then move on. You have to practise the phrase correctly more times than you got it wrong, otherwise you've actually practised the mistake. If you stuff it up five times, you haven't practised properly until you've played it right at least six times.

If this is the case for individuals, how much more is it the case for groups, where the interaction between us creates complex systems of complex systems? Feedback loops inculcate particular ways of being and doing, because we're always learning from each other, modelling our behaviour on those around us, and on our assumptions of their expectations of us. Behaviour creates norms and norms create behaviour, institutions and culture self-perpetuate in reinforcing cycles.

The most remarkable analysis of this that I've seen is in research by the Common Cause Foundation, who study the way values underpin our behaviour and behaviour activates or deactivates those values.[5] Through deep research across cultures and countries over decades, they have shown how, when we are thinking in terms of 'self-transcendence values' – such as care for others, care for the natural world, equality, social justice – we are less likely to behave in a selfish or dominating manner. Equally, when we are thinking in terms of 'self-enhancement values' – such as wealth, authority and social status – we're less likely to behave in generous, caring, trusting ways. So far so relatively obvious. Then we add the social layer.

It's remarkable how easily our behaviour is influenced by those around us. If we see someone helping an injured person get up off the ground, we're more likely to stop and pick up a pen someone dropped. If we see someone grabbing the last biscuit, we're more likely to walk past a fallen runner. Indeed, Common Cause has identified that much of our behaviour is guided less by the internal values we consider ourselves driven by than by the values we think those around us hold.[6] In fact, as their research shows, most people consider themselves primarily driven by altruistic values but think that most other people are more selfish. And there's good reason for that – the myth of human selfishness, as we've discussed, has been deliberately cultivated over centuries, and we're bombarded by it every day – in advertising, in the news, from politicians and businesspeople. This has evolved into a cultural norm of self-interest, leading people to suppress their own compassion, to feel embarrassed to show care, to deny altruistic motivations in others and search for self-interested explanations for their behaviour. This norm has a tremendously powerful effect on our behaviour, which in turns feeds the further development and entrenchment of social norms.

So we have to be very careful not to practise mistakes.

I'm not arguing for perfectionism, as that can lead to paralysis. I'm asking for a genuine and honest evaluation of what kinds of tactics and strategies add to the change we need, and what hold it back. Some activities create better alternative ways of being, and some undermine those alternatives. Some cultivate the conditions for those alternatives to grow, while some poison the soil. Some withdraw consent from existing systems of power while others embed consent ever deeper. Some build trust in each other and in new ways of being, while some undermine that trust. Can we be better at thinking through and critiquing our work in these terms? Can we be more ecological about it, considering the interplay between change and change-making, between policies and approaches, between means and ends?

Because of the power of practice and norms, it is tremendously difficult to work for social change from within a system that has evolved to uphold the status quo, and easy to fall into the trap of replicating what we want to replace. American activist and author, adrienne maree brown, puts this in particularly stark terms: 'We have lived through a good half century of individualistic linear organizing (led by charismatic individuals or budget-building institutions), which intends to reform or revolutionize society, but falls back into modelling the oppressive tendencies against which we claim to be pushing.'[7] At the worst end, we see examples of racist and sexist leadership in social change organisations. More systemically, too much campaigning buys into existing systems of power, emphasising the cultural norms of domination and disconnection.

Let's look at the earlier critique of both reformism and revolution from this perspective. If revolution pits people and groups against one another in a culture of coercion, domination, and violence, what alternatives are we practising? Are we cultivating the conditions of growth for something we don't want? And the revolutionary search for a single 'historical subject' – the working class – capable of driving change effectively erases the diversity of alternatives we would get through a more intersectional approach of many subjects creating many alternatives. Equally, reformist supplicant politics practises the behaviour of consent to the existing system instead of withdrawing it. By putting faith in those in power, it undermines trust in each other, sometimes explicitly calling for coercive responses to restrain untrustworthy people.

Neither, of course, can we just 'buy out' of the existing system, start to build our own and ignore the old one. We have to actively dismantle the master's house, but we can also reuse the bricks and timbers as we build our own. Both Barcelona en Comú and Voices for Indi creatively reimagine the role of government and parliament in enabling rather than blocking change, for example. Similarly, there's the recuperation of corporations, with workers taking them over as cooperatives instead of abandoning them.

Another mistake we often practise is sliding into attacking and dividing, instead of cultivating trust, which is so crucial for the new system – crucial in its own right, crucial for cultivating conditions for trust-based alternatives to grow, and crucial for withdrawing consent from a system that relies on dividing us.

Right-wing politicians and commentators have made a big deal about so-called 'cancel culture', which is ironic given their long history of publicly attacking, bullying and de-platforming people who express progressive ideas. But their critique contains a kernel of truth. In parts of progressive movements, there is a tendency to blame individuals rather than seeing their behaviour as driven by the system. This can drive people away instead of helping them recognise injustices, change their behaviour, and help change the system. It drives us apart instead of cultivating trust. If we want to cultivate the conditions for alternative ways of being to grow, we need to shift from calling out to calling in, encouraging people to join us, and believing in people's capacity for change. We've seen this tendency in the way environmentalists too easily criticise people for their consumption choices, instead of keeping the focus on the systemic drivers of those behaviours. The culture of attacking people for not strictly obeying pandemic lockdown orders follows a similar pattern, often failing to take into consideration social, physical and economic reasons why people may need to go out. This takes the focus off those systemic drivers that need to be changed, and sows distrust in the community. It convinces us that most people around us are selfish and can't be trusted, which feeds the values and norms of selfish individualism.

This reflects probably the most common mistake we fall into, and one which is the focus of Common Cause's work. Because we assume that people are selfish, campaigns for progressive causes are very often framed in those terms. We call for protection of the Great Barrier Reef because of its financial value to the tourism industry, or of old growth forests because we can sell the carbon credits they hold. We promote the arts because of the investment they drive, and we seek an increase to welfare payments because people will be able to buy more and keep business booming. We keep making these mistakes despite the fact that they are devastating to the strategic changes we need to make.

Here's the crucial flipside to the Common Cause research: one of the most powerful tools we have to change our behaviour is to change our opinions and expectations of each other. Trust breeds trust. Kindness begets kindness. Sharing encourages reciprocal sharing. And the best way to cultivate that virtuous cycle is to practise it together. This is what we're doing when we take part in a Buy Nothing group or join an urban farm. It's what happens in citizens' assemblies and workers' cooperatives. It's what communities are doing all around the globe. It's how we practise living democracy – by living it.

## Living. Democracy.

In a hall in the Upper Hunter Valley, a community riven by disagreement over fossil fuel extraction is meeting to discuss their future. A quietly-spoken, unassuming woman takes the podium. People shuffle uncomfortably, but if Amanda Cahill is nervous she doesn't show it. She asks them to share among themselves what their community has going for it, what its strengths are. She tells them about other communities, in Australia and around the world, that have faced these confronting times and found their way through them constructively and cooperatively. She leads them to their own conclusions so gently and effectively that they beg her to repeat the workshop three times that weekend!

In an area that consistently elects climate-denying fossil fuel promoters, plans are laid for a community renewable energy cooperative, farm gates are locked against coal and gas corporations, and a divided community forges a common path with confidence and cohesion. Change is brewing.

Across the world in north-east Syria, in towns all but destroyed by violent oppression and sectarian fighting, sites of revolutionary battles for decades, a community is meeting. Seats scrape as the co-chairs call the session to order, and discussion begins around water supply, fixing potholes, and school timetables. Any age, any gender, any religion or none, any ethnic background, everyone is welcome to have their say, share ideas, and work towards constructive solutions. In Rojava, against a backdrop of war, poverty and historical divides, they are building their better world, living it day by day, with new communities asking to join their municipal confederation. Change is growing.

These are models of change-making born of panarchical rather than hierarchical power. They're rejecting revolutionary fighting that seeks to replace one 'power over' with another. They're moving beyond tactics and strategies focussed on politics as a communications challenge, persuading people to agree with and vote for policies and messages carefully crafted by someone else far away. They're dissolving and distributing power by actively enabling people to find real agency in their lives. Embodying Angela Davis's advice that 'you can't simply invite people to join you and be immediately on board, particularly when they were not necessarily represented during the earlier organizing processes',[8] they're starting with an open heart, a set of questions, and a deep belief in people, and they're supporting communities to find their own way together. They're building a living practice of democracy, and, by living it, bringing it to life.

Elinor Ostrom developed a model for how this works. She wrote of how, in systems based on trust, you have to carefully cultivate that trust through positive tit-for-tat exchanges, scaffolding those exchanges with democratically-developed rules and procedures as you go, and constantly checking if it's working, renewing the trust. It's this process, building flexible institutional structures around the behaviours and norms we develop in practice, that sees us forge the path from community projects to transformative, systemic change.

Activist and blogger, Sophia Burns, encapsulated this idea of scaffolding beautifully in a piece written shortly after Donald Trump's election:

> It begins with dropping conventional activism and finding ways to build institutions that can weave into ... people's daily lives. It begins with taking on small projects that win credibility and expand capacity (then using that expanded credibility and capacity to take on larger and more daring projects, repeating the cycle and growing a base). It begins with strategy.[9]

As Burns and Ostrom explained, and communities from Barcelona to Kurdistan to Wangaratta are showing, that iterative process of seeding, tending, cultivating and growing is crucial. We practise behaviours with each other. We listen and watch and respond. We set expectations of each other and ourselves, monitoring and re-evaluating as we go. We turn the practices into new norms and institutions, replacing the old ones on the way.

In this way, the journey is the destination, the means is the end. We change the world, while operating in it as it currently is, by living in it as we wish it to be, making life better in our communities as we work to make life better for everyone.

And that simple act, living as we wish to live together,

can be a truly transformative one, particularly at a time when dominating power is already shaky. Remember what Ester Boserup told us: that the simplest way to control people is to 'deprive [us] of the right to be independent cultivators'? What if we take back that right, and start to cultivate what we want? What if, through community-sharing economies we demonstrate that we can create genuine abundance and make life better than capitalism can? What if, through community cohesion, we show we can keep people safer than the state can? What if, through community assemblies, we give people first-hand experience of a better way of making decisions than adversarial politics? What if, just as the systems of power that caused the mess we're in are collapsing, we create cohesive, coherent, ecological communities all over the world that do the job better?

Crucially, this will involve multiple interwoven paths, not a one-size-fits-all solution imposed from on high. Each community, each group, needs to find its own way, and many of us will follow several different paths at the same time. We'll learn from each other, cross-pollinating as we practise these different ways, each project filling a particular niche as a complex, interconnected ecology develops.

Countless seeds of living democracy already exist, all over the world. Whether it's your local food co-op or a renewable energy cooperative, a verge garden run by a few neighbours or a regional community-supported agriculture scheme, a discussion group for a city block or a suburb-wide community assembly, a mutual aid group or a Barefoot Patrol, we need to plant more of these seeds, everywhere we can, save the seeds of their flowers, and scatter them ever more widely.

As those seedlings grow, we need to help them regenerate

the health of the democratic soils, so they can support new plants to grow. We need to use the tools we can, whether that be protesting, getting elected, or channelling funds, using space or using our voices to tell the stories, so the plants can grow into bushes and trees and the change can start to cascade up.

Along the way, we'll have to weed the ground and remove invasive species that make it harder for our ecosystem to flourish, like political donations, advertising, violent policing, and extreme wealth. We'll have to build one of those predator-proof fences, with anti-corruption bodies and truth and reconciliation commissions.

Soon, the forest will be teaming with life, and the living practice of democracy will have fostered a new political culture. We'll have replaced our energy, transport and food systems with ecologically sustainable alternatives, by growing them from the ground up and removing the political barriers that held them back. We'll have remodelled labour and redesigned corporate structures, by taking the lead ourselves, doing it better as the old models drive themselves to extinction. We'll have ended structural prejudice, de-colonised, and re-imagined the nation by bringing people together honestly and openly, celebrating our differences while finding our common purpose, learning from Indigenous elders how to appreciate that resilience comes from interdependent diversity.

And, biggest of all, we will discover how to institutionalise living power in a living democracy. Recognising Hannah Arendt's brilliant insight that 'all political institutions ... petrify and decay as soon as the living power of the people ceases to uphold them',[10] and panarchy's lesson that we need 'adaptive ways to deal with surprise and the unpredictable',[11] we will avoid setting our systems in stone. We'll establish an array of feedback mechanisms to help us constantly renew trust and update our rules. We'll challenge domination and hierarchy wherever it arises. We'll balance stabilisation with destabilisation, creating a complex system of complex systems with the flexibility to help us survive and thrive together in the difficult years ahead.

Here in the interregnum, as the old world is dying, we'll midwife the new world, wean it, set it on its feet to toddle, and watch it learn to run.

How we live influences how we believe we can live, which influences how we live. So let's do it. Let's live democracy.

# THE
# BEGINNING

# THERE'S NO TIME LEFT
# NOT TO DO EVERYTHING

'Isn't it too late for that?'

We were at the National Climate Emergency Summit in Melbourne, in that fleeting moment in February 2020 while the horrific summer of fire and smoke was still lingering in our clothes and minds, and before the COVID pandemic arrived. We'd spent two days discussing the need for emergency-scale climate action and how to make it happen.

I was on a panel about citizen action, arguing for what this book proposes – that we need to cultivate grassroots democracy and sharing economies, embedding ecological values through community-building projects, as a critical path to urgent and deep climate action. The question was put to me: 'Isn't it too late for the deep change you're talking about? Don't we just need governments to declare an emergency and get on with it?'

In over two decades working for climate action, I've tried pretty much everything. I've done doorknocking, marches and stalls. I've lobbied governments and corporations, through meetings, letter-writing, and public engagement. I've been involved in blockading coal infrastructure. I've worked in parliaments to negotiate better legislation, I've run for election and I've disrupted parliament from the public gallery. I've published research papers and press releases and opinion pieces. I've helped build alliances with students and unions and faith groups. I've worked in the community, taking practical action to reduce emissions. I've joined a renewable energy cooperative. I've spent painstaking hours taking political journalists through the details of reports from the Intergovernmental Panel on Climate Change. I've even written songs about it, and convinced other musicians to become advocates.

Over the years, when I've suggested that we need to think bigger than stopping this mine, taxing or regulating these companies, or electing these people, and start working for systemic change, the response from Big Important Men (almost always men) in the climate movement has far too often been a dismissive 'we don't have time for that'. It's been easily a decade since I was first told that – a decade in which progress on climate action has continued to be ... well, glacial is no longer the right word.

So I was maybe a bit heated when I threw the question back to the room: 'Does anyone here think that's actually going to happen?' Does anyone think that there is any realistic chance that the current federal government, or the next one, will declare a climate emergency and act on it with the seriousness and urgency that that requires?

Nervous tittering. One or two shouts of 'No!' Not a single person raised their hand. Among the 250 passionate climate activists in the room, nobody – not even the questioner – said 'yes'.

We all know it, don't we? We don't have time to keep demanding that governments do what we know they won't do.

We don't have time not to rewrite the rules. We don't have time not to change everything.

The climate emergency is here. Ecological collapse is well underway. Shit is hitting the fan. No matter what we do now, the loss we face in the years ahead will be immeasurably immense, and the grief will push us to breaking point. And, at the same time, the potential is extraordinary!

Because the things we have to do to turn around our destruction of the natural world are also what we have to do to enable us to survive what's coming, and to address the interwoven social, economic and political crises. We're in the same state with the attacks on democracy, with spiralling inequality, with the rise of the politics of hate. Participatory democracy, cultivationist economy, systems of coexistence, and interdependence with nature – these are the solutions to our crises *and* our tools for survival. This can genuinely be the most exciting of times to be alive, because we have the social, technological and political capacity to do extraordinary things, and because the institutions and norms that have constrained us for so long are all up for grabs.

It's the end of the world as we know it. It doesn't have to be the end of the world.

So often these days, I hear people mutter darkly that we're utterly screwed. I hear talk of survivalism, or of emergency suspension of democracy. And it's no surprise, really. Our system is designed to steal our hope of change.

But there is always hope. Particularly when you consider the speed of ecological change compared to the speed of human life. We're taught to think of climate collapse as a *Day After Tomorrow* scenario – suddenly, from one day to the next, the end of the world will have arrived. In reality, it's a process over years. And a slow apocalypse gives us time to decide how we will live through it, and that in turn shapes the apocalypse. It's like bending the curve of a pandemic. Or the arc of history.

We've already lost so much, and there's a lot more we can't save. Grief for what we're losing is real, and is a vital emotion for us to grapple with. But doomism, revelling in the idea that we're screwed, is unhelpful. So is speculating about survivalism, finding a bolthole in Tasmania or New Zealand.

While grief can lead us to act, doomism and survivalism shut off the possibility of action. They assume that there's no longer any chance of preventing catastrophe, that there's nothing left to be done. While the scientists whose research I read and who I speak to are increasingly desperate, none condone this view. All argue that, even if we were to pull out all stops now and drive the fastest and largest transition in human history, we will still face severe impacts; but, if we act fast, it doesn't have to mean extinction. The worst thing to do would be to cut off that option and give in to those who want to keep milking profits out of the destruction of our only home. That only makes it less likely that any of us will survive. Survivalist retreat, of course, by definition, is only available to a select few, and any safety is illusory and temporary. Talking in those terms divides our society even further, making the *Mad Max* scenario of societal collapse even more likely.

Which brings us back to climate emergency responses. As we've seen, in the face of emergencies, people and communities have an extraordinary instinct to reach out and help each other. And those in power have a strong reflex to slam the gates, shut down democracy, use the moment to seize even more power. Too many campaigners, including speakers at that Melbourne Climate Emergency Summit, are willing to countenance the idea that we should be open to the suspension of democracy, because humans can survive tyranny, but we can't survive the climate crisis.

These ideas open the door to a very dark future. It is genuinely not far-fetched to imagine governments suspending planning laws to ram through construction of nuclear power stations on the outskirts of cities, and waste dumps on Aboriginal land; enforcing energy efficiency by cutting power supplies to poorer areas for hours each day; banning all protest and enforcing broad social compliance through militarised policing; closing the borders and deporting or imprisoning undesirable people in a population control exercise. This is what I call the 'Margaret Atwood scenario'. It's scary because it's plausible. Like Atwood says of *The Handmaid's Tale*, all of the aspects of this story have been done somewhere already. It could happen.

Climate emergency responses that shut down democracy are no true solution for the majority of humanity. Like survivalism, they divide our society even further, making it less likely any of us will survive. But emergency responses don't need to limit democratic participation. In fact, the more inclusive and decentralised they are, the more effective they tend to be, as long as they're well coordinated.

We're entering an era of rolling crises. If we're to survive, it will only be together. It will only be by using the coming years to cultivate trust and social cohesion while learning to live within natural limits. It will be by acting as though this is an emergency, with community-driven emergency responses that give us hope by creating hope. It will be by living democracy.

The way we confront the climate crisis, and all the other crises we face, is by creating a world in which we can survive it.

People always ask me, what can I do myself in the face of such huge challenges? What's the most important thing I can do on my own?

My only response is, whatever you do, don't do it on your own! Find others. Make something more complex and wonderful together.

There's no time left not to do everything, but we don't all have to do everything ourselves! It's through cultivating the ecosystem of each of us doing our part as the old world collapses that the new world will emerge.

So what are you going to do?

Are you good with your hands? Can you fit draft-excluders on windows and doors? As well as doing them in your own place, how about organising some working bees in the community, showing people how to do it themselves, and offering people in your street to come and do it for them? Make sure you help out renters, older people, young families, and those who often lack both support and connection. And get one of your participants to write up what you did and share it as a guide for others.

Is there a Buy Nothing group where you live? Find out about it and join it if it exists. If not, set one up! It's incredibly easy. And a lot of fun.

Many of us can't install solar panels ourselves, but anyone can get involved in a renewable energy cooperative, and groups like the Coalition for Community Energy can help. There might already be one nearby in planning that you could join. Or how about checking with the local bowling club or school if they can host it?

Are you into gardening? Or do you have a bit of land others can use? Turning our yards and verges and balconies over to urban food production might be one of the most important things we can do to both tackle the climate crisis and help us survive and thrive. There are gardening groups all over the place, and you can find advice easily online. Or see if someone else wants to make use of your land, and turn it into an anarchist plot!

Are you involved in a business that could be a cooperative? Organisations like the Business Council for Co-operatives and Mutuals can advise on what needs to be done. Make sure that, as you do, you write social and ecological goals into your governing documents, not just profit.

What are you passionate about in your community? What really bugs you? Could you start a walking school bus? Does a bike path need improving? Is there some open space that could use bush regeneration? Start conversations about it! Host a meet-up to talk it over. It might turn into something amazing. It might fizzle out, and that's fine too. See what happens next!

Do you know the First Nations people whose land you live on? Have you met the custodians? Sit down and have a yarn with them. Learn some language. Listen. Ask what you can do for them. Understand how their survival can point the way for all of us.

Start a community citizens' assembly. Work out what you want to do together. Do it. Work out what you want to do next. Do that, too!

Join, start or replicate a community cooperative organising

platform, where everyone can find people and projects near them and get involved.[1]

Write to your members of parliament, tell them what you're doing, and explain that the community expects them to get on board.

If they don't, run for election.

Occupy your member of parliament's office, or a coal corporation's, or a bank's.

Get your union to start building momentum towards a general strike.

Or help out from the peace and quiet of your own home or a community centre's back room, doing research, data entry, filing, accounting, whatever suits your skills.

Vital roles exist in doing all this and more. And in helping to mobilise and coordinate it. Bringing these projects together is the future of campaigning organisations and politics, pivoting from the broad but shallow community mobilising we do so well now into deep community building.

Instead of recruiting people to our 'mass movement' to 'demand' policy change, failing to get that change, and having to reach out again to ask for the next thing, community building recruits people to get involved long term in these fun, creative, mutually beneficial activities, projects that make our lives better while also benefiting the community and the environment. And it cultivates those projects as the seeds of a new set of democratic institutions, grown from the grassroots up.

David Graeber wrote, 'To create a new world, we can only start by rediscovering what is and has always been right before our eyes.'[2]

Everything in this book has already been done. By far the biggest challenge is believing we can do it, and trusting ourselves and each other enough to start, and to stick at it.

If nothing else, we'll make life better, more fun, more connected, more worth living.

If we do it well, we'll tame the crises we face. We'll reduce the pressures on the ecosystems we are part of and cannot live without, and slowly start to regenerate them. We'll lessen the social and economic inequities that pit us against each other, and create shared abundance, social cohesion and better communities.

If we do it really well, we will thrive in a flourishing new political and economic system, built around ecological principles, as the destructive system withers away.

All of a sudden, the impossible will have become inevitable.

And then it'll happen.

Before we know it, we'll be living democracy.

# NOTES

**Introduction: To not simply survive but thrive**

1  'Greta Thunberg to world leaders: "How dare you? You have stolen my dreams and my childhood"', *Guardian News*, YouTube, youtube.com/watch?v=TMrtLsQbaok (accessed 8/2/22).

2  I hasten to add that Thunberg has a brilliant, intuitively ecological grasp of politics and how change happens. Her statement that 'we need a system change rather than individual change, but you cannot have one without the other' is a point which many fail to grasp: @gretathunberg, Twitter 24/6/2019, twitter.com/GretaThunberg/status/1142829435504254977 (accessed 8/2/22).

3  Sherryn Groch, 'Climate anxiety spikes as Canberra students gear up for school strike', *Canberra Times*, 27/11/2019.

4  Janine Israel, 'Sustainability expert Michael Mobbs: I'm leaving the city to prep for the apocalypse', *Guardian Australia*, 29/9/2019.

**Part 1: Where are we coming from?**
**An ecological many-festo**

1  This reimagining of lines from *The Communist Manifesto* first appeared in a different form as *A Many-festo of Polyphonic Tenderness*, a 'Dispatch from the future' I wrote as part of the Assembly for the Future in 2020, thethingswedidnext.org/dispatches-from-the-future (accessed 8/2/22).

2  Friedrich Engels, *The Part Played by Labour in the Transition from Ape to Man*, 1876, quoted in 'Friedrich Engels: Can humanity conquer nature?', Climate and Capitalism, climateandcapitalism.com/2012/03/01/worth-framing (accessed 8/2/22).

3  Gerry Stoker, Mark Evans and Max Halupka, 'Trust and democracy in Australia', Democracy 2025, University of Canberra and Museum of Australian Democracy, democracy2025.gov.au/documents/Democracy2025-report1.pdf (accessed 8/2/22).

4   One of the best explorations of this is Johann Hari, *Lost Connections*, Bloomsbury, 2018.
5   I highly recommend Kimberlée Crenshaw, *On Intersectionality: Essential writings*, The New Press, 2019.

**What on earth is 'ecology'?**

1   I am indebted here to numerous conversations, including advice from Professor Rob Heinsohn, Dr Erik Doerr, Margaret Blakers (OAM), Professor Euan Ritchie and Dr Michelle Maloney, as well as books including Tim Low, *Where Song Began: Australia's birds and how they changed the world*, Penguin, 2014; Timothy Morton, *Being Ecological*, Pelican, 2018; Lance H Gunderson and CS Holling (eds), *Panarchy: Understanding transformations in human and natural systems*, Island Press, 2002; and Merlin Sheldrake, *Entangled Life: How fungi make our worlds, change our minds, and shape our futures*, The Bodley Head, 2020.
2   Morton, pp 74–75.
3   Charles Darwin, *The Descent of Man*, 1871, Ch 4, infidels.org/library/historical/charles_darwin/descent_of_man/chapter_04.html (accessed 8/2/22).
4   Morton, p 153.
5   Donella Meadows, *Leverage Points: Places to intervene in a system*, The Sustainability Institute, 1999, donellameadows.org/wp-content/userfiles/Leverage_Points.pdf (accessed 8/2/22).

**The evolution of anti-ecology**

1   This phrase is borrowed from Christopher Hill, *The World Turned Upside Down: Radical ideas during the English revolution*, Penguin, 1972.
2   Thomas Hobbes, *Leviathan*, Clarendon Press, 1651, files.libertyfund.org/files/869/0161_Bk.pdf (accessed 8/2/22).
3   John Locke, *Two Treatises of Government, Second Treatise of Government*, 1689, gutenberg.org/files/7370/7370-h/7370-h.htm (accessed 8/2/22).
4   Quoted in Carolyn Merchant, 'The Death of Nature', in Michael E Zimmerman, J Baird Callicott, George Sessions, Karen J Warren and John Clark (eds), Environmental Philosophy: From animal rights to radical ecology, Prentice Hall, 2001, p 278.
5   Yuval Noah Harari, *Sapiens: A brief history of humankind*, Random House, 2014, p 35.
6   Tyson Yunkaporta, *Sand Talk: How Indigenous thinking can save the world*, Text Publishing, 2019, pp 30–32.
7   Mary Graham, 'Some thoughts about the philosophical underpinnings of Aboriginal worldviews', *Worldviews: Environment, culture, religion*, 3, 1999, pp 105–18.
8   Williams credits Stan Grant and John Rudder, *A New Wiradjuri Dictionary*, Restoration House, 2010.

9    Tjanara Goreng Goreng, *Aboriginal Law and Culture Presentation*, presented to a Green Institute seminar, 7/7/2020, greeninstitute.org.au/inspiration-on-indigenous-democracy (accessed 8/2/22).

10   Yunkaporta, p 95.

11   Bruce Pascoe, *Dark Emu: Black Seeds: Agriculture or accident?*, Magabala Books, 2014.

12   David Graeber and David Wengrow, *The Dawn of Everything: A new history of humanity*, Farrar, Straus and Giroux, 2021, p 25.

13   Graeber and Wengrow, p 115.

14   James C Scott, *Against The Grain: A deep history of the earliest states*, Yale University Press, 2017, p 8.

15   Scott, p 155.

16   Ester Boserup, *The Conditions of Agricultural Growth*, Aldine, 1965, p 73.

17   Karl Polanyi, *The Great Transformation: The political and economic origins of our time*, Farrer and Rinehart, 1944.

18   Naomi Klein, *This Changes Everything: Capitalism vs the climate*, Allen Lane, 2014, p 159.

19   For a brilliant easy read about this history, see Raj Patel and Jason W Moore, *A History of the World in Seven Cheap Things: A guide to capitalism, nature, and the future of the planet*, Verso, 2018. For deeper theory, see Cedric J Hill, *Black Marxism: The making of the Black radical tradition*, University of North Carolina Press, 1983.

20   Hill.

21   GH Sabine (ed), *The Works of Gerrard Winstanley*, Cornell University Press, 1941, pp 42–43, quoted in Hill, p 224.

22   Charles Darwin, *The Descent of Man*, 1871, Ch 4, infidels.org/library/historical/charles_darwin/descent_of_man/chapter_04.html (accessed 8/2/22).

23   Peter Kropotkin, *Mutual Aid: A factor of evolution*, BiblioLife, 1891.

24   Kropotkin.

25   Peter Kropotkin, 'Letter to the Workers of Western Europe', in Peter Kropotkin, *Kropotkin's Revolutionary Pamphlets*, Dover Publications, 1970, p 254.

26   See, for example, Renfrey Clarke, 'The ecological disaster that was the USSR', *Socialist Alliance*, Vol 11, No 7, December 2011, socialist-alliance.org/alliance-voices/ecological-disaster-was-ussr-0 (accessed 8/2/22).

27   Benito Mussolini (October 1925), quoted in Ian Kershaw, *To Hell and Back: Europe 1914–1949*, Penguin Books, 2016, p 275.

28   For an eye-watering collection of direct quotes from Garrett Hardin and background to his views, see Southern Poverty Law Centre, splcenter.org/fighting-hate/extremist-files/individual/garrett-hardin (accessed 8/2/22).

29   Friedrich A Hayek, *The Road to Serfdom*, Routledge, 1944, p 217.

30   See Rutger Bregman, *Human Kind: A hopeful history*, Bloomsbury Publishing, 2019, Chs 7 and 8.

31    Margaret Thatcher, 'Interview for "Woman's Own" ("No Such Thing as Society")', 1987, in 'Speeches, interviews and other statements', Margaret Thatcher Foundation, margaretthatcher.org/speeches (accessed 25/2/22).

32    See Clayton R Critcher and David Dunning, 'No good deed goes unquestioned: Cynical reconstructuals maintain belief in the power of self-interest', *Journal of Experimental Social Psychology*, No 6, 2011, p 1212.

33    See Jason Hickel, 'It's not thanks to capitalism that we're living longer, but progressive politics', *Guardian Australia*, 22/11/2019, theguardian.com/commentisfree/2019/nov/22/progressive-politics-capitalism-unions-healthcare-education (accessed 8/2/22).

34    See David Graeber and Andrej Grubačić, 'Introduction from forthcoming new edition of Kropotkin's *Mutual Aid: An illuminated factor of evolution*', Truthout, truthout.org/articles/david-graeber-left-us-a-parting-gift-his-thoughts-on-kropotkins-mutual-aid (accessed 8/2/22).

35    Donella Meadows, *Thinking in Systems: A primer*, Chelsea Green Publishing, 2008, p 80.

36    See Drew Westen, *The Political Brain: The role of emotion in deciding the fate of the nation*, Public Affairs Books, 2007.

37    See Ed Yong, *I Contain Multitudes: The microbes within us and a broader view of life*, Ecco Press, 2018.

38    See Paul Mason, *Postcapitalism: A guide to our future*, Allen Lane, 2015; and McKenzie Wark, *Capital Is Dead; Is this something worse?*, Verso, 2019.

### Seeds: The means of reproduction

1    See, for example, Jedediah Britton-Purdy, 'Environmentalism's racist history', *The New Yorker*, 13/8/2015, newyorker.com/news/news-desk/environmentalisms-racist-history (accessed 8/2/22).

2    Bureau of Ocean Energy Management, *Record of Decision for Gulf of Mexico Outer Continental Shelf Oil and Gas Lease Sale 257*, 2021, p 7.

3    David Crowe, 'Albanese pledges carbon cuts while backing coal exports for "decades"', *Sydney Morning Herald*, 29/2/2020.

4    Simon Copland, 'Belittling the Canberra convoy protesters will just push ostracised people further into their bunkers', *Guardian Australia*, 16/2/2022.

5    Hannah Arendt, *The Origins of Totalitarianism*, Harcourt, Brace and Co, 1951.

6    Andrej Grubačić, 'David Graeber left us a parting gift – His thoughts on Kropotkin's "Mutual Aid"', *Truthout*, 4/9/2020, truthout.org/articles/david-graeber-left-us-a-parting-gift-his-thoughts-on-kropotkins-mutual-aid (accessed 8/2/22).

7    Ariel Salleh, *Ecofeminism as Politics*, Zed Books, 1997, 2017, p xx.

8    Salleh, p xxii.

9    Jeff Sparrow, 'It's either Adani or the Great Barrier Reef. Are we willing to fight for a wonder of the world', *Guardian Australia*, 7/4/2017, theguardian.com/commentisfree/2017/apr/07/its-either-adani-or-the-great-barrier-reef-are-we-willing-to-fight-for-a-wonder-of-the-world (accessed 8/2/22).

10 Arundhati Roy, 'Another world is not only possible, she is on her way', *Truthout*, 18/4/2014.

**Part 2: Where are we going?**
**Doing democracy**

1 Frances Moore Lappé, *EcoMind: Changing the way we think to create the world we want*, Nation Books, 2011, p 153.

2 Tim Low, *Where Song Began: Australia's birds and how they changed the world*, Penguin, 2014, p 53.

3 Elinor Ostrom, 'A general framework for analyzing sustainability of social-ecological systems', *Science*, Vol 325, Issue 5939, July 2009, p 420.

4 Tyson Yunkaporta, *Sand Talk: How Indigenous thinking can save the world*, Text Publishing, 2019, pp 15–16.

5 Yunkaporta, p 55.

6 I'm immensely grateful to several staff members for conversations about the project. In addition, see Tessy Britton and Laura Billings, *Designed To Scale: Mass participation to build resilient neighbourhoods*, Civic Systems Lab, 2017, drive.google.com/file/d/0B28SOnHQM5HVV0pyT2p1NGNvQk0/view (accessed 8/2/22), and No Author, *Tools to Act: Building a participatory ecosystem in Barking and Dagenham through the Every One Every Day initiative*, 2019, participatorycity.org/tools-to-act (accessed 8/2/22).

7 I'm indebted to fascinating conversations in Barcelona in March 2017, with Jaime Palomera, Francesca Bria and Giacomo Dalisa, for this detail.

8 Personal communication, Amanda Cahill, 2/11/2020.

9 Personal communication, Denis Ginnivan and Helen Haines MP, 11/5/2021.

10 Jonathan Sri, Councillor for the Gabba Ward, jonathansri.com/about (accessed 8/2/22).

11 G1000 Foundation for Future Generations press release, German-speaking Community of Belgium becomes world's first region with permanent citizen participation drafted by lot: Ambitious model for innovating democracy designed by G1000, 26 February 2019, foundationfuturegenerations. org/files/documents/news/20190226_dgpermanentcitizensassembly_ pressrelease.pdf (accessed 8/2/22).

12 Amanda Cahill, *What Queensland Wants: Regional perspectives on building a stronger economy*, The Next Economy Consultation Report, August 2020, nexteconomy.com.au/work/what-queensland-wants-report (accessed 8/2/22).

13 Personal communication, Amanda Cahill, 2/11/2020.

14 Elinor Ostrom, *Beyond Markets and States: Polycentric governance of complex economic systems*, Nobel Prize Lecture, 8 December 2009, p 435, nobelprize. org/uploads/2018/06/ostrom_lecture.pdf (accessed 8/2/22).

15 Yunkaporta, p 131.

16 Lappé, p 153–54.

17 Elinor Ostrom, *Governing the Commons: The evolution of institutions for collective action*, Cambridge University Press, 1990, p 90.
18 Yunkaporta, pp 31–32.
19 John Dryzek and Jonathan Pickering, *The Politics of the Anthropocene*, Oxford University Press, 2019, p 17.
20 Personal communication, Simon Niemeyer, 13/7/2021.
21 Chantal Mouffe, *Deliberative Democracy or Agonistic Pluralism*, Institute for Advanced Studies, Vienna, 2000.
22 Murray Bookchin, *The Next Revolution: Popular assemblies and the promise of direct democracy*, Verso, 2015, p 71.
23 Bookchin, p 38.
24 Ostrom, 1990, p 135.
25 Ostrom, 1990, p 136.
26 See Lance H Gunderson and CS Holling (eds), *Panarchy: Understanding transformations in human and natural systems*, Island Press, 2002, p 85.
27 Quoted in Howard Zinn, *A People's History of the United States: 1492–present*, HarperPerennial, 1995, p 94.
28 Bookchin, p 68.
29 Gunderson and Holling, p 32.
30 Ostrom, 1990, pp 207–10.
31 Lappé, p 153.
32 Bookchin, p 60.

**Exercising economy**

1 2011 Census Borough Analysis, p 32, lbbd.gov.uk/sites/default/files/attachments/2011-Census-Borough-Analysis.pdf (accessed 8/2/22).
2 Henry David Thoreau, *Walden, or Life in the Woods*, Harper and Row, 1965, p 23.
3 See, for example, Samuel Alexander and Brendan Gleeson, *Degrowth in the Suburbs: A radical imaginary*, Palgrave Macmillan, 2018, and Jason Hickel, *Less is More: How degrowth will save the world*, Windmill Books, 2021.
4 Robert F Kennedy, *Remarks at the University of Kansas*, 18/3/1968, jfklibrary.org/learn/about-jfk/the-kennedy-family/robert-f-kennedy/robert-f-kennedy-speeches/remarks-at-the-university-of-kansas-march-18-1968 (accessed 8/2/22).
5 Kate Raworth, *Doughnut Economics: Seven ways to think like a 21st century economist*, Random House, 2017.
6 Bob Brown, 'Green Oration', 2012, quoted in Paddy Manning, *Inside the Greens: The origins and future of the party, the people and the politics*, Black Inc Books, 2019, p 297.
7 Murray Bookchin, *The Next Revolution: Popular assemblies and the promise of direct democracy*, Verso, 2015, p 19.
8 See Mariana Mazzucato, *The Value of Everything: Making and taking in the global economy*, Public Affairs, 2018.

9    No Author, *Tools to Act: Building a participatory ecosystem in Barking and Dagenham through the Every One Every Day initiative*, 2019, participatorycity.org/tools-to-act (accessed 8/2/22).

10   For example, 'Local currency models', Schumacher Center for a New Economics, centerforneweconomics.org/apply/local-currencies-program/local-currency-models (accessed 8/2/22); Phil England, '10 steps to creating your own local currency', *The Ecologist*, 8/6/2010, theecologist.org/2010/jun/08/10-steps-creating-your-own-local-currency (accessed 8/2/22); and Charles Eisenstein, '*Design and strategy principles for local currency*', Charles Eisenstein blog, January 2012, charleseisenstein.org/essays/design-and-strategy-principles-for-local-currency (accessed 8/2/22).

11   I've written a detailed analysis of the destructive role of advertising in our economy: Tim Hollo, 'Confronting advertising: The elephant in the bus shelter', *Green Agenda*, 4/9/2016, greenagenda.org.au/2016/09/confronting-advertising-the-elephant-in-the-bus-shelter (accessed 8/2/22).

12   Tim Hollo, 'Keeping Canberra ad free – New poll massively backs campaign', The Green Institute, 19/2/2018, greeninstitute.org.au/keeping-canberra-ad-free (accessed 8/2/22).

13   David Evan Harris, 'São Paulo: A city without ads', AdBusters, 3/8/2007, web.archive.org/web/20160418175040/https://www.adbusters.org/article/sao-paulo-a-city-without-ads (accessed 8/2/22).

14   Arwa Mahdawi, 'Can cities kick ads? Inside the global movement to ban urban billboards', *Guardian Australia*, 12/8/2015, theguardian.com/cities/2015/aug/11/can-cities-kick-ads-ban-urban-billboards (accessed 8/2/22).

15   Rory Mulholland, 'Grenoble to replace street advertising with trees and "community spaces"', *The Telegraph*, 24/11/2014, telegraph.co.uk/news/worldnews/europe/france/11250670/Grenoble-to-replace-street-advertising-with-trees-and-community-spaces.html (accessed 8/2/22).

16   Mahdawi.

17   James Turner, 'We replaced 68 tube adverts with cats. Here's why...', *Medium*, 12/9/2016, medium.com/on-advertising/why-we-just-replaced-68-tube-adverts-with-cat-pictures-9ed1ae1177d0 (accessed 8/2/22).

18   No author, *Advertising Shits in Your Head*, Dog Section Press, 2017 issue. com/dogsectionpress/docs/advertising_shits_in_your_head (accessed 8/2/22).

19   Elisha Portelli, '"You belong to us": The experience of conditional welfare and its brief suspension', in Tim Hollo (ed), *Unconditionally: COVID response and the future of welfare*, The Green Institute, November 2021, greeninstitute.org.au/publications/can-we-imagine-a-future-in-which-welfare-is-unconditional (accessed 8/2/22).

20   Elise Klein, 'Australia's COVID Basic Income: what can we learn?', in Hollo, 2021.

21   See, for an excellent summary, Maiy Azize, 'The state of welfare: Reimagining support in the wake of COVID-19', *Green Agenda*, Spring 2020,

greenagenda.org.au/2020/11/the-state-of-welfare-reimagining-support-in-the-wake-of-covid-19 (accessed 8/2/22).

22    Shalailah Medhora, 'Over 2000 people died after receiving Centrelink robo-debt notice, figures reveal', *ABC JJJ Hack*, 18/2/2019, abc.net.au/triplej/programs/hack/2030-people-have-died-after-receiving-centrelink-robodebt-notice/10821272 (accessed 8/2/22).

23    I acknowledge here the impact on my thinking of Manus Prison Theory, as developed and explained in Behrouz Boochani, *No Friend but the Mountains: Writing from Manus Prison*, Picador Australia, 2018.

24    Verity Burgmann, Ray Jureidini and Meredith Burgmann, 'Doing without the boss: Workers' control experiments in Australia in the 1970s', *Labour History*, No 103, November 2012, pp 103–22.

25    Matthew Yglesias, 'Elizabeth Warren has a plan to save capitalism', *Vox*, 15/8/2018, vox.com/2018/8/15/17683022/elizabeth-warren-accountable-capitalism-corporations (accessed 8/2/22).

26    Pablo Solón, *Vivir Bien: Old cosmovisions and new paradigms*, Great Transition Initiative, February 2018, greattransition.org/publication/vivir-bien (accessed 8/2/22).

27    See George Lakey, *Viking Economics*, Melville House, 2017.

28    See Marina Sitrin and Dario Azzellini, *They Can't Represent Us: Reinventing democracy from Greece to Occupy*, Verso, 2014.

29    Hazel Sheffield, 'The Preston model: UK takes lessons in recovery from rust-belt Cleveland', *Guardian Australia*, 11/4/2017, theguardian.com/cities/2017/apr/11/preston-cleveland-model-lessons-recovery-rust-belt (accessed 8/2/22).

30    Martin Neil Baily and Nicholas Montalbano, *Post-crisis, Community Banks are Doing Better than the Big Four by Some Measures*, Brookings Institution, 2015, brookings.edu/research/post-crisis-community-banks-are-doing-better-than-the-big-four-by-some-measures (accessed 8/2/22).

31    See Certified B Corporation, bcorporation.com.au (accessed 8/2/22).

32    Yglesias.

33    Rajeev Syal, 'Employees to be handed stake in firms under Labour plan', *Guardian Australia*, 24/9/2018, theguardian.com/politics/2018/sep/23/labour-private-sector-employee-ownership-plan-john-mcdonnell (accessed 8/2/22).

34    Sarah Hansen, 'Richest Americans – including Bezos, Musk and Buffett – paid federal income taxes equaling just 3.4% of $401 billion in new wealth, bombshell report shows', *Forbes*, 8/6/2021.

35    Nassim Khadem, 'More big companies paid no tax during the COVID crisis, ATO transparency data reveals', *ABC*, 10/12/2021.

36    No author, *Poverty in Australia*, Australian Council of Social Service, 2020, povertyandinequality.acoss.org.au/poverty (accessed 8/2/22).

37    Yanis Varoufakis, 'After the virus: How to design a post-capitalist world', *The Saturday Paper*, 7/11/2020, thesaturdaypaper.com.au/

opinion/topic/2020/11/07/after-the-virus-how-design-post-capitalist-world/160466760010658 (accessed 8/2/22).

38    @Mikel_Jollet, Twitter, twitter.com/Mikel_Jollett/
status/1241843944238923777?s=20 (accessed 8/2/22).

39    Suzanne Simard, David A Perry, Melanie D Jones, David D Myrold, Daniel M Durall and Randy Molina, 'Net transfer of carbon between ectomycorrhizal tree species in the field', *Nature*, 388, 1997, pp 579–82.

40    David Graeber, *Debt: The first 5000 years*, Melville House Publishing, 2011.

41    Astra Taylor and David Graeber, *Democracy May Not Exist, But ...*, London Review of Books podcast, lrb.co.uk/podcasts-and-videos/podcasts/at-the-bookshop/astra-taylor-and-david-graeber-democracy-may-not-exist-but (accessed 8/2/22).

**Practicing peace**

1    Hannah Arendt, 'Reflections on violence', *Journal of International Affairs*, Vol 23, No 1, Political Conflict: Perspectives on Revolution, 1969, p 21.

2    Murray Bookchin, *The Next Revolution: Popular assemblies and the promise of direct democracy*, Verso, 2015, p 38.

3    Quoted in Arendt, p 12.

4    Tyson Yunkaporta, *Sand Talk: How Indigenous thinking can save the world*, Text Publishing, 2019, p 244.

5    Ursula Le Guin, *The Ones Who Walk Away from Omelas*, learning.hccs.edu/faculty/emily.klotz/engl1302-6/readings/the-ones-who-walk-away-from-omelas-ursula-le-guin/view (accessed 8/2/22).

6    Martin Luther King, Jr, *Nobel Peace Prize Lecture*, 11/12/1964, nobelprize.org/prizes/peace/1964/king/lecture (accessed 8/2/22).

7    Rutger Bregman, *Human Kind: A hopeful history*, Bloomsbury Publishing, 2019, Ch 4.

8    David Graeber, *The Utopia of Rules: On technology, stupidity, and the secret joys of bureaucracy*, Melville House, 2015, pp 67–68.

9    Judith Butler, 'Judith Butler on the case for nonviolence', *Lithub*, 18/2/2020, lithub.com/judith-butler-on-the-case-for-nonviolence (accessed 8/2/22).

10    Yunkaporta, p 34.

11    Bregman, p 362.

12    Arendt, p 19.

13    Richard Jackson, 'Bringing pacifism back into international relations', *Social Alternatives*, Vol 33, No 4, 2014, p 63.

14    Jackson, p 64.

15    Angela Y Davis, *Freedom is a Constant Struggle: Ferguson, Palestine, and the foundations of a movement*, Haymarket Books, 2016, p 85.

16    Davis, p 108.

17    Davis, p 85.

18    Martin Luther King, Jr, *A Letter from Birmingham*, 16/4/1963, africa.upenn.edu/Articles_Gen/Letter_Birmingham.html (accessed 8/2/22).

19 Paddy Manning, *Inside the Greens: The origins and future of the party, the people and the politics*, Black Inc Books, 2019, pp 124–25.

20 Petra Kelly, *Fighting For Hope*, Chatto and Windus, 1984, p 46.

21 Kelly, pp 73–74.

22 Marcia Langton, 'Aborigines and policing: Aboriginal solutions from the Northern Territory communities', *Australian Aboriginal Studies*, 1992, Vol 2, p 6.

23 Huibert Oldenhuis with Rolf Carriere, Mel Duncan, Ellen Furnari, Anne Frisch and Thor Wagstrom, *Unarmed Civilian Protection: strengthening civilian capacities to protect civilians against violence*, UNITAR/Nonviolent Peace Force, no date, nonviolentpeaceforce.org/images/UCP_Course_Manual.pdf (accessed 8/2/22).

24 Srdja Popovic, *Blueprint for Revolution*, Scribe, 2015, pp 177–80.

25 No Author, *Tools to Act: Building a participatory ecosystem in Barking and Dagenham through the Every One Every Day initiative*, 2019, participatorycity.org/tools-to-act (accessed 8/2/22).

26 Kelly, p 74.

27 Jessica Bennett, 'What if instead of calling people out, we called them in', *New York Times*, 19/11/2020, nytimes.com/2020/11/19/style/loretta-ross-smith-college-cancel-culture.html (accessed 8/2/22).

28 Popovic, pp 59–64.

29 Arendt, p 11.

30 Jackson, p 64.

31 Maria Stephan and Erica Chenoweth, 'Why civil resistance works: The strategic logic of nonviolent conflict', *International Security*, Vol 33, No 1, 2008, pp 7–44.

32 Erica Chenoweth and Maria Stephan, 'How the world is proving Martin Luther King right about nonviolence', *Washington Post*, 19/1/2016, washingtonpost.com/news/monkey-cage/wp/2016/01/18/how-the-world-is-proving-mlk-right-about-nonviolence (accessed 8/2/22).

33 Explore an amazing encyclopedia of nonviolence: Beautiful Trouble, beautifultrouble.org (accessed 8/2/22).

34 Arendt, p 20.

35 Arendt, p 16.

36 Arendt, pp 15–16.

37 Derecka Purnell, 'How I became a police abolitionist', *The Atlantic*, 6/7/2020, theatlantic.com/ideas/archive/2020/07/how-i-became-police-abolitionist/613540/ (accessed 8/2/22).

38 Graeber, p 73.

39 Stuart Schrader, 'Defund the global policeman', *N+1 Magazine*, Fall 2020, nplusonemag.com/issue-38/politics/defund-the-global-policeman (accessed 8/2/22).

40 Purnell.

41 Madison Pauly, 'What a world without cops would look like', *Mother Jones*,

2/6/2020, motherjones.com/crime-justice/2020/06/police-abolition-george-floyd (accessed 8/2/22).

42  Purnell.

43  'PACER program, making a difference in our community', ACT Emergency Services Agency, 10/7/2020, esa.act.gov.au/pacer-program-making-difference-our-community (accessed 8/2/22).

44  Harry Blagg and Giulietta Valuri, 'Self-policing and community safety: The work of Aboriginal Community Patrols in Australia', *Current Issues in Criminal Justice*, Vol 15, No 3, 2004, p 207.

45  Davis, p 27.

46  Davis, p 4.

47  Tony Marshall, 'The evolution of restorative justice in Britain', *European Journal on Criminal Policy and Research*, Vol 4(4), p 37.

48  Barcelona en Comú, with Debbie Bookchin and Ada Colau, *Fearless Cities: A guide to the global municipalist movement*, New Internationalist Publications, 2019, p 147.

49  Arendt, p 2.

50  Arendt, p 12.

51  Oldenhuis.

52  Sara Koopman, 'Alter-geopolitics: Other securities are happening', *Geoforum*, 42, 2011, p 281.

53  Progressive International, *Declaration*, September 2020, cloud.progressive.international/s/F767W5iQ2GCN3ee#pdfviewer (accessed 8/2/22).

**Knowing nature**

1  Edward O Wilson, *Biophilia*, Harvard University Press, 1984.

2  Theodore Roszak, ME Gomes and AD Kanner (eds), *Ecopsychology: Restoring the earth, healing the mind*, Sierra Club Books, 1995.

3  Richard Louv, *Last Child in the Woods: Saving our children from nature-deficit disorder*, Algonquin Books, 2005.

4  See, for example, Mathew P White, Ian Alcock, James Grellier, Benedict Wheeler, Terry Hartig, Sara L Warber, Angie Bone, Michael Depledge and Lora E Fleming, 'Spending at least 120 minutes a week in nature is associated with good health and wellbeing', *Nature: Scientific Reports*, 9, 7730, 2019; Richard Mitchell and Frank Popham, 'Effect of exposure to natural environment on health inequalities: An observational population study', *Lancet*, 372(9650), 2008, pp 1655–60; Meredith A Repke, Meredith S Berry, Lucian G Conway, Alexander Metcalf, Reid M Hensen and Conor Phelan, 'How does nature exposure make people healthier?: Evidence for the role of impulsivity and expanded space perception', *PloS one,* Vol 13(8), 22/8/2018.

5  Tonia Gray, 'Being in nature is good for learning, here's how to get kids off screens and outside', *The Conversation*, 26/10/2018, theconversation.com/being-in-nature-is-good-for-learning-heres-how-to-get-kids-off-screens-and-outside-104935 (accessed 8/2/22).

6    Vaclav Havel, *The Art of the Impossible*, Knopf, 1997.

7    It's worth reading about the Griffins' philosophy: 'Philosophy', Walter Burley Griffin Society, griffinsociety.org/philosophy (accessed 8/2/22).

8    Jacqui Meyers, Drew Devereux, Tom Van Niel and Guy Barnett, *Mapping surface urban heat in Canberra*, CSIRO Land and Water, 2017, environment. act.gov.au/_data/assets/pdf_file/0005/1170968/CSIRO-Mapping-Surface-Urban-Heat-In-Canberra.pdf (accessed 8/2/22).

9    Department of Economic and Social Affairs, '68% of the world population projected to live in urban areas by 2050, says UN', United Nations, 16/5/2018, un.org/development/desa/en/news/population/2018-revision-of-world-urbanization-prospects.html (accessed 8/2/22).

10   *2071.0 – Census of Population and Housing: Reflecting Australia – Stories from the Census, 2016*, Australian Bureau of Statistics, 12/7/2018, abs.gov. au/ausstats/abs@.nsf/Lookup/by%20Subject/2071.0~2016~Main%20 Features~Small%20Towns~113 (accessed 8/2/22).

11   Amelia Thorpe, 'A day for turning parking spaces into pop-up parks', *The Conversation*, 14/9/2014, theconversation.com/a-day-for-turning-parking-spaces-into-pop-up-parks-65164 (accessed 8/2/22).

12   Alex Morss, '"Not just weeds": How rebel botanists are using graffiti to name forgotten flora', *Guardian Australia*, 2/5/2020, theguardian.com/ environment/2020/may/01/not-just-weeds-how-rebel-botanists-are-using-graffiti-to-name-forgotten-flora-aoe (accessed 8/2/22).

13   Anthony Scully, 'Newcastle bowling clubs switch to solar in community-led initiative to reduce energy consumption', *ABC Newcastle*, 20/8/2020, abc. net.au/news/2020-08-20/newcastle-town-bowling-clubs-go-solar/12574850 (accessed 8/2/22).

14   For example, Jensen Montambault, Myriam Dormer, Jacob Campbell, Naureen Rana, Sara Gottlieb, John Legge, Deron Davis and Mohamad Chakaki, 'Social equity and urban nature conservation', *Conservation Letters*, October 2017.

15   Aiden Ricketts and Annie Kia, 'Enabling emergence: The Bentley Blockade and the struggle for a gasfield free Northern Rivers', *The Commons Social Change Library*, 2018.

16   Don Driscoll, Bob Pressey, Euan Ritchie and Noel D Preece, 'Research reveals shocking detail on how Australia's environmental scientists are being silenced', *The Conversation*, 9/9/2020, theconversation.com/research-reveals-shocking-detail-on-how-australias-environmental-scientists-are-being-silenced-140026 (accessed 8/2/22).

17   Lisa Cox, '"Fantasy documents": Recovery plans failing Australia's endangered species', *Guardian Australia*, 20/2/2018, theguardian.com/ environment/2018/feb/20/fantasy-documents-recovery-plans-failing-australias-endangered-species (accessed 8/2/22).

18   Quentin Grafton, Luc Doyen, Christophe Béné, Edoardo Borgomeo, Kate Brooks, Long Chu, Graeme S Cumming, John Dixon, Stephen Dovers,

Dustin Garrick, Ariella Helfgott, Qiang Jiang, Pamela Katic, Tom Kompas, L Richard Little, Nathanial Matthews, Claudia Ringler, Dale Squires, Stein Ivar Steinshamn, Sebastián Villasante, Sarah Wheeler, John Williams and Paul R Wyrwoll, 'Realizing resilience for decision-making', *Nature Sustainability*, Vol 2, October 2019, pp 907–908.

19    Jade Macmillan, 'Scott Morrison announces $2 billion Climate Solutions Fund to reduce Australia's emissions', *ABC*, 25/2/2019.

20    Adam Gartrell, 'Great Barrier Reef valued at $56 billion by Deloitte economists', *Sydney Morning Herald*, 26/6/2017, smh.com.au/environment/great-barrier-reef-valued-at-56-billion-by-deloitte-economists-20170625-gwy2yj.html (accessed 8/2/22).

21    *Environmental Planning and Biodiversity Conservation Act 1999* (Cth), s 3A(a).

22    Christopher Stone, 'Should trees have standing? Towards legal rights for natural objects', *Southern California Law Review*, 45, 1972, p 450.

23    See, Peter Burdon (ed), *Exploring Wild Law: The philosophy of Earth jurisprudence*, Wakefield Press, 2011; Peter Burdon, 'Wild Law and the Project of Earth Democracy', in Michelle Maloney and Peter Burdon (eds), *Wild Law in Practice: Law, Justice and Ecology*, Routledge Press, 2014; Michelle Maloney, 'Rights of Nature, Earth democracy and the future of environmental governance', in Tim Hollo (ed), *Rebalancing Rights: Communities, corporations, and nature*, The Green Institute, 2019.

24    Diane Evers, Second Reading Speech, Rights of Nature and Future Generations Bill 2019, Parliament of Western Australia Hansard, 28/11/2019, p 9513a.

25    No author, 'Blue Mountains council resolves to integrate Rights of Nature into operations and planning', *Blue Mountains Gazette*, 15/4/2020, bluemountainsgazette.com.au/story/6721668/blue-mountains-council-resolves-to-integrate-rights-of-nature-into-operations-and-planning (accessed 8/2/22).

## Part 3: How do we get there?
### Making the impossible inevitable

1    No author, 'First same-sex marriages take place', *RTE News*, 17/11/2015, rte.ie/news/2015/1117/742465-same-sex-couple-marriage (accessed 8/2/22).

### Cycles of change, collapse and renewal

1    I am grateful for this section for numerous conversations with First Nations people, including Dr Goreng Goreng, Diyan Coe, and Shane Mortimer.

2    I am grateful for this section for conversations with Euan Ritchie and Erik Doerr; also Graham Readfearn, 'Decline in bogong moth numbers leaves mountain pygmy possums starving', *Guardian Australia*, 24/2/2019, theguardian.com/environment/2019/feb/25/decline-in-bogong-moth-numbers-leaves-pygmy-mountain-possums-starving (accessed 8/2/22).

3   Melissa Clarke, 'The sudden death of the snow gums', *ABC*, 10/3/2021, abc.net.au/news/2021-03-10/sudden-death-of-snow-gums-longicorn-beetle/13226128?nw=0 (accessed 8/2/22).

4   Grant Williamson, Gabi Mocatta, Rebecca Harris and Tomas Remenyi, 'Yes, the Australian bush is recovering from bushfires – but it may never be the same', *The Conversation*, 19/2/2020, theconversation.com/yes-the-australian-bush-is-recovering-from-bushfires-but-it-may-never-be-the-same-131390 (accessed 8/2/22).

5   Charles Massy, *Call of the Reed Warbler: A new agriculture – A new Earth*, University of Queensland Press, 2017.

6   Lance H Gunderson and CS Holling (eds), *Panarchy: Understanding transformations in human and natural systems*, Island Press, 2002, p 9.

7   Gunderson and Holling, p 26.

8   Gunderson and Holling, p xxii.

9   Kelly Clancy, 'Survival of the friendliest', *Nautilus Magazine*, 22/8/2019, nautil.us/issue/75/story/survival-of-the-friendliest-rp (accessed 8/2/22).

10  For an excellent history of this process, see Christine Milne, *An Activist Life*, University of Queensland Press, 2017, Ch 12.

11  Gunderson and Holling, p 6.

12  Hannah Arendt, 'Reflections on violence', *Journal of International Affairs*, Vol 23, No 1, Political Conflict: Perspectives on Revolution, 1969, p 15.

**It's the end of the world as we know it and I feel fine**

1   James C Scott, *Against The Grain: A deep history of the earliest states*, Yale University Press, 2017, in particular p 185 and pp 210–16.

2   'Australia Talks', *ABC*, 2021, australiatalks.abc.net.au (accessed 22/2/22).

3   'Edelman Trust Barometer 2020', Institute of Business Ethics, ibe.org.uk/resource/edelman-trust-barometer-2020.html (accessed 8/2/22).

4   Martin Gilens and Benjamin I Page, 'Testing theories of American politics: Elites, interest groups, and average citizens', *Perspectives on Politics*, September 2014, p 564.

5   Anne Applebaum, 'The bad guys are winning', *The Atlantic*, 15/11/2021, theatlantic.com/magazine/archive/2021/12/the-autocrats-are-winning/620526 (accessed 8/2/22).

6   Jedediah Britton-Purdy, 'The only treatment for coronavirus is solidarity', *Jacobin*, 13/3/2020, jacobinmag.com/2020/03/coronavirus-donald-trump-solidarity-profits (accessed 8/2/22).

7   Rebecca Solnit, *Hope in the Dark: Untold histories, wild possibilities*, Canongate, 2005.

**The journey is the destination**

1   Barcelona en Comú, with Debbie Bookchin and Ada Colau, *Fearless Cities: A guide to the global municipalist movement*, New Internationalist Publications, 2019, p 145.

2    I'm grateful for this section for conversations with key participants, Denis Ginnivan and Helen Haines MP, as well as Professor Carolyn Hendriks, who has studied Voices for Indi.

3    Personal communication, Helen Haines MP, 11/5/2021.

4    Personal communication, Denis Ginnivan, 11/5/2021.

5    See Common Cause, commoncausefoundation.org (accessed 8/2/22) for further explanation and detailed research.

6    Common Cause Foundation, *Perceptions Matter*, 2016.

7    adrienne maree brown, *Emergent Strategy: Shaping change, changing worlds*, AK Press, 2017, p 16.

8    Angela Y Davis, *Freedom is a Constant Struggle: Ferguson, Palestine, and the foundations of a movement*, Haymarket Books, 2016, p 25.

9    Sophia Burns, 'Strategize, don't moralize', *Gods and Radicals*, 6/4/2018, godsandradicals.org/2018/04/06/strategize-dont-moralize (accessed 8/2/22).

10    Hannah Arendt, 'Reflections on violence', *Journal of International Affairs*, Vol 23, No 1, Political Conflict: Perspectives on Revolution, 1969, p 15.

11    Lance H Gunderson and CS Holling (eds), *Panarchy: Understanding transformations in human and natural systems*, Island Press, 2002, p 19.

**Part 4: The beginning**
**There's no time left not to do everything**

1    For example, bHive Cooperative, bhive.coop (accessed 8/2/22).

2    David Graeber and Andrej Grubačić, 'Introduction from the forthcoming *Mutual Aid: An illuminated factor of evolution*', *Truthout*, truthout.org/articles/david-graeber-left-us-a-parting-gift-his-thoughts-on-kropotkins-mutual-aid (accessed 8/2/22).

# ACKNOWLEDGMENTS

This book was written on the lands of the Ngunnawal and Ngambri people, where I am privileged to live. I acknowledge and celebrate their deep and continuing connection with the land and recognise how much we have to learn from them about caring for country and living democracy.

My family is my core, my heart. Without them, this book would not exist. Jimmy and Maxie, you are my impetus to keep going, and I hope the book helps you to see a positive future. Lorana, you are my constant inspiration and constant support. Thank you all for putting up with the year of me 'not writing a book' with so many laughs and so much love. Huge love and thanks also to my mum for lovingly fostering my curiosity about the world, my dad for unstinting belief in me, and my brother for your warm encouragement, your reassuring presence, and for all the music.

This book had many parents, but without the Greens family it would never have even started. I want to particularly thank Christine Milne, who has been a boss, a friend, a mentor and an inspiration, as well as Scott Ludlam and Margaret Blakers, for their wisdom, advice and trust. My immense gratitude goes to the board and staff of the Green Institute, especially Elissa Jenkins, for their trust and patience.

Millie Rooney and Mark Chenery went way above and beyond, providing detailed and superb feedback on early drafts from their deep expertise and experience. I cannot imagine this book without their involvement, input and encouragement. Ecologists Rob Heinsohn, Erik Doerr and Euan Ritchie provided me with crucial advice and constructive critique along the way. And Amanda Cahill provided invaluable inspiration and advice.

A long list of other wonderful people – friends, colleagues, and co-conspirators – have encouraged me, stretched my thinking, challenged me and brought ideas to my attention over many years. Often I haven't recognised until much later how important those ideas were and how much they've influenced me. Among these are Clare Ozich, Holly Hammond, Imogen Ebsworth, Michael Croft, Mary Graham, Felicity Gray, Simon Copland, Michelle Maloney, Helen Oakey, Frances MacGuire, Maiy Azize, Nicola Paris, Rosanne Bersten, David Paris, Peter Burdon, Hannah Parris, Eleanor Glenn, Jonathan Sri, Alex Kelly, Josh Wyndham-Kidd, Indra Esguerra, Oliver Woldring, Rachel Siewert, Berish Bilander, Tim Dunlop, Tjanara Goreng Goreng, Danielle Celermajer, Arnagretta Hunter, Felicity Ruby and Carlos Morreo.

I want to especially acknowledge Imogen and Clare for urging me to think beyond the state, Alex for taking me out of my creative comfort zone, Mary and Tjanara for introducing me to Indigenous political theory, Tim for encouraging me to actually write a book and connecting me with NewSouth, Hannah for pestering me to read Elinor Ostrom, and Peter for the same with Hannah Arendt.

# Acknowledgments

Jessica Perini was a wonderful hands-on editor, and Elspeth Menzies and Phillipa McGuinness from NewSouth were brilliantly supportive and encouraging publishers. The work and advice of all three made this a far better book. No – it made a book from a collection of thoughts.

Thanks to REM and Universal Music Publishing for permission to use the fabulous line 'It's the end of the world as we know it and I feel fine', from the song 'It's The End Of The World As We Know It', words and music by Thomas William Berry, Peter Lawrence Buck, Michael E. Mills, John Michael Stripe, copyright Night Garden Music E, Universal Tunes, Universal/MCA Music Publishing Pty. Ltd.

Finally, I acknowledge all those living democracy around the world. Thank you for your inspiration, and for leading the way to the next world.

# INDEX

# Index

# Index

# Index